INTERNATIONAL
HUMAN RIGHTS

Fromm, 20

my paper
forgive, 49

DILEMMAS IN WORLD POLITICS

Series Editor

George A. Lopez, University of Notre Dame

Dilemmas in World Politics offers teachers and students of international relations a series of quality books on critical issues, trends, and regions in international politics. Each text examines a "real world" dilemma and is structured to cover the historical, theoretical, practical, and projected dimensions of its subject.

FORTHCOMING

*Democracy and Democratization: Processes and Prospects
in a Changing World,* Second Edition, Georg Sørenson

Southern Africa in World Politics, Janice Love

Russia and the World, Andrew C. Kuchins

INTERNATIONAL HUMAN RIGHTS, SECOND EDITION

■ ■ ■

Jack Donnelly

University of Denver

WestviewPress

A Division of HarperCollins*Publishers*

Dilemmas in World Politics

Copyright © 1998 by Westview Press, A Division of HarperCollins Publishers, Inc.

Published in 1998 in the United States of America by Westview Press, 5500 Central Avenue, Boulder, Colorado 80301-2877, and in the United Kingdom by Westview Press, 12 Hid's Copse Road, Cumnor Hill, Oxford OX2 9JJ

A CIP catalog record for this book is available from the Library of Congress.
ISBN 0-8133-9969-6 (pbk.)

The paper used in this publication meets the requirements of the American National Standard for Permanence of Paper for Printed Library Materials Z39.48-1984.

10   9   8   7   6   5   4   3   2   1

Contents

□ □ □ **8 International Human Rights
in a Post–Cold War World** **149**

Ideology and Intervention, 149
Sovereignty, Power, and Interdependence, 151
Democracy and Human Rights, 153
Markets and Human Rights, 159
International Human Rights Policy
in a New World Order, 161

□　□　□

Tables and Boxes

Tables

Boxes

□　□　□

Acknowledgments

Writing for a general audience of intelligent but not necessarily informed readers is a challenge that I hope I am beginning to master with this second edition. Much of the credit belongs to friends, colleagues, and editors who have helped with various aspects of this manuscript. The bulk of the new work in this second edition was done while I was a visiting professor at Bar Ilan University, enjoying the hospitality of the Department of Political Studies and its chair, Bernie Susser. George Lopez, the editor of the Dilemmas in World Politics series, and Jennifer Knerr, who initially commissioned the book for Westview, have been immensely helpful and supportive, despite my tardiness, through both editions. The manuscript is clearer and more precise as a result of the careful and thoughtful copyediting of Marian Safran and Michele Wynn. Jacek Lubecki and Dan Wessner provided exemplary research assistance. And I received helpful substantive comments from Joanne Bauer, Dave Forsythe, Andrew Nathan, Eduardo Saxe, and Michael Stohl. Thanks to all of you, and to the many teachers who used the first edition and thus created a demand for this second edition.

As has so often been the case over the past fifteen years, I owe a special debt to Rhoda Howard. After struggling through two full drafts of the first edition, she read the new chapters in this second edition and offered characteristically pointed and helpful suggestions. By the third edition, her prodding may finally force me to get it right.

Jack Donnelly

□ □ □

Acronyms

AI	Amnesty International
ANC	African National Congress
AOHR	Arab Organization for Human Rights
APDH	Permanent Assembly for Human Rights
ARENA	National Republican Alliance
ASEAN	Association of Southeast Asian States
CADHU	Argentine Human Rights Commission
CAT	Committee Against Torture
CCP	Chinese Communist Party
CEDAW	Committee on the Elimination of Discrimination Against Women
CELS	Center for Legal and Social Studies
CERD	Committee on the Elimination of Racial Discrimination
CIA	Central Intelligence Agency
COMADRES	Committee of Mothers of Political Prisoners, Disappeared, and Assassinated in El Salvador
CONADEP	National Commission on Disappeared Persons (Sábato Commission)
COPACHI	Committee of Cooperation for Peace
CRC	Committee on the Rights of the Child
CSCE	Conference on Security and Cooperation in Europe
CVR	Commission for Truth and Reconciliation
EC	European Community
ECOSOC	Economic and Social Council
EEC	European Economic Community
ERP	Revolutionary Army of the People
ESMA	Navy Mechanics School
EU	European Union
FDR	Democratic Revolutionary Front
FEDEFAM	Federation of Families of Disappeared Persons and Political Prisoners
FSLN	Sandinista National Liberation Front

G7	Group of Seven
GA	(United Nations) General Assembly
HRC	Human Rights Committee
IACHR	Inter-American Commission of Human Rights
IFOR	multilateral implementation force (in the former Yugoslavia)
ILO	International Labor Organization
IMF	International Monetary Fund
JNA	Yugoslav National Army
MFN	most-favored nation
MNCs	multinational corporations
NAACP	National Association for the Advancement of Colored People
NGOs	nongovernmental organizations
NSM	National Security Memorandum
OAS	Organization of American States
OAU	Organization of African Unity
OSCE	Organization for Security and Cooperation in Europe
PLO	Palestine Liberation Organization
SAPs	structural adjustment programs
SERPAJ	Service for Peace and Justice
SFOR	stabilization force (in the former Yugoslavia)
UK	United Kingdom
UN	United Nations
UNPAs	United Nations Protected Areas
UNPROFOR	United Nations Protection Force (in the former Yugoslavia)
WTO	World Trade Organization

INTERNATIONAL HUMAN RIGHTS

□ □ □

Introduction:
A Note to the Reader

This is a book about the international relations of human rights since the end of World War II, that is, the ways in which states and other international actors have addressed human rights. Although wide-ranging, the topic is narrower than some readers might expect.

Life, liberty, security, subsistence, and other things to which we have human rights may be denied by an extensive array of individuals and organizations. "Human rights," however, are usually taken to have a special reference to the ways in which states treat their own citizens. For example, domestically, we distinguish muggings and private assaults, which are not typically considered human rights violations, from police brutality and torture, which are. Internationally, we distinguish terrorism, war, and war crimes from human rights issues, even though they both lead to denials of life and security. Although the boundaries are not always entirely clear—for example, disappearances became an important form of human rights abuse in the 1970s (see Chapter 3) when perpetrators attempted to obscure the nature of their actions by operating at the boundary between private violence (murder) and state terrorism—the distinction is part of our ordinary language and focuses our attention on an important set of political problems.

No single book can cover all aspects of the politics of human rights. My concern will be *international* human rights policies, a vital and increasingly well-established area of policy and inquiry. This does not imply that international action is the principal determinant of whether human rights are respected or violated. In fact, much of the book demonstrates the limits of international action.

Nonetheless, one of this book's distinctive features, as opposed to most other discussions of international human rights, is its substantial attention to the domestic politics of human rights. Chapter 3 provides a relatively detailed look at human rights violations in the Southern Cone of South America. In addition, briefer domestic case studies of South Africa, Central America, China, and the former Yugoslavia appear in Chapters 4–7.

Another distinctive feature of this book, along with the other volumes in the Dilemmas in World Politics series, is a relatively extensive emphasis on theory. Chapter 2 addresses philosophical issues of the nature, substance, and source of human rights; the place of human rights in the contemporary international society of states; and the theoretical challenges posed to the very enterprise of international human rights policy by arguments of radical cultural relativism and political realism (realpolitik, or "power politics"). Like the domestic case studies, this discussion may appear to be more than is strictly necessary in a book on international human rights. Both the case studies and the theory, however, provide important background, context, and insights. I encourage readers at least to look them over, even—perhaps especially—if at the outset those issues do not seem central to their own concerns.

I have tried to write a book that assumes little or no background knowledge. Anyone with an interest in the topic, regardless of age or experience, should find this book accessible. I have tried, however, not to write a *textbook*, a term that has justly acquired pejorative overtones. I have tried not to "write down," either in style or in substance. Furthermore, although I have made an effort to retain some balance in the discussion, I have not expunged my own views and interpretations.

Textbook presentations of controversial issues—when they are not entirely avoided—tend to involve bland and noncommittal presentations of "the two sides" to an argument. By contrast, I have often laid out and defended one interpretation and given lesser (or even scant) attention to alternative views. I have made great efforts to be accurate and fair. But there is no false pretense of "objectivity."

I draw the reader's attention to the discussion questions for each chapter, which appear at the end of the book. There is almost a short chapter's worth of material in these questions, which often frame alternative interpretations and highlight controversial claims in the main body of the text. These are an integral part of the book and provide at least a partial corrective to any "imbalance" in the main text.

Unlike many authors of introductory books, I have not set out with the principal goal of providing information—although there is a lot of straightforward factual information for the reader to absorb. Neither do I aim to convey the received wisdom on the subject—although this book does provide an overview of the kinds of issues typically addressed, and some important perspectives that have been commonly adopted, in the study of international human rights. Rather, I hope to get you to think about why and how human rights are violated, what can (and cannot) be done about such violations through international action, why human rights remain such a small part of international relations, and what might be done about that. These are pressing political issues that merit, even demand, thought and attention.

ONE

□ □ □

Human Rights as an Issue
in World Politics

Before World War II, human rights were rarely discussed in international politics. Most states violated human rights systematically. Racial discrimination pervaded the United States. The Soviet Union was a totalitarian secret-police state. Britain, France, the Netherlands, Portugal, Belgium, the United States, and Spain maintained colonial empires in Africa, Asia, and the Caribbean. And the political history of most Central and South American countries was largely a succession of military dictatorships and civilian oligarchies.

Such phenomena troubled many people. They were not, however, considered a legitimate subject for international action. Rather, human rights were viewed as an internal (domestic) political matter, an internationally protected exercise of the sovereign prerogatives of states. Even genocidal massacres, such as Russian pogroms against the Jews or the Turkish slaughter of Armenians, drew little more than polite statements of disapproval. Less egregious violations were typically not even considered a fit subject for diplomatic conversation.

As we will see in more detail in Chapter 2, international relations have for the past three centuries been organized around the principle of sovereignty. States, the principal actors in international relations, are seen as **sovereign,** that is, subject to no higher political authority. The duty correlative to the right of **sovereignty** is **nonintervention,** the obligation not to interfere in matters that are essentially within the domestic jurisdiction of sovereign states. Human rights, which typically involve a state's treatment of its own citizens in its own territory, were traditionally seen as just such a matter of domestic jurisdiction. One purpose of this book is to chronicle a fundamental change in this dominant international understanding of the range of state sovereignty over the past fifty years.

In the nineteenth and early twentieth centuries, the European Great Powers and the United States did occasionally intervene in the Ottoman and Chinese empires to rescue nationals caught in situations of civil strife and to establish or protect special rights and privileges for Europeans and Americans. Rarely, though, did they intervene to protect foreign nationals from their own government. In fact, human rights were seldom even a topic of diplomatic discussion. Likewise, the "humanitarian law" of war, expressed in documents such as the 1907 Hague Conventions, limited only what a state could do to *foreign* nationals, not its own nationals (or peoples over whom it exercised colonial rule).

The principal exception was the campaign against slavery. The major powers recognized an obligation to abolish the slave trade at the Congress of Vienna in 1815. A comprehensive treaty to abolish the slave trade was (finally) concluded in 1890. But a treaty to abolish slavery, as opposed to international trade in slaves, was not drafted until 1926. After World War I, the International Labor Organization (ILO) dealt with some workers' rights issues, and the League of Nations had limited powers to protect ethnic minorities in selected areas.[1] With these marginal exceptions, however, human rights were not an accepted subject of international relations prior to World War II. In assessing current international human rights activity, we must keep in mind this starting point.

THE EMERGENCE OF INTERNATIONAL HUMAN RIGHTS NORMS

A problem often becomes the subject of international action only after a dramatic event crystallizes awareness. For example, the discovery of the Antarctic ozone hole contributed significantly to the recent upsurge of international environmental action. The catalyst that made human rights an issue in world politics was the Holocaust, the systematic murder of millions of innocent civilians by Germany during World War II.

The human rights response of the victorious Allies was shameful. Before the war, little was done to aid Jews trying to flee Germany and the surrounding countries. In fact, some who escaped were denied refuge by Allied governments, including the United States. During the war, no effort was made to impede the functioning of the death camps. For example, the Allies did not even target the railway lines that brought hundreds of thousands to the slaughter at Auschwitz. The world watched—or, rather, turned a blind eye to—the genocidal massacre of 6 million Jews and half a million Gypsies, and the deaths of tens of thousands of Communists, Social Democrats, homosexuals, church activists, and just ordinary decent people who refused complicity in the new politics and technology of barbarism.

BOX 1.1   Treaties as a Source of International Law

Lawmaking treaties such as the 1948 Genocide Convention and the 1966 International Human Rights Covenants typically are drafted by an international organization or conference and then presented to states for their consideration—or as international lawyers put it, they are "opened for signature and ratification." Neither the drafting of a treaty nor its approval by the United Nations or another international organization gives it legal effect. For a treaty to be binding, it must be accepted by sovereign states. And it is binding only on those states that have formally and voluntarily accepted it.

Signing a treaty is a declaration by a state that it intends to be bound by the treaty. That obligation, however, only becomes effective after the treaty has been *ratified* or acceded to according to the constitutional procedures of that country. (In the United States, the president signs a treaty and then transmits it to the Senate for ratification, for which a two-thirds vote is required.) States that have ratified or acceded to a treaty are said to be *parties* to the treaty. Typically a specified number of states must become parties before the treaty becomes binding. When sufficient ratifications have been filed, the treaty is said to enter into force.

Only as the war came to an end were Allied leaders and citizens, previously preoccupied with military victory, willing to begin to confront this horror. But in international relations, they were forced to face the Holocaust armed only with their moral sensibilities. As we have seen, international law and diplomacy before the war had not addressed human rights.

The first step in filling this void came with the Nuremberg War Crimes Trials (1945–1946), at which leading Nazis were prosecuted under the novel charge of crimes against humanity. Human rights really emerged as a standard subject of international relations, though, in the United Nations (UN). The Covenant of the League of Nations did not mention human rights. The Preamble of the Charter of the United Nations, by contrast, includes a determination "to reaffirm faith in fundamental human rights." Article 1 lists "encouraging respect for human rights and for fundamental freedoms for all" as one of the organization's principal purposes. And the United Nations moved quickly to elaborate international human rights standards.

On December 9, 1948, the Convention on the Prevention and Punishment of the Crime of Genocide was opened for signature (see Box 1.1).

On the following day, the UN General Assembly (GA) unanimously adopted the **Universal Declaration of Human Rights**,[2] which even today provides the most authoritative statement of international human rights norms. This vital document is reprinted as the Appendix, and its main provisions are summarized in Table 1.1.

TABLE 1.1   Internationally Recognized Human Rights

The International Bill of Human Rights recognizes the rights to:
  Equality of rights without discrimination (D1, D2, E2, E3, C2, C3)
  Life (D3, C6)
  Liberty and security of person (D3, C9)
  Protection against slavery (D4, C8)
  Protection against torture and cruel and inhuman punishment (D5, C7)
  Recognition as a person before the law (D6, C16)
  Equal protection of the law (D7, C14, C26)
  Access to legal remedies for rights violations (D8, C2)
  Protection against arbitrary arrest or detention (D9, C9)
  Hearing before an independent and impartial judiciary (D10, C14)
  Presumption of innocence (D11, C14)
  Protection against ex post facto laws (D11, C15)
  Protection of privacy, family, and home (D12, C17)
  Freedom of movement and residence (D13, C12)
  Seek asylum from persecution (D14)
  Nationality (D15)
  Marry and found a family (D16, E10, C23)
  Own property (D17)
  Freedom of thought, conscience, and religion (D18, C18)
  Freedom of opinion, expression, and the press (D19, C19)
  Freedom of assembly and association (D20, C21, C22)
  Political participation (D21, C25)
  Social security (D22, E9)
  Work, under favorable conditions (D23, E6, E7)
  Free trade unions (D23, E8, C22)
  Rest and leisure (D24, E7)
  Food, clothing, and housing (D25, E11)
  Health care and social services (D25, E12)
  Special protections for children (D25, E10, C24)
  Education (D26, E13, E14)
  Participation in cultural life (D27, E15)
  A social and international order needed to realize rights (D28)
  Self-determination (E1, C1)
  Humane treatment when detained or imprisoned (C10)
  Protection against debtor's prison (C11)
  Protection against arbitrary expulsion of aliens (C13)
  Protection against advocacy of racial or religious hatred (C20)
  Protection of minority culture (C27)

Note: This list includes all rights that are enumerated in two of the three documents of the International Bill of Human Rights or have a full article in one document. The source of each right is indicated in parentheses, by document and article number. D = Universal Declaration of Human Rights. E = International Covenant on Economic, Social, and Cultural Rights. C = International Covenant on Civil and Political Rights.

FROM COLD WAR TO COVENANTS

Following the adoption of the Universal Declaration, human rights continued to be discussed at the United Nations. The momentum of the immediate postwar years, however, was not sustained. The rise of the **cold war,** the ideological and geopolitical struggle between the United States and the Soviet Union, brought this initial progress to a halt.

After the descent of the Iron Curtain in Central and Eastern Europe in 1948 and the final Communist victory in China in 1949, human rights increasingly became just another arena of superpower struggle. For example, in the late 1950s the Commission on Human Rights, under Western (U.S.) control, extensively discussed freedom of information (a right that the Soviets systematically violated) but ignored all economic and social rights, as well as most other particular civil and political rights. Conversely, the Soviets tried to focus attention on racial discrimination and unemployment in the capitalist West. Although each side pointed to real abuses, charges of human rights violations were largely tactical maneuvers in a broader political and ideological struggle.

Furthermore, both superpowers regularly revealed a flagrant disregard for human rights. For example, in Guatemala in 1954 the United States overthrew the freely elected government of Jacobo Arbenz Guzmán, in part because of its redistributive policies that aimed to better implement economic and social rights. This ushered in thirty years of military rule that culminated in the systematic massacre of tens of thousands of Guatemalans in the early 1980s. Elsewhere as well, the United States not only tolerated gross and systematic violations of human rights in "friendly" (anticommunist) countries but often warmly embraced the responsible regimes. Likewise, the Soviets forcibly insisted upon one-party totalitarian dictatorships in their sphere of influence. For example, Soviet tanks rolled into Hungary in 1956 to put an end to liberal political reforms and (re)impose totalitarian dictatorship.

The impact of the cold war is also evident in the derailing of work on further elaborations of international human rights standards. Because the Universal Declaration of Human Rights is a resolution of the UN General Assembly, not a treaty, it is not per se legally binding (see Box 1.2).

Its drafters intended to follow the declaration with a covenant (treaty) that would give human rights binding force in international law. Although largely complete by 1953, the covenant was tabled for more than a decade, in large measure because of ideological rivalry over the status of economic and social rights.

Progress again began to be made in the early 1960s, in part as a result of the one line of effective UN human rights activity in the 1950s, namely, decolonization. In 1945, when the United Nations was founded, most of

---

BOX 1.2   Sources of International Law

The two main sources of international law are treaties and custom. Other sources—for example, the writings of publicists, general principles of law recognized in the domestic law of most states, national and international judicial decisions, or *jus cogens* (overriding international norms, very much like the classical idea of the natural law)—are either of lesser importance or their status is a matter of controversy.

Treaties are essentially contractual agreements of states to accept certain specified obligations. The process by which treaties become binding is briefly discussed in Box 1.1.

Customary rules of international law are well-established state practices to which a sense of obligation has come to be attached. One classic example often used in teaching international law in the United States is the case of *The Scotia*. The U.S. Supreme Court decided in 1871 that it had become a binding customary practice of the international law of the sea that ships show colored running lights in a pattern originally specified by Great Britain, and the court awarded damages on the basis of this unwritten, customary law. In the area of human rights, a U.S. District Court held in the 1980 case of *Filartiga v. Peña-Irala*, brought by the family of a Paraguayan torture victim, that torture was a violation of customary international law.

Some lawyers have argued that the Universal Declaration of Human Rights has, over time, become a part of customary international law, or at least strong evidence of custom. Even if this is true, the universal declaration per se does not establish international legal obligations. That task was reserved by its drafters for a later treaty, which was ultimately adopted by the UN General Assembly in 1966, and entered into force in 1976.

Africa and Asia were under Western colonial rule. The process of decolonization that began in 1947 with the independence of Indonesia and India accelerated dramatically in Africa in the late 1950s and 1960s. UN membership doubled in barely a decade, and by the mid-1960s, Afro-Asian states formed the largest voting bloc in the UN.

These countries, which had suffered under colonial domination, had a special interest in human rights. They found a sympathetic hearing from some Western European and Latin American countries. The UN thus began to reemphasize human rights. In 1965, the International Convention on the Elimination of All Forms of Racial Discrimination was opened for signature and ratification. And in December 1966, the **International Human Rights Covenants** were finally completed. (In deference to the lingering cold war, the single treaty envisioned in 1948 was broken into two, the International Covenant on Economic, Social, and Cultural Rights and the International Covenant on Civil and Political Rights.)

The Covenants, together with the Universal Declaration, represent an authoritative statement of international human rights norms, standards of behavior to which all states should aspire. These three documents, which are referred to collectively as the **International Bill of Human Rights,** present a summary statement of the minimum social and political guarantees recognized by the international community as necessary for a life of dignity in the contemporary world. They are summarized in Table 1.1.

The very comprehensiveness of the Covenants, however, meant that further major progress in international action on behalf of human rights would lie primarily in implementing (or monitoring the implementation of) these standards—an area in which the United Nations had been, and still is, far less successful.

THE 1970S:
FROM STANDARD SETTING TO MONITORING

The existence of international norms does not in itself give the United Nations the authority to inquire into how states implement (or do not implement) them. Through the Universal Declaration and the Covenants, states have agreed to follow international human rights standards. But they did not authorize the UN to investigate their compliance with these standards.

This began to change in the late 1960s. In 1967, Economic and Social Council Resolution 1235 authorized the Commission on Human Rights to discuss human rights violations in particular countries. In 1968, a Special Committee of Investigation was created to consider human rights in the territories occupied by Israel after the 1967 war. In the same year, the UN Security Council imposed a mandatory blockade on the white minority regime in Southern Rhodesia. The 1965 racial discrimination convention, which requires parties to file periodic reports on implementation, came into force in 1969. And in 1970, Economic and Social Council Resolution 1503 authorized the Commission on Human Rights to conduct confidential investigations of complaints that suggested "a consistent pattern of gross and reliably attested violations of human rights and fundamental freedoms."

Each of these efforts was limited or partial. The procedures authorized by Resolution 1503 have had little demonstrable, concrete impact. The implementation provisions of the racial discrimination convention are extremely weak (see Chapter 4). The initiatives in Southern Africa and the Occupied Territories reflected the special political concerns of the newly dominant Afro-Asian bloc. Optimists could argue that these developments provided precedents for stronger action. Their significance, though, was largely symbolic: the UN was at last beginning to move, however tentatively, from merely setting standards to examining how those standards were implemented by states.

The severe structural constraints on the UN need to be emphasized. The United Nations is an intergovernmental organization, established by a treaty (the UN Charter) among sovereign states. Its members are sovereign states. Delegates to the United Nations represent states, not the international community, let alone individuals whose rights are violated. Like other intergovernmental organizations, the UN has only those powers that states—which are also the principal violators of human rights—give it. Thus, perhaps more surprising than the limits on its human rights monitoring powers is the fact that the UN actually acquired even these limited powers. Although of little comfort to victims, a balanced assessment of the human rights achievements of the UN and other intergovernmental organizations cannot ignore the central fact of state sovereignty and the restrictions it imposes.

Modest monitoring progress continued in the 1970s. In response to the 1973 military coup in Chile (see Chapter 3), the UN created an Ad Hoc Working Group on the Situation of Human Rights in Chile. In 1976, the International Human Rights Covenants entered into force; that is, following the ratification of thirty-five states, the Covenants became binding legal obligations for those states. This led to the creation of the Human Rights Committee (HRC), charged with monitoring implementation of the International Covenant on Civil and Political Rights (see Chapter 4).

The 1970s also saw human rights explicitly introduced into the bilateral foreign policies of individual countries, beginning in the United States. In 1973, Congress recommended linking U.S. foreign aid to the human rights practices of recipient countries. In 1975, this linkage was made mandatory: U.S. foreign aid policy was required to take into account (although not necessarily be determined by) the human rights practices of recipient countries. Such legislation was both nationally and internationally unprecedented. When Jimmy Carter became president in 1977, the executive branch also became generally supportive of pursuing human rights in foreign policy. Although practice still regularly fell short of rhetoric, these American initiatives helped to open space for new ways of thinking about and acting on international human rights concerns (see Chapter 5).

The 1970s also saw substantial growth in the number and activities of human rights **nongovernmental organizations (NGOs),** private associations that engage in political activity. Such groups act as advocates for victims of human rights violations by publicizing violations and lobbying to alter the practices of states and international organizations.

Best known is Amnesty International (AI), which was founded in 1961, received the Nobel Peace Prize in 1977, and has an international membership of more than 1 million people. AI's best-known activity is letter writing on behalf of individual prisoners of conscience, incarcerated for their beliefs or nonviolent political activities. In its first thirty years, it investigated the cases of over forty-two thousand individual prisoners. Amnesty International also publishes an annual report, special reports on individual countries, and occasional reports on torture and other general issues of concern. In addition, its representatives testify before national legislatures and intergovernmental organizations and publicize human rights issues through public statements and appearances in the media.

The private status of NGOs allows them to operate free of the political control of states. And unlike even states with active international human rights policies, human rights NGOs do not have to take into account other foreign policy objectives. Therefore, they are often better able to press human rights concerns.

NGOs, however, must rely on the power of publicity and persuasion. They lack the resources of even weak states. States remain free to be unpersuaded. And many states have used their powers of coercion against the members of human rights NGOs, turning them into new victims.

Nonetheless, human rights NGOs have played an important role in legitimating international concern with human rights. NGO lobbying helped to assure that human rights language was included in the United Nations Charter. Since then, NGOs have become regular, active, and occasionally influential participants in the human rights work of the UN. For example, national and international campaigns by Amnesty International played an important role in UN initiatives on torture in the 1970s and 1980s.

NGOs have also helped to incorporate concern for human rights into the foreign policies of individual states. For instance, Amnesty's Dutch section contributed to the drafting of the 1979 White Paper that made human rights a formal part of the foreign policy of the Netherlands. In the United States, AI has been especially active on Capitol Hill, lobbying, testifying, and providing information and support to sympathetic members of Congress and their staffs. In Australia, there is even an Amnesty International group in the Parliament. And national human rights NGOs, such as the American Civil Liberties Union in the United States, have been involved in the domestic politics of numerous states.

THE 1980S:
FURTHER GROWTH AND INSTITUTIONALIZATION

Multilateral, bilateral, and nongovernmental human rights activity continued to increase, more or less steadily, through the 1980s. Norms continued to be developed. In December 1979, the Convention on the Elimination of Discrimination Against Women was opened for signature and ratification. This wide-ranging treaty, addressing systematic discrimination against one-half the population of the globe, in every country of the world, was the first major human rights treaty to emerge from the UN since the Covenants in 1966. Drafting of the Convention Against Torture and Other Cruel, Inhuman, or Degrading Treatment or Punishment was completed in 1984. The General Assembly adopted a Declaration on the Right to Development in 1986. The decade came to a close with the Convention on the Rights of the Child in November 1989.

In the area of monitoring, the Human Rights Committee began to review periodic reports submitted under the International Covenant on Civil and Political Rights. The Committee on Economic, Social, and Cultural Rights was created in 1986 to improve reporting and monitoring in this important area. The Commission on Human Rights undertook "thematic" initiatives on disappearances, torture, and summary or arbitrary executions. Furthermore, a larger and more diverse group of countries came under commission scrutiny.

The process of incorporating human rights into bilateral foreign policy also accelerated in the 1980s. For example, the Netherlands and Norway have had particularly prominent international human rights policies (see Chapter 5). Both the Council of Europe and the European Community (EC) introduced human rights concerns into their external relations (see Chapter 5). A few Third World countries, such as Costa Rica, have also emphasized human rights in their foreign policies.

Perhaps more surprising was the persistence of the issue of human rights in U.S. foreign policy. Ronald Reagan campaigned for the presidency in 1980 against Carter's human rights policy. His revival of the cold war against the Soviet "evil empire" led many people to fear (or hope) that human rights would again be forced to the sidelines. And U.S. international human rights policy did become less evenhanded and more controversial in the 1980s. Nonetheless, when George Bush took office in 1989, human rights had a secure (although hardly uncontroversial) and well-institutionalized place in U.S. foreign policy. The Bureau of Human Rights and Humanitarian Affairs was increasingly seen as an integral part of the State Department rather than as an unwanted intrusion. Regular, continuing action on behalf of international human rights had bipartisan support in Congress.

The 1980s also saw a dramatic decline in the fortunes of repressive dictatorships. Throughout Latin America, military regimes that had appeared unshakable in the 1970s crumbled in the 1980s. By 1990, elected governments held office in every continental country in the Western Hemisphere (although the democratic credentials of some, such as Paraguay, remained extremely suspect). In addition, there were peaceful transfers of power after elections in several countries in 1989, including Argentina, Brazil, El Salvador, and Uruguay.

In Asia, the personalist dictatorship of Ferdinand Marcos was overthrown in the Philippines in 1986. South Korea's military dictatorship was replaced by an elected government in 1988. Taiwan ended four decades of imposed single-party rule. In Pakistan, Benazir Bhutto was elected president in December 1988, ending a dozen years of military rule. Asia, however, also presented the most dramatic human rights setback of the decade—the June 1989 massacre in Beijing's Tiananmen Square (see Chapter 6).

The changes with the greatest international impact, however, occurred in Central and Eastern Europe. Soviet-imposed regimes in East Germany and Czechoslovakia crumbled in fall 1989 in the face of peaceful mass protests. In Hungary and Poland, where liberalization had begun earlier in the decade, Communist Party dictatorships also peacefully withdrew from power. Even Romania and Bulgaria ousted their old Communist governments (although their new governments include numerous former Communists with tenuous democratic credentials). In the USSR, where glasnost (openness) and perestroika (restructuring) had created the international political space for these changes, the Communist Party fell from power after the abortive military coup of August 1991, and the Soviet Union was dissolved four months later.

THE 1990S:
CONTINUITY AND CHANGE IN THE POST–COLD WAR ERA

With the collapse of the Soviet empire, the cold war international order crumbled. Although this has certainly altered the context for international human rights, the "new world order" proclaimed by President George Bush has proved not entirely new and often rather disorderly. A region-by-region review shows mostly gradual, but generally positive, change.

In Latin America and Central and Eastern Europe, the progress of the 1980s has largely been maintained. In many cases, such as El Salvador and Hungary, liberalization has substantially deepened. In a few countries, such as the Czech Republic and perhaps Argentina, something close to full democratization seems to have been achieved. In most of the former Soviet republics, however, the commitment to and understanding of both democracy and human rights of the countries' elected leaders (and most of their opponents) is hardly inspiring. In several Latin American countries as well, such as Guatemala and Paraguay and to a lesser extent Mexico and El Salvador, elected governments provide a sort of liberalized, semiauthoritarian rule.

In Sub-Saharan Africa, where one-party and no-party states remained the norm throughout the 1980s, political liberalization has been widespread. Although progress has been less consistent (and usually less deep) than in much of Latin America, relatively open multiparty elections are becoming common. In March 1991, Benin's Nicephore Soglo became the first candidate in the history of mainland Africa to defeat an incumbent president in a democratic election. Even more dramatic was the November 1991 defeat of Kenneth Kaunda, Zambia's president for the first twenty-five years of its independence. And the end of apartheid in South Africa was a dramatic change indeed.

But Nigeria, Africa's most populous country, remains under military rule. Zaire has just emerged from four decades of suffering under the personalist dictatorship of Mobutu Sese Seko. In Mauritania, policies of forced relocation and state-sponsored ethnic violence and repression continue, as does genocide in Rwanda and Burundi and a brutal civil war in Liberia. Furthermore, most African countries still systematically infringe on a number of internationally recognized civil and political rights, and most are experiencing a second decade of stagnation or decline in the enjoyment of economic, social, and cultural rights.

In Asia, the picture remains mixed but improved. South Korea and Taiwan have made significant progress toward establishing democratic, rights-protective regimes. Cambodia, with a substantial assist from the United Nations, has cast off Vietnamese occupation and freely elected a government that, although politically precarious, is by far the most liberal it has seen in decades. Tentative and partial but real liberalization has occurred in Vietnam. And India, for all its problems, remains the world's largest multiparty electoral democracy.

China, however, despite its substantial economic opening and reform, remains a highly repressive, Stalinist party state. Burma continues to push aside its internal democracy movement and international pressures for liberalization. Pakistan and, even more so, Afghanistan are racked by ethnic and religious violence. North Korea continues to be arguably the world's most closed and politically backward state. And some, especially in Singapore, Malaysia, China, and Indonesia, have begun to argue that international human rights standards do not apply in their entirety in Asia.

The mixed pictures in Africa and Asia are, sadly, far more encouraging than those in the Middle East. Hafiz al-Assad's brutal dictatorial rule continues in Syria, as does Saddam Hussein's in Iraq. Libya remains subject to Muammar Qadaffi's personalist dictatorship. Religious intolerance and the suppression of all dissent remain the norm in Iran. The Gulf States remain as closed and undemocratic as ever. Increasingly violent Islamic fundamentalist movements have led to growing repression in Egypt and military dictatorship and shockingly brutal civil war in Algeria. In Yemen, earlier progress has largely been reversed. The new Palestinian entity, run by Yasir Arafat's Palestine Liberation Organization (PLO), has shown little more concern for human rights than the former Israeli occupiers. In Saudi Arabia, very modest reforms to increase input into the decisionmaking process were instituted in 1992, in the aftermath of the Gulf War, but they do not even extend to the toleration of independent human rights NGOs: in April 1993, the founders of the Committee for the Defense of Legitimate Rights were removed from their jobs and jailed. Modest liberalization in the monarchies of Jordan and Morocco, including unusually free elections in 1993, are about the only examples of substantial progress in the region.

A similar pattern of solidifying past gains coupled with modest progress in selected areas is apparent at the international level. Perhaps most striking was the decisive rebuff of arguments by China and other countries at the World Human Rights Conference in Vienna in 1993 against the full implementation of internationally recognized human rights in the short and medium term. And the very decision to hold the World Conference indicates the growing force of the idea of international human rights. Such events, particularly when coupled with the changes in national practices already noted, signify a deepening penetration of the international consensus on human rights norms, which was often shallow in the 1970s and 1980s.

This deepening penetration of international norms can be seen in the United States as well. Although probably the most vocal proponent of international human rights in the 1970s and 1980s, the United States steadfastly refused to be bound by international human rights treaties in its own practice. In 1992, however, the Senate finally ratified the International Covenant on Civil and Political Rights (but not the International Covenant on Economic, Social, and Cultural Rights). And in 1994, the United States also become a party to the conventions on torture and women's rights.

Multilateral institutions continue to function at least as well as they did in the past. At the United Nations, there has even been a noticeable decline in political partisanship. And the creation, at the end of 1993, of a high commissioner for human rights has the potential to increase both the scope and depth of multilateral monitoring (although the high commissioner's activities to date have been modest).

In bilateral relations, human rights continue to become a more deeply entrenched and less controversial foreign policy concern. In contrast to the 1970s and early 1980s, when debate often focused on whether human rights should be an active foreign policy concern, today the question is usually which rights to emphasize in which particular cases. Furthermore, nongovernmental human rights organizations and advocates have become a significant part of the political landscape in a growing number of countries in the Third World and former Soviet bloc.

International human rights today are not only more frequently discussed in a wider range of countries, but they are treated as an ordinary part of international relations. States that are targets of international human rights pressure continue to appeal to sovereignty. But almost all other states have rebuffed claims, made perhaps most strenuously by China, that human rights practices are not a legitimate concern of foreign states and international organizations.

More dramatic changes in the international politics of human rights have come in response to a series of post–cold war political and humanitarian crises. After repelling the Iraqi invasion of Kuwait, the United Nations set up security zones in northern Iraq to protect Iraqi Kurds against their own government. In the face of the complete breakdown of centralized political authority in Somalia, the United Nations launched a massive, militarized humanitarian relief mission that saved hundreds of thousands of Somalis from starvation and civil war. The United States, the Organization of American States (OAS), and the United Nations mobilized substantial political pressure, instituted economic sanctions, and successfully threatened armed force to remove military rule in Haiti.

Perhaps the most dramatic progress has been in international responses to genocide. During the cold war era, genocide and politicide, in places such as Burundi, East Pakistan (Bangladesh), Cambodia, and Uganda, was met by verbal expressions of concern but little concrete action (except by neighboring states—India, Vietnam, and Tanzania—with a strong selfish interest in intervening). But the international tribunals for the former Yugoslavia and Rwanda, created in 1991 and 1994, have revived the Nuremberg precedent. And the General Assembly's decision at the end of 1995 to create an international criminal tribunal suggests a deeper normative transformation.

Of no less importance has been the post–cold war penetration of human rights into other areas of international concern, most notably multilateral peacekeeping. Until the late 1980s, peacekeeping operations were scrupulously organized and operated to avoid direct reference to human rights. This reflected the politicized nature of UN human rights discussions and the desire of most states to avoid creating precedents for UN field action on behalf of human rights. In recent years, however, the link between human rights and international peace and security, which has been a central part of United Nations rhetoric since the drafting of the Charter, has finally become part of UN practice.

UN peacekeeping operations in Namibia, El Salvador, Cambodia, Somalia, Northern Iraq, Mozambique, Bosnia, Croatia, and Guatemala have had explicit human rights responsibilities, and the operations in Haiti and Rwanda had primarily human rights mandates. The tasks of these peacekeeping forces have included monitoring the activities of the police and security forces, verifying the discharge of human rights undertakings in agreements ending civil wars, supervising elections, encouraging authorities to adopt and comply with international human rights treaties, and providing human rights education. In El Salvador, Haiti, Guatemala, and Rwanda, peacekeepers have even had explicit mandates to investigate human rights violations.

Bosnia (see Chapter 7) and Rwanda are the two clearest cases of the convergence of human rights, humanitarian, and peacekeeping concerns and activities. The UN sent peacekeepers to Rwanda in fall 1993 and again in June 1994 (two months after the death of President Habyarimana touched off the resumption of the civil war that led to the massacre of over half a million civilians and forced 2 to 3 million people to flee their homes). Both were tragically belated efforts, and the first mission in particular was denied the resources necessary to succeed as the crisis worsened. Nonetheless, these were operations that would have been inconceivable during the cold war. And in Bosnia, although international interventions have been criticized as too little, too late, the humanitarian efforts on behalf of Sarajevo and other protected enclaves were substantial and sustained, despite the costs and dangers. Furthermore, extensive UN, U.S., and European diplomatic and political efforts produced the Dayton Agreements of November 1995, which have stopped the fighting and established a (precarious) political foundation for the country.

Such events—especially in the context of the already noted continuing national political progress, international normative deepening, and the maturing of human rights as an international issue—have been taken by many to suggest a qualitative transformation of the international politics of human rights in the 1990s. These arguments will be examined in Chapters 6–8. But whatever we conclude about the character of changes in the post–cold war politics of human rights, not only do human rights have a firm place in international relations, in sharp contrast to just a half century ago, but their place is more prominent than at any other time in modern history.

TWO

□ □ □

Theories of Human Rights

The preceding chapter reviewed major developments in the international politics of human rights over the past fifty years. This chapter examines three sets of theoretical issues:

1. philosophical theories of human rights,
2. the place of human rights in international society, and
3. political realism and cultural relativism, which challenge the very idea of international human rights policies.

THE NATURE OF HUMAN RIGHTS

The term **human rights** indicates both their nature and their source: they are the rights that one has simply because one is human. They are held by all human beings, irrespective of any rights or duties individuals may (or may not) have as citizens, members of families, workers, or parts of any public or private organization or association. They are universal rights.

If all human beings have them simply because they are human, human rights are held equally by all.[1] And because being human cannot be renounced, lost, or forfeited, human rights are inalienable. Even the cruelest torturer and the most debased victim are still human beings. In practice, not all people *enjoy* all their human rights, let alone enjoy them equally. Nonetheless, all human beings *have* the same human rights and hold them equally and inalienably.

What exactly does it mean to have a right? In English, "right" has two principal moral and political senses.

"Right" may refer to what *is* right, the right thing to do. For example, we say that it is right to help the needy and wrong (the opposite of right)

18

to lie, cheat, or steal. The focus here is on the righteousness of the required action and on the duty-bearer's obligation to do "what is right."

"Right" may also refer to a special entitlement that one has to something. In this narrower sense, we speak of having, claiming, exercising, enforcing, and violating rights.[2] The focus is on the relationship between right-holder and duty-bearer. Many things to which people do not *have* a (human) right would nevertheless *be* right for every human being to have or enjoy: for example, to be treated with consideration and respect by strangers or to have a loving and supportive family.

Both rights, in the sense of entitlement, and considerations of righteousness create relations between those who have a duty and those who are owed or benefit from that duty. Rights, however, involve a special set of social institutions, rules, or practices. Rights place right-holders and duty-bearers in a relationship that is largely under the control of the right-holders, who may ordinarily exercise their rights as they see fit. Furthermore, claims of rights ordinarily take priority over ("trump") other kinds of demands, including righteousness.

If Anne has a right to x with respect to Bob, it is not simply desirable, good, or even merely right that Anne enjoy x. She is *entitled* to it. Should Bob fail to discharge his obligations, besides acting improperly and harming Anne, he violates her rights. This makes him subject to remedial claims and sanctions that she largely controls.

Anne does not merely benefit from Bob's obligation. She may assert her right to x. If he still does not discharge his duty, she may press further claims against Bob (or excuse him), largely at her discretion. She is in charge of the relationship, as suggested by the language of "exercising" rights. Rights empower, in addition to benefiting, their holders.

Although rights do not have absolute priority, they do typically have prima facie priority over competing claims. Likewise, although there are limits, discretionary exercise is a central and distinguishing feature of rights. The power and control of rights in ordinary circumstances are precisely what make them so valuable to right-holders.

Human rights are a special type of right. Most fundamentally, they are paramount moral rights. In the preceding chapter, we saw that human rights are recognized in international law. Most countries also recognize many of these rights in their legal systems. As a result, the same "thing"—for example, food or protection against discrimination—is often guaranteed by several different types of rights.

One "needs" *human* rights principally when they are not effectively guaranteed by national law and practice. If one can secure food or equal treatment through national legal processes, one is unlikely to advance human rights claims. One still has those human rights, but they are not likely to be used (as human rights). For example, in the United States racial discrimination is prohibited by constitutional and statutory law. Discrimination on the basis of sexual preference is not prohibited in most jurisdictions. Therefore, gay rights activists frequently claim a human right to nondiscrimination. Racial minorities, by contrast, usually claim legal and constitutional rights—"civil rights."

Human rights is the language of victims and the dispossessed. Human rights claims are used principally to seek to alter legal or political practices. Claims of human rights thus aim to be self-liquidating. To assert one's human rights is to attempt to change political structures and practices so that it will no longer be necessary to claim those rights (as human rights). For example, the struggle against apartheid in South Africa was a struggle to change South African laws and practices so that average South Africans could turn to the legislature, courts, or bureaucracy should they be denied, for example, equal protection of the laws or political participation.

Human rights thus provide a moral standard of national political legitimacy. Chapter 1 suggested that they are also emerging as an international political standard of legitimacy. Only when citizens no longer need to assert their human rights regularly against their government is that government likely to be considered fully legitimate in the contemporary world.

THE SOURCE OR JUSTIFICATION OF HUMAN RIGHTS

How does being human give rise to rights? To answer this question we need a theory of human nature. Although I despair of being able to offer one, I can point out some basic distinctions that provide useful insights.

Theories of human nature deal with how we define, or what it means to be, "human." In a very crude way, we can say that a scientific approach to human nature involves an empirical investigation of the psychobiological makeup of human beings. A moral or philosophical approach focuses on what it means to be a person, a *human* being capable of reflective action and subject to the constraints of morality. Although moral theories may be constrained by science, they address different issues.

Those who seek to ground human rights in science usually speak of basic human needs. But any list of needs that can plausibly claim to be empirically established provides an obviously inadequate list of rights: life, food, protection against cruel or inhuman treatment, and perhaps companionship. The problem may lie in contingent shortcomings of our current scientific procedures or knowledge. I would argue, however, that science is in principle incapable of providing the appropriate kind of theory of human nature. We have human rights not to what we need for health but to what we need for a life of dignity.

An anthropological approach that seeks to ground human rights on cross-cultural consensus faces equally serious problems. History is replete with societies based on hierarchies of birth, gender, wealth, or power. Likewise, many cultures have sanctioned slavery, infanticide, blood feuds, and the execution of dissidents. American history is marked by systematic torture and execution of religious deviants (witches); enslavement of and then legal discrimination against African Americans; barbarous treatment of native peoples; denial of political participation, property rights, and even legal personality to women; and repression of political dissidents (especially communists).

The human nature that is the source of human rights rests on a moral account of human possibility. It indicates what human beings might become, not what they have been historically or "are" in some scientifically determinable sense. Human rights rest on an account of a life of dignity to which human beings are "by nature" suited. If the rights specified by the underlying theory of human nature are implemented and enforced, they should help to bring into being the envisioned type of person, one who is worthy of such a life. The effective implementation of human rights thus resembles a self-fulfilling moral prophecy.

Unfortunately, no philosophical theory of human nature has widespread acceptance. Although consensus is no measure of truth, without consensus any particular theory—and any action based on it—is vulnerable to attack. The problem is even more severe when we recognize that many moral theories, and their underlying theories of human nature, deny human rights.

For example, Marxism explains moral beliefs in terms of class structure and struggle, which are determined by the means and mode of production. Radical behaviorists see human personality as the result of conditioning. In both cases, "human nature" is the result of historical processes that shape human beings into socially prescribed molds, rather than the reflection of an inherent essence or potential. For adherents of either theory, talk of equal and inalienable rights held by all people simply because they are human is pointless. "Simply because they are human" probably makes no sense and certainly has no substantive moral implications.

Utilitarianism, which achieved its classic formulations in the works of Jeremy Bentham and John Stuart Mill in the first half of the nineteenth century, is also at odds with human rights. Utilitarians hold that the moral quality of an act is a function of its good or bad consequences (utility). Good and bad, in turn, are matters of pleasure and pain (which are usually understood in subtle and expansive terms). The principle of utility, or what Bentham called the greatest happiness principle, requires us to act so as to maximize the balance of pleasure over pain. For a utilitarian, statements about human rights are at most a convenient shorthand for noting the tendency of certain acts to produce pleasure or pain. Human rights have no independent moral status or force.

Moral or political theories that emphasize differences between communities are also likely to be incompatible with the idea of human rights.

Classical Greeks considered themselves inherently superior to "barbarians" (non-Greeks), who were not entitled to the same treatment as Greeks. The American notion of manifest destiny or the British colonial ideology of the white man's burden justified barbarous treatment of non-white peoples on the grounds of the superior virtue or moral development of Americans or Englishmen. Nazi Germany provides an even more extreme version of the denial of rights to "inferior races" on grounds of moral and political superiority. More recently, ethnic cleansing in the former Yugoslavia has been based on a claim of unbridgeable qualitative differences between groups. In Israel today, some Zionists and settler communities argue for unbridgeable cultural differences that require rigid physical and political separation and the subordination of Palestinian rights to the apparently "higher" demands of Jewish security.

But there are also a variety of bases for justifying human rights. Human rights have often been held to be given by God. Alan Gewirth has argued that we have human rights to those things that are necessary in order to act as a moral agent.[3] In my own work, I have tried to give an account of human rights as the social and political guarantees necessary to protect individuals from the standard threats to human dignity posed by the modern state and modern markets.[4]

Human rights might also be seen as a political specification of Immanuel Kant's **categorical imperative.** In his *Grounding for the Metaphysics of Morals*, Kant argued that there is one supreme principle of morality, namely, the duty to treat people as ends, never as means only. This duty (or imperative), Kant argued, is categorical, without exception. A list of human rights can be seen as a political specification of what it means to treat all human beings as ends.

We thus have a considerable variety of possible moral justifications, as well as an array of theories that deny or radically devalue human rights. In what follows I will assume that there are human rights, that is, that we have accepted some sort of philosophical defense. This theoretical evasion is justified by the fact that almost all states acknowledge the existence of human rights. In other words, this assumption is relatively unproblematic for our purposes here, namely, studying the international politics of human rights.

LISTS OF HUMAN RIGHTS

Despite the absence of philosophical consensus, there is, as we saw in Chapter 1, an international *political* consensus on the list of rights in the Universal Declaration of Human Rights and the International Human Rights Covenants (see Table 1.1 and the Appendix). This consensus draws theoretical support from the fact that it can be derived from a plausible and attractive philosophical account, namely, the requirement that the state treat each person with equal concern and respect.[5] Consider the Universal Declaration of Human Rights.

One must be recognized as a person (Universal Declaration, Article 6) in order to be treated with any sort of concern or respect. Personal rights to nationality and to recognition before the law, along with rights to life and to protection against slavery, torture, and other inhuman or degrading practices, can be seen as legal and political prerequisites to recognition and thus respect (Articles 3–5, 15). Rights to equal protection of the laws and protection against racial, sexual, and other forms of discrimination are essential to *equal* respect (Articles 1, 2, 7).

Equal respect for all persons will be at most a hollow formality without the freedom to choose and act on one's own ideas of the good life. Freedoms of speech, conscience, religion, and association, along with the right to privacy, guarantee a private sphere of personal autonomy (Articles 12, 18–20). The rights to education and to participate in the cultural life of the community provide a social dimension to personal autonomy (Articles 26, 27). The rights to vote and to freedom of speech, press, assembly, and association guarantee political autonomy (Articles 18–21).

Rights to food, health care, and social insurance (Article 25) make equal concern and respect a practical reality rather than a mere formal possibility. The right to work is a right to economic participation very similar to the right to political participation (Article 23). A (limited) right to property may be justified in such terms (Article 17).

Finally, the special threat to personal security and equality posed by the modern state requires legal rights to constrain the state and its functionaries. These include rights to be presumed innocent until proven guilty, due process, fair and public hearings before an independent tribunal, and protection from arbitrary arrest, detention, or exile (Articles 8–11). Anything less would allow the state to treat citizens with differential concern or respect.

The idea of equal concern and respect certainly is philosophically controversial. It does, however, have a certain inherent plausibility. It is closely related to the basic fact that human rights are equal and inalienable. It even offers an attractive interpretation of the claim in the International Human Rights Covenants that the rights recognized "derive from the inherent dignity of the human person."

There are also powerful practical reasons for adopting the list of human rights in the Universal Declaration and the Covenants. To act internationally on the basis of a different list would risk the charge of imposing one's own biased preferences instead of widely accepted international standards.

Although almost all states have explicitly endorsed the list provided by the Universal Declaration—whatever their actual practices may be—there have been three principal exceptions in recent years.[6] First, some fundamentalist Muslim states, supported by the Vatican and its allies at recent women's conferences, have denounced the principle of prohibiting legal and political distinctions on the basis of sex. Such arguments will be briefly addressed later in this chapter. Second, some Asian commentators have argued that international human rights norms are in important ways incompatible with Asian values, which ought to receive priority. These arguments will be considered at the end of Chapter 6. Finally, many American and British conservatives have argued that economic, social, and cultural rights are not really *human* rights.

Such critics argue that **economic, social, and cultural rights,** entitlements to socially provided goods, services, and opportunities such as food, health care, social insurance, and education, are less important than **civil and political rights,** such as due process, freedom of speech, and the right to vote. The right to paid holidays (Universal Declaration, Article 24) is an often-cited example.

But the full right recognized in the Universal Declaration—the right to "rest, leisure, and reasonable limitation of working hours and periodic holidays with pay"—is very important. Consider the horrors of sixty-hour workweeks, fifty-two weeks a year, in nineteenth-century factories or twentieth-century sweatshops. In addition, one can point to even more minor civil and political rights. For example, Article 10 of the International Covenant on Civil and Political Rights proclaims the right of juveniles to separate prison facilities. In every country of the world, far fewer people have suffered from penal confinement as juveniles in the company of adult criminals than from the denial of reasonable rest and leisure. In any case, the right to paid holidays is hardly the typical economic and social right. Consider, for example, the rights to food, housing, health care, work, and social security.

Arguments of practicality, which are often advanced against economic and social rights, are more complex. For example, Maurice Cranston argued that "there is nothing especially difficult about transforming political and civil rights into positive rights" but that in most countries it is "utterly impossible" to realize most economic and social rights.[7] In fact, though, the victims of repression in countries such as Nazi Germany, the Soviet Union, apartheid-era South Africa, and contemporary China and North Korea have found it extremely difficult to transform internationally recognized civil and political rights into effective rights in national law.

Conversely, many of the impediments to implementing economic and social rights are political. For example, there is already enough food in the world to feed every person. Universal implementation of the right to food would "only" require redistributing existing supplies. Of course, health care and social services at the level provided in much of Western Europe cannot be universally implemented. That level has yet to be reached even by the United States. Nonetheless, almost all countries can make major improvements, at relatively modest cost, in realizing most economic and social rights.

It is also often argued that there is a qualitative difference between "negative" civil and political rights and "positive" economic and social rights. Negative rights require only the forbearance of others to be realized. Violating a negative right thus involves actively causing harm, a sin of commission. Positive rights require that others provide active support. Violating a positive right involves only failing to provide assistance, a (presumably lesser) sin of omission.

All human rights, however, require both positive action and restraint by the state if they are to be effectively implemented. Some rights, of course, are relatively positive. Others are relatively negative. But this distinction does not correspond to the division between civil and political rights and economic and social rights.

The right to vote requires extensive positive endeavors, not forbearance, on the part of the government. So do the rights to due process, trial by a jury of one's peers, and access to legal remedies for violations of basic rights. Even the right to nondiscrimination may require—beyond refraining from discriminating—extensive, difficult, and costly state intervention (e.g., affirmative action) if individuals are to be effectively protected against discrimination. "Simply" refraining usually means assuring that certain things are not done, which can require considerable work over an extended period of time. In fact, were it easy to abstain, the right in question probably would not be very important (in that context).

The (social) right to marry and found a family is no less negative than the right to freedom of religion. The rights to participate in the cultural life of the community and to share in the benefits of science and technology are as negative (or positive) as the right to nondiscrimination. In many countries, the right to food would be more widely realized if governments would simply refrain from encouraging the production of cash crops such as coffee, cocoa, and fruits for export.

The moral basis of the positive-negative distinction is also questionable. Does it really make a moral difference if one kills someone through neglect or by positive action? What if the neglect is knowing and willful? Consider, for example, leaving an injured man to die; refusing to implement relatively inexpensive health care or nutrition programs for needy and malnourished children; or the fact that a black infant in the United States is twice as likely to die as a white infant.

Another way to approach the question of the status of economic, social, and cultural rights is to ask what a life with only civil and political rights would look like. Without minimum economic and social guarantees, a life of dignity is clearly impossible, especially in modern market economies. Even the Reagan administration stressed the importance of a "safety net" of economic and social rights for the "deserving poor."

Finally, we should note that most critics of economic and social rights destroy their own arguments by defending a right to property. This is an *economic* right, not a civil and political right—and a rather extravagant economic right at that. Furthermore, standard defenses of a right to property support other economic and social rights. For example, the right to work no less than the right to property allows economic participation in society and provides personal economic security.

There are, of course, differences between economic and social rights and civil and political rights. But there are no less important differences within each broad class of rights, as well as important similarities across these classes. For example, the (civil and political) right to life and the (economic and social) right to food can be seen as different means to protect the same value. Categorical distinctions, let alone blanket denials, simply do not withstand scrutiny.

HUMAN RIGHTS AND THE SOCIETY OF STATES

Having surmounted, or at least disposed of, some of the more pressing philosophical questions, we can now turn to the place of human rights in the theory of international relations.

Sovereignty, Anarchy, and International Society

The modern international system is often dated, somewhat arbitrarily, to 1648, when the Treaty of Westphalia ended the Thirty Years' War. As we saw in Chapter 1, however, human rights have been an issue in international relations for barely fifty years. The absence of human rights from modern international relations for its first three centuries was the direct result of an international order based on sovereign territorial states.

To be sovereign is to be subject to no higher power. In early modern Europe, sovereignty was a personal attribute of rulers. For example, Thomas Hobbes wrote of "princes and other persons of sovereign authority." In many other times and places, as in medieval Europe, no (earthly) power was considered to be sovereign. In contemporary international relations, sovereignty is seen as an attribute of territorial states.[8]

International relations are structured around the legal fiction that states have exclusive jurisdiction over their territory, its occupants and resources, and the events that take place there. Practice typically falls far short of pre-cept, as usually is the case with political principles. Nonetheless, the basic norms, rules, and practices of contemporary international relations rest on state sovereignty and the formal equality of (sovereign) states.

Nonintervention is the duty correlative to the right of sovereignty. Other states are obliged not to interfere with the internal actions of a sov-ereign state. Because human rights principally regulate the ways states treat their own citizens within their own territory, international human rights policies would seem to involve unjustifiable intervention.

A principal function of international law, however, is to overcome the initial presumption of sovereignty. A **treaty** is a contract between states to accept mutual obligations, that is, restrictions on their sovereignty. For ex-ample, a treaty of alliance may oblige a state to aid an ally that is attacked. Such a state is no longer (legally) free to choose whether or not to go to war. Through the treaty, it has voluntarily relinquished some freedom of action. International law, including international human rights law, is the record of restrictions on sovereignty accepted by states.

The choice of sovereignty as an ordering principle is conditioned by the fact that the realm of international relations is anarchic, a political arena without formal hierarchical relations of authority and subordination. But **anarchy,** the absence of hierarchical political rule, does not necessarily im-ply chaos, the absence of order. In addition to international law, states reg-ulate their interaction through institutionalized practices such as diplo-macy, balance of power, and recognition of spheres of influence. Although there is no international government, there is rule-governed social order. International relations take place within an anarchical society of states.[9]

The international society of states of the eighteenth, nineteenth, and early twentieth centuries gave punctilious respect to the sovereign prerog-ative of each state to treat its own citizens as it saw fit. Today, however, as we saw in Chapter 1, there is a substantial body of international human rights law. States have become increasingly vocal in expressing, and some-times even acting on, their international human rights concerns. In addi-tion, human rights NGOs, which seek to constrain the freedom of action of rights-violating states, have become more numerous and more active.

This reflects (and has helped to create) a transformed understanding of the place of individuals in international relations. States have traditionally been the sole subjects of international law, the only actors with interna-tional legal standing (the right to bring actions in international tribunals). The rights and interests of individuals could traditionally be protected in international law only by states acting on their behalf. Although even the International Bill of Human Rights does not empower individuals to act against states, contemporary international human rights law (see Chapter 4) has given individuals and their rights a place in international relations.

It has also introduced a new conception of international legitimacy. Traditionally, a government was considered legitimate if it exercised authority over its territory and accepted the international legal obligations that it and its predecessors had contracted. What it did at home was largely irrelevant. Today, human rights provide a standard of moral legitimacy that has been (very incompletely) incorporated into the rules of the international society of states.

Consider the almost universal negative reaction to the Tiananmen massacre in 1989, when Chinese troops fired on unarmed student demonstrators and brutally crushed China's emerging democracy movement. China's diplomatic isolation reflected this new, human rights–based understanding of legitimacy. But, as we shall see in considerable detail in Chapter 6, that isolation lasted only a year or two. Even the strongest supporters of sanctions were not willing to allow Chinese brutality to interfere with long-term economic and security interests.

This tension is characteristic of the current state of international human rights. The future of international human rights activity can be seen as a struggle over balancing the competing claims of sovereignty and international human rights and the competing conceptions of legitimacy that they imply.

Three Models of International Human Rights

The universality of human rights fits uncomfortably with a political order structured around sovereign states. Universal moral rights seem better suited to a cosmopolitan conception of world politics, which sees individuals more as members of a global political community ("cosmopolis") than as citizens of states. Instead of thinking of international relations (the relations between nation-states), a cosmopolitan thinks of a global political process in which individuals and other nonstate actors are important direct participants. We thus have three competing theoretical models of the place of human rights in international relations, each with its own conception of the character of the international community.

The traditional **statist** model sees human rights as principally a matter of sovereign national jurisdiction. Statists readily admit that human rights are no longer the exclusive preserve of states and that the state is no longer the sole significant international actor (if it ever was). They nonetheless insist that human rights remain primarily a matter of sovereign national jurisdiction and (ought to continue to be) a largely peripheral concern of international (interstate) relations. For statists, there is no significant, independent international community, and certainly no international body with the right to act on behalf of human rights.

A **cosmopolitan** model starts with individuals rather than states—which are often "the problem" for cosmopolitans. Cosmopolitans see the state challenged both from below, by individuals and NGOs, and from above, by the truly global community (not merely international organizations and other groupings of states). International action on behalf of human rights is relatively unproblematic in such a model. In fact, cosmopolitans largely reverse the burden of proof, requiring justification for *non*intervention in the face of gross and persistent violations of human rights.

The space toward the center of the continuum defined by statism and cosmopolitanism is occupied by what we can call **internationalist** models. "The international community," in an internationalist model, is essentially the society of states (supplemented by NGOs and individuals, to the extent that they have been formally or informally incorporated into international political processes). International human rights activity is permissible only to the extent authorized by the norms of the society of states. These norms, however, may vary considerably across particular international societies. Consider, for example, the difference noted earlier between the late nineteenth and late twentieth centuries. Therefore, we need to distinguish strong and weak internationalism, based on the distance from the statist end of the spectrum.

Each of these three models can be read as making descriptive claims about the place that human rights do have in international relations or as making prescriptive claims about the place they ought to have. For example, a statist might argue (descriptively) that human rights are in fact peripheral in international relations, or (prescriptively) that they ought to be peripheral, or both.

Cosmopolitanism, however, has little descriptive power. States and their interests still dominate world politics. The international political power of individuals, NGOs, and other nonstate actors is real, and appears to be growing, but is still relatively small—and power is a relative notion. The global political community (as opposed to the international society of states) is at best rudimentary. The cosmopolitan model, if more than a prescription about what is desirable, rests on predictions of the direction of change in world politics.

If the world envisioned by cosmopolitans has yet to come into being, that envisioned by statists is in part a thing of the past. Although accurate even into the 1970s, the statist model of international human rights today is at best a crude first approximation. Furthermore, it misleadingly directs attention away from two decades of significant, cumulative change.

Some sort of internationalist model—or a very heavily hedged statism—provides the most accurate description of the place of human rights in contemporary international relations. I began to lay out the evidence for this claim in Chapter 1. Much of Chapters 4–8 in effect show that a relatively weak internationalist model, with modest international societal constraints on state sovereignty, describes the nature of the contemporary international politics of human rights and is likely to continue to do so for at least the next several years.

Current descriptive power, however, is no guarantee of future accuracy. And it does not mean that internationalism is the best, or even a good, way to treat human rights in international relations. Nonetheless, as Chapters 4–8 will show in detail, the international human rights reality that we face today is one of considerable state sovereignty, with modest limits rooted in the international society of states.

REALISM AND HUMAN RIGHTS

Before leaving the discussion of theory, we need to consider two common theoretical challenges to even this limited concern with international human rights, namely, political **realism,** or **realpolitik** (power politics), and cultural relativism.

The theory of realpolitik is an old and well-established theory of international relations, typically traced back to figures such as Niccolo Machiavelli in the early sixteenth century and Thucydides, whose *History* chronicles the great wars between Athens and Sparta in the final decades of the fifth century B.C. Realism stresses "the primacy in all political life of power and security."[10] Because men are egoistic and evil and because international anarchy requires states to rely on their own resources even for defense, realists argue that "universal moral principles cannot be applied to the actions of states."[11] To pursue a moral foreign policy would be not only foolishly unsuccessful but would leave one's country vulnerable to the power of self-interested states.

Realists argue that only considerations of the national interest should guide foreign policy. And the national interest, for the realist, must be defined in terms of power and security. For example, George Kennan, one of the architects of postwar U.S. foreign policy and one of the most respected recent realist writers, argued that a government's "primary obligation is to the *interests* of the national society it represents . . . its military security, the integrity of its political life and the well-being of its people." "The process of government . . . is a practical exercise and not a moral one."[12] As for international human rights policies,

> it is difficult to see any promise in an American policy which sets out to correct and improve the political habits of large parts of the world's population. Misgovernment . . . has been the common condition of most of mankind for centuries and millennia in the past. It is going to remain that condition for long into the future, no matter how valiantly Americans insist on tilting against the windmills.[13]

Such arguments do contain a kernel of truth. The demands of morality often do conflict with the national interest defined in terms of power. But *all* objectives of foreign policy may compete with the national interest thus defined. For example, arms races may contribute to the outbreak of war. Alliances may prove dangerously entangling. For example, the European alliance system of the early twentieth century transformed a regional dispute between Austria-Hungary and Russia into a devastating world war that removed Austria-Hungary from the map. Realists, however, rightly refuse to conclude from this that we should eschew arms or allies. They should also abandon their categorical attacks on morality in foreign policy. A valuable caution against moralistic excess has been wildly exaggerated into a general principle, even a law, of politics.

Realist arguments against morality in foreign policy also appeal to the special office of the statesman. For example, Herbert Butterfield argued that although a man may choose to sacrifice himself in the face of foreign invasion, he does not have a "right to offer the same sacrifice on behalf of all his fellow-citizens or to impose such self-abnegation on the rest of his society."[14] But nonmoral objectives as well may be pursued by statesmen with excessive zeal, and equally deadly consequences. And most moral objectives can be pursued at a cost far less than national survival. This certainly is true of many international human rights goals. For example, the United States could reduce or eliminate aid to most Third World countries on human rights grounds with little or no discernible impact on U.S. national security or major U.S. economic interests.

In addition, there is no reason a country cannot, if it wishes, include human rights or other moral concerns in its definition of the national interest. Security, independence, and prosperity may be unavoidable necessities of national political life. But governments need not limit themselves to these necessities. Even if the primary obligation of governments must be to the national interest defined in terms of power, this need not be their sole, or even ultimate, obligation.

Appeals to the anarchic structure of international relations will not rescue realist amoralism. For example, Robert Art and Kenneth Waltz claimed that "states in anarchy cannot afford to be moral. The possibility of moral behavior rests upon the existence of an effective government that can deter and punish illegal actions."[15] This is obviously false, even if we set aside their confusion of morality and law. Just as individuals may behave morally without government to enforce moral rules, so moral behavior is possible in international relations.

The costs of moral behavior are typically greater in an anarchic system of self-help enforcement. Nonetheless, states can often act on moral concerns with safety, and sometimes even with success. In particular instances there may be good policy reasons to pursue amoral, or even immoral, policies. There are, however, no good general theoretical reasons for amoral policies to be required, or even the norm.

CULTURAL RELATIVISM AND
UNIVERSAL HUMAN RIGHTS

Realist arguments are often reinforced by **relativist** arguments that moral values are historically or culturally specific rather than universal. For example, Kennan argued that "there are no internationally accepted standards of morality to which the U.S. government could appeal if it wished to act in the name of moral principles."[16] Many nonrealists share such relativist skepticism.

It is often claimed that there are a variety of distinctive and defensible conceptions of human rights that merit our respect and toleration even if we disagree with them. One standard form of this argument, which was particularly prominent in the 1980s, was the claim that there are "three worlds" of human rights.[17] The "Western" (First World) approach, it is asserted, emphasizes civil and political rights and the right to private property. The "socialist" (Second World) approach emphasizes economic and social rights. The "Third World" approach emphasizes self-determination and economic development. Furthermore, both the socialist and the Third World conceptions are held to be group oriented, in contrast to the fundamental individualism of the "Western" approach.

The reality of Western practice over the past half century, however, has been quite different. The West may have neglected economic and social rights in the nineteenth and early twentieth centuries.[18] But that anyone looking at the welfare states of Western Europe over the past half century can be expected to take such a description of the Western approach seriously, to put it bluntly, boggles the mind. In fact, the liberal democratic welfare states of Western (and especially northern) Europe are the countries that have taken most seriously the interdependence and indivisibility of all human rights. And it is in these countries that we find the most complete realization of internationally recognized economic, social, and cultural rights.

Conversely, as we saw in 1989, citizens in the former Soviet bloc, when given the opportunity, demanded their civil and political rights. Far from being a superfluous bourgeois luxury, Eastern Europeans no less than Western Europeans see civil and political rights as essential to a life of dignity. And the dismal state of Soviet bloc economies suggests that the sacrifice of civil and political rights probably did not even facilitate the long-term realization of economic and social rights.

The recent wave of liberalizations and democratizations likewise suggests that the so-called Third World conception of human rights has little basis in local values. Ordinary citizens in country after country have found that internationally recognized civil and political rights are essential to protecting themselves against repressive economic and political elites. When given the chance, they have in effect declared that sacrifices made in the name of development, self-determination, or national security were not chosen but were imposed through force and the systematic violation of civil and political rights.

Political histories, cultural legacies, economic conditions, and human rights problems certainly differ in these three "worlds." For that matter, there is considerable diversity even within each "world," especially the Third World. Cultural relativity is a fact. Social institutions and values have varied, and continue to vary, with time and place. Nonetheless, I will argue that contemporary international human rights norms have near universal applicability, requiring only relatively modest adjustments in the name of cultural diversity.

Moral relativism, the belief that moral values (and thus conceptions of human rights) are determined by history, culture, economics, or some other independent social force, is best seen as a matter of degree. At one extreme is a **radical relativism** that sees culture (or history, or economics) as the source of all values.[19] Such a position in effect denies the very idea of human rights, for it holds that there are no rights that everyone is entitled to equally, simply as a human being. Radical relativism can be ignored once we have decided, as we have above, that there *are* human rights, rights that all human beings have, independent of society (and thus irrespective of their particular history or culture).

At the other end of the spectrum lies radical **universalism,** the view that all values, including human rights, are entirely universal, in no way subject to modification in light of cultural or historical differences. In its pure form, radical universalism would hold that there is only one set of human rights that applies at all times and in all places. But to insist that all human rights be implemented in identical ways in all countries would be wildly unrealistic, and most people would find such a demand morally and politically perverse.

Rejecting the two end points of the spectrum leaves us with a considerable variety of "relativist" positions, which can be roughly divided into two ranges. *Strong relativism* holds that human rights (and other values) are principally, but not entirely, determined by culture or other circumstances. "Universal" human rights serve as a check on culturally specific values. The emphasis, however, is on variation and relativity. *Weak relativism* reverses the emphasis. Universal human rights are held to be subject only to secondary cultural modifications. I will defend a form of weak cultural relativism on both descriptive and prescriptive grounds.

Internationally recognized human rights represent a good first approximation of the guarantees necessary for a life of dignity in the contemporary world of modern states and modern markets. In all countries, the unchecked power of the modern state threatens individuals, families, groups, and communities alike. Likewise, national and international markets, whether free or controlled, threaten human dignity in all countries. The Universal Declaration and the Covenants provide a generally sound approach to protecting human dignity against these threats.

For example, it is difficult to imagine defensible arguments in the contemporary world to deny rights to life, liberty, security of the person, or protection against slavery, arbitrary arrest, racial discrimination, and torture. The rights to food, health care, work, and social insurance are equally basic to any plausible conception of equal human dignity.

Universality, however, is only an initial presumption. Deviations from international human rights norms may be justified, even demanded. For example, the free and full consent of spouses in marriage (Universal Declaration, Article 16) reflects a culturally specific conception of marriage that it would be unreasonable to apply everywhere without exception. This does not mean that we should approve of forced marriages. It does, however, suggest that we tolerate some notions of consent that would be unacceptable in the contemporary West.

The possibility of justifiable modifications, however, must not obscure the fundamental universality of international human rights norms. Deviations should be rare. And the need to keep their cumulative impact minor suggests that substantial variations are likely to be legitimate only in relatively specific and detailed matters of implementation.

We can distinguish three levels at which the substance of a human right can be specified. At the top are what we can call "concepts," very general formulations such as the rights to political participation or work. Little cultural variability at this level is justifiable.[20] Below these are what we can call "interpretations." For example, a guaranteed job and unemployment insurance are two interpretations of the right to work. Some interpretative variability seems plausible for most internationally recognized human rights. And at a still more detailed third level, there is room for considerable variation in the particular form in which an interpretation is implemented.

Suppose that we interpret the right to political participation as a right to vote in open and fair elections. Members of the legislature might be chosen through winner-take-all elections in local districts or by a system in which people vote for party lists and seats in the legislature are awarded proportional to the national vote. Such variations of form should usually be considered permissible, as long as they tend to realize a defensible interpretation of the governing concept.

These guidelines will not provide clear answers in all important cases. They do, however, have strong and generally clear implications. In Chapter 6, we will consider in greater detail arguments for a distinctive Asian conception of human rights. To illustrate my argument here, I want to consider the claim of many religious fundamentalists, especially among monotheistic revealed religions of the Near East (Judaism, Christianity, and Islam), that men and women do not have the same rights, that each sex has its own particular, and largely complementary, social and political rights and responsibilities.

The weak relativist position sketched above would reject such an argument. The claim that because of ascriptive characteristics such as age, sex, race, or family one is not entitled to the same basic human rights as members of other groups is incompatible with the very idea of human rights. This does not imply that all differences based on gender are incompatible with human rights. For example, dress codes to protect public morals and decency, such as the Muslim requirement that women wear veils in public or the Western requirement that women (but not men) cover their chests in public, clearly lie within the realm of permissible distinctions. But the claim that one group in society has radically different basic rights from another group—for example, that it can deny the rights to vote, speak, and assemble freely to women, deny women full and equal legal personality, or award otherwise identical men and women different treatment in social insurance schemes—is not a culturally different conception of human rights but a (partial) rejection of the very idea of *human* rights.

Human rights do not require cultural homogenization. If women *choose* to vote as their husbands do or choose a private family life instead of a public life and work outside of the home, human rights require that such choices be respected. But when they are imposed—and especially when those who define and enforce differential rights receive preferred treatment—they involve unacceptable violations of human rights.

Such an argument does not imply wanton cultural imperialism. The legacy of imperialism demands that Westerners in particular show special caution and sensitivity when dealing with clashing cultural values. Caution, however, must not be confused with inaction. Even if we are not entitled to impose our values on others, they are our own values. Sometimes they may demand that we act on them even in the absence of agreement by others. And if the practices of others are particularly objectionable—consider, for example, societies in which it is traditional to kill the first-born child if it is female or the deeply rooted tradition of anti-Semitism in the West—even strongly sanctioned traditions may deserve neither our respect nor our toleration.

THREE

□　□　□

The Domestic Politics of
Human Rights: The Case of
the Southern Cone

Although this book deals primarily with the international politics of human rights, national politics largely determines how human rights are protected or violated in a world of sovereign states. National case studies can both illustrate this important point and provide concreteness to the notion of "human rights violations." This chapter looks in some detail at violations in the Southern Cone of South America. Chapters 4 and 5 will examine more briefly human rights violations in South Africa and Central America, two cold war focal points for international human rights action. Chapters 6 and 7 consider China and the former Yugoslavia, two prominent post–cold war examples.

The geographical area known as the Southern Cone of South America includes the countries of Argentina, Chile, Paraguay, and Uruguay, as well as southern Brazil. In this chapter, we will look at three of these countries, Argentina, Chile, and Uruguay, which for convenience I will refer to as the countries of the Southern Cone. They suffered under a distinctive style of intensely repressive military rule in the 1970s and 1980s and provided an impetus for some important developments in international human rights policies.

POLITICS BEFORE THE COUPS

In Chile, military rule had been rare since the mid-nineteenth century. After World War II, a stable three-party democratic system emerged. And in 1970, Salvador Allende became the world's first freely elected Marxist president. Allende dramatically intensified the economic and social reforms begun under his Christian Democratic predecessor, Eduardo Frei. Large agricultural estates were expropriated. Key private industries and banks were nationalized, including Chile's (largely U.S.-owned) copper industry. Social services were expanded.

These changes were both lavishly praised and reviled, both within Chile and abroad. The resulting ideological polarization helped to set the stage for a military coup in September 1973. Allende was assassinated and a repressive military regime was installed that ruled until 1990.

In Uruguay, the military had not intervened in politics since the 1860s. Furthermore, beginning in the first two decades of the twentieth century, under President José Batlle y Ordoñez, Uruguay implemented a series of model social and political reforms that created a widely admired democratic welfare state that provided education and health care for all. The system, however, began to collapse in the late 1960s.

Political stalemate between its two dominant parties weakened Uruguay's government. The economy faced high inflation and labor unrest. And the Tupamaros were waging a dramatic campaign of guerrilla terrorism. In response, civil liberties were temporarily suspended in 1968, 1970, and 1971 and were even more seriously restricted in 1972. In June 1973, President Bordaberry suspended most remaining constitutional rights, closed the National Assembly, and for three years provided a public face for the military government—until he too was forced from office.

Argentina has a more checkered political history. Following independence in 1821–1822, Argentine politics were noted for violent struggles among provincial bosses (caudillos) and for leadership in the capital, Buenos Aires. Later in the century, however, a less violent political order emerged. Argentina even experienced a period of democratic rule from 1916 until 1930.

After World War II, populist leader Juan Perón ruled Argentina as an elected president for a decade. In 1955, however, he was overthrown in a military coup, and civilian governments were also prevented from completing their terms in office by coups in 1966 and 1973. But the military was not even able to impose its preferred candidates when the country returned to civilian rule. Marcelo Cavarozzi aptly characterized this alternation of ineffective civilian and military regimes as the "failure of 'semidemocracy.'"[1]

In the mid-1970s, an already unstable political situation was made much worse by the incompetence and corruption of the civilian government. Meanwhile, the Argentine state and society were under guerrilla attacks by the Montoneros and the Revolutionary Army of the People (ERP). The political Right, with the support of the military and security forces, responded with assassinations of leftist students, lawyers, journalists, and trade unionists, in addition to guerrillas. In October 1975, five months before the overthrow of the civilian government, Army Commander in Chief Jorge Rafael Videla warned that "as many people will die in Argentina as is necessary to restore order."[2] The following year, Videla, who had become president, delivered on his promise of violence, if not order.

TORTURE AND DISAPPEARANCES

A distinguishing feature of repression in the Southern Cone was the extensive use of **disappearances**, that is, extrajudicial detentions, usually accompanied by torture, often followed by death.[3] The politics of disappearances were most highly developed in Argentina.

> Task forces of the armed services . . . were detailed to arrest suspected subversives without warrant; to avoid identification of the captors; to take the detainees to clandestine detention camps, generally within military or police facilities; and to disclaim any knowledge of the whereabouts of their prisoners. In those camps, prisoners were interrogated under the most severe forms of torture. . . . The camps were deliberately shielded from any judicial or administrative investigation so that the torturers could be free to use any methods, and to deny even the existence of their prisoners, without fear of punishment. . . . The overwhelming majority of those who entered the system of "disappearances" were never seen alive again.[4]

After the return of civilian government, the Argentine National Commission on Disappeared Persons (CONADEP, the Sábato Commission) documented 8,960 disappearances, a figure that probably underestimates the total by one-third or more. The commission identified 340 clandestine detention and torture centers, involving about 700 military officers and organized in 5 zones, 35 subzones, and 210 areas. The kidnappers operated with such impunity that only one disappearance in ten occurred in unknown circumstances. Three-fifths took place in the home of the victim, with witnesses present during the abduction. The mere passing of an unmarked green four-door Ford Falcon, the car of choice of the arresting squads, was enough to spread terror.

The Navy Mechanics School (ESMA) in Buenos Aires was Argentina's most important clandestine detention center. Torture at ESMA became a routinized, bureaucratic activity. A trip to ESMA typically began with "Caroline," a thick broom handle with two long wires running out the end. The victim was stripped and tied to a steel bed frame. "Caroline" was attached to a box on a table that supplied the current. Then the electricity was applied to the victim, who often was periodically doused with water to increase the effects.

It was unhurried and methodical. If the victim was a woman they went for the breasts, vagina, anus. If a man, they favored genitals, tongue, neck. . . . Sometimes victims twitched so uncontrollably that they shattered their own arms and legs. Patrick Rice, an Irish priest who had worked in the slums and was detained for several days, recalls watching his flesh sizzle. What he most remembers is the smell. It was like bacon.[5]

Children were tortured in front of their parents, and parents in front of their children. Some prisoners were kept in rooms no longer or wider than a single bed. And the torture continued for days, weeks, months, even years, until the victim was released or, more often, killed. The sadistic brutality did not always even end with the death of the victim. "One woman was sent the hands of her daughter in a shoe box." The body of another woman "was dumped in her parents' yard, naked but showing no outward signs of torture. Later the director of the funeral home called to inform her parents that the girl's vagina had been sewn up. Inside he had found a rat."[6]

Most bodies, however, were never recovered. At ESMA, which also served as a disposal site for other naval camps, corpses were initially buried under the sports field. When this was filled, the bodies were burned daily, at 5:30 in the afternoon, usually after having been cut up with a chain saw. Finally, those in charge of destroying the evidence of their crimes hit on the idea of aerial disposal at sea. Once they had mastered the currents—at first bodies washed up in Buenos Aires, then in Montevideo—there was no trace to be found. Other units encased their victims in cement and dumped them in the river. The army's preferred method seems to have been to drive the corpses to the cemetery and register them as "NN," Name Unknown.

Repression in Chile was very similar, although the number of deaths was much lower. The Uruguayan style, however, was significantly different. Almost all the disappeared reappeared, usually in prison, after having been severely tortured. Only forty-four Uruguayans who disappeared in Uruguay remained unaccounted for at the end of military rule. The per capita rate of permanent disappearances in Uruguay was only about one-fifth the Chilean rate and one-twentieth that of Argentina. But about sixty thousand people, roughly 2 percent of the population, were detained, giving Uruguay the highest per capita rate of political prisoners and torture victims in all of Latin America. Virtually everyone in the country knew someone who had been detained—an extraordinarily powerful technique of state terror.

Uruguay developed a grotesque division of labor between clandestine detention centers, which specialized in physical abuse, and official prisons, which specialized in psychological abuse. The prison regimen was carefully calculated to dehumanize and break people who had already suffered excruciating physical torture. Prisoners were never referred to by name, always by number or insulting epithet: "cockroach," "rat," "apesto" (diseased one). Peepholes and listening devices were common, and broken prisoners were used as informants. Cell mates were often chosen on the basis of psychological profiles in order to cause one another the most annoyance. Even families were incorporated into the routine of torture. For example, children were sometimes permitted to visit their parents once a month, but only if the parent demonstrated no sign of affection.

Prisoners were allowed outside only one hour a day. When they were in their cells, they were often required to stand except during designated sleeping hours. Every aspect of existence was regulated by ominously arbitrary rules. Violations were typically punished by isolation in a windowless cell with a bare electric light bulb that burned twenty-four hours a day. In the most extreme case, nine top Tupamaro leaders, following months of vicious physical torture, were kept in complete solitary confinement for over a decade. One spent an extended period of his confinement at the bottom of a dry well. Mauricio Rosencof reported: "In over eleven and a half years, I didn't see the sun for more than eight hours altogether. I forgot colors—there were no colors."[7]

THE NATIONAL SECURITY DOCTRINE

Some of the brutality reflected simple sadism.

> At ESMA the complete licence they [the torturers] had to do what they wanted with their prisoners seems to have acted on them like an addiction. Sometimes they would stay in the torture room for a full 24 hours, never taking time off or resting; or else they would go home, and then return a couple of hours later, as though the atmosphere of cruelty and violence had drawn them back.[8]

But much of the violence was the work of professionals pursuing what they saw as defense of the nation.

National security doctrines, which drew heavily on French and U.S. counterinsurgency doctrines of the 1950s and 1960s, provided an all-encompassing ideological framework for the military regimes of the Southern Cone. The state was viewed as the central institution of society. The military in turn was seen as the central institution of the state, the only organization with the combined insight, commitment, and resources needed to protect the interests and values of the nation.

The "Subversive" Threat

The nation and its values were seen as under assault from an international conspiracy that was centered on, but by no means limited to, international communism. For example, a diagram used at Argentina's Air Force Academy[9] depicts a tree of subversion with three roots: Marxism, Zionism, and Freemasonry. Progressive Catholicism appears at the top, and new growths at the bottom include human rights organizations, women's rights, pacifism, nonaggression, disarmament, the Rotary Club, Lions Club, and junior chambers of commerce. The main branches off the trunk are Communist parties, the extreme totalitarian Right (nazism and fascism), Socialist parties, liberal democracy, revolutionary front parties, Protestants, sectarians and anti-Christians, armed revolutionary organizations, and "indirect aggression." The branches off the limb of "indirect aggression" are particularly striking: drug addiction, alcoholism, prostitution, gambling, political liberalism, economic liberalism, lay education, trade union corruption, "hippieness," pornography, homosexuality, divorce, art, newspapers, television, cinema, theater, magazines, and books.

All-out war was the only "reasonable" response to such a pervasive threat. The process would not always be pretty, especially when applied to the agents of "indirect aggression." But even if many "subversives" were more misdirected or gullible than malicious, they were still guilty and had to be treated as such. As General Iberico Saint Jean, military governor of Buenos Aires, put it in May 1976, "First we will kill all the subversives; then we will kill their collaborators; then ... their sympathizers; then ... those who remain indifferent; and finally we will kill the timid."[10]

The metaphor of disease was also common. "Subversives" were an infection, the armed forces the nation's antibodies. An infected member of the body politic had to be isolated (detained) to stop the spread of the disease. If treatment was possible, so much the better—although even a cure might be painful (torture). If the member was beyond repair, though, permanent surgical removal (death) was demanded. What mattered was the long-run health of the body politic, not its individual members.

This paranoid vision helps to explain the wide range of victims. Violence against terrorists was not unexpected; in both Argentina and Uruguay it had been official policy even before the coups. Most of the disappeared, though, had no connection at all to the guerrillas.[11] Yet they too were considered guilty because of their "dangerous" political views.

Uruguay carried this ideology to its totalitarian extreme, creating Certificates of Democratic Background. An "A" rating indicated political reliability. A "B," or suspect, rating subjected one to police scrutiny and harassment. Those rated "C"—sometimes for an "offense" as minor as having been involved in a protest march twenty years earlier—were absolutely banned from public employment, a serious penalty in a country where the state was the largest employer. Many had trouble finding even private-sector jobs because hiring a "C" (or even a "B") citizen often led to harassing government audits and ominous questions about the employer's own loyalty.

The military sought to penetrate and "purify" all aspects of Uruguayan life. Each school received a new, politically reliable director. Every class had a "teacher's aide" to take notes on the behavior of students and teachers. A permit was required to hold a birthday party. Elections for captains of amateur soccer teams were supervised by the military, which could veto the results. A public performance of Ravel's Piano Concerto for the Left Hand was banned because of its sinister title.

Economic Reform and Economic and Social Rights

National purification also had a major economic dimension. In Chile, the Pinochet government tried to reverse not only Allende's reforms but also those of the 1960s as well. In 1975 the junta applied "Shock Treatment" (*Plan Shock*). Government spending declined by more than one-fourth and public investment was cut in half. Uruguay and Argentina pursued similar plans somewhat less vigorously. The aim was to privatize the economy and weaken or destroy organized labor, which was seen as a focal point for subversion. (In Argentina, for example, as many as half of the disappeared were labor activists.)

This forced march toward "free" markets produced a rapid decline in living standards. For example, real wages in Chile were one-third lower in 1976 than in 1970. Infant mortality increased dramatically.[12] But after the initial shock, there was limited economic recovery, especially in Chile. Although most of the benefits of growth were concentrated in the hands of a small elite, employment and wages increased while inflation declined. Economic success helped to calm at least some of the discontent with military rule. In fact, all three military governments relied on economic success to deflect attention from, or compensate for, political repression.

The beneficiaries of the national security state were somewhat less clear than the victims. Some members of the upper and middle classes profited from the privatization of the economy and the lifting of government controls. Industrialists seem to have strongly supported military control over labor. But neither local industrialists nor multinational corporations seem to have had much influence on economic policies. Furthermore, many local industrialists were left extremely vulnerable to foreign competition.[13] And although the military amply rewarded itself—for example, between 1968 and 1973, Uruguayan spending on education declined from 24.3 percent to 16.6 percent of the budget, while military spending rose from 13.9 percent to 26.2 percent—economic advantage seems to have been a secondary concern.[14] In their economic policies as much as in their political strategies, ideology was central to the policies of the military regimes of the Southern Cone.

HUMAN RIGHTS NGOS

If the Southern Cone provides a particularly striking example of human rights violations, it also provides a moving example of resistance. On April 30, 1977, fourteen middle-aged women, frustrated in their search for their disappeared children, met publicly in the Plaza de Mayo (the main square of Buenos Aires) in front of the Casa Rosada (the president's residence and the seat of government). The weekly Thursday afternoon vigil of the Mothers of the Plaza de Mayo—white scarves on their heads, silently walking around the square—became a symbol of both the cruelty of the military regime and the refusal of at least some ordinary people to bow to repression.

Although subject to harassment and even attack—nine people associated with the mothers, including two French nuns, permanently disappeared on December 10, 1977, after evening mass—the mothers persevered and grew in numbers and in strength. By 1980, they had almost five thousand members and were able to set up a small office.

The following summer, similar groups from several Latin American countries joined to form Federation of Families of Disappeared Persons and Political Prisoners (FEDEFAM). Its first president was Lidia Galletti, one of the leaders of the mothers. Patrick Rice, the Irish priest mentioned earlier who survived his trip to ESMA, became its volunteer secretary, operating out of a small office with a borrowed typewriter in Caracas, Venezuela. FEDEFAM became an important source of information and a focus for concerted international action by relatives' groups throughout Central and South America.

The Grandmothers of the Plaza de Mayo were organized in October 1977 to deal with one of the most bizarre aspects of Argentina's "Dirty War," the traffic in children. Young children and infants were occasionally picked up with their parents. Others were born while their mothers were in captivity. The total numbered around eight hundred. They were usually given or sold to childless military couples. One torturer estimated that about sixty babies passed through ESMA and that all but two—whose heads were smashed against the wall in efforts to get their mothers to talk—were sold.[15] Even today, the grandmothers continue to try to trace and recover these victims.

Several other human rights NGOs operated in Argentina. For example, the Center for Legal and Social Studies (CELS) was established in summer 1979 to investigate individual cases involving the security forces. Within a year of its founding, CELS had become affiliated with both the Geneva-based International Commission of Jurists and the New York-based International League for Human Rights. The Argentine Human Rights Commission (CADHU) was formed in 1975 to protest right-wing death-squad killings. It was forced into exile in 1976 but opened branches in Geneva, Mexico, Rome, and Washington to spread information about the nature of the repression in Argentina. Adolfo Pérez Esquivel, a leader of the Service for Peace and Justice (SERPAJ), received the Nobel Peace Prize in 1980, three years after having been imprisoned and tortured by the military regime. Important work was also done by the Permanent Assembly for Human Rights (APDH) and the Families of Those Detained and Disappeared for Political Reasons.

But the Argentine Catholic Church, despite the disappearance or assassination of two bishops and twenty priests, nuns, and seminarians, was never a vocal critic of the military. Although SERPAJ was a religious organization and the Ecumenical Movement for Human Rights was active, the church as an institution was not part of the opposition. In fact, some military chaplains actively participated in the system of torture.

In Chile, by contrast, the church was at the center of the human rights movement. The Committee of Cooperation for Peace (COPACHI) was formed in October 1973, the month after the coup, under the joint leadership of the bishops of Chile's Catholic and Lutheran churches. A month later, a legal-aid organization was established in space provided by the Catholic Church. By August 1974, COPACHI had more than one hundred employees in the capital of Santiago alone.

When Pinochet ordered COPACHI dissolved in November 1975, the Catholic Church responded by organizing the Vicaría de la Solidaridad (Vicariate of Solidarity).[16] The Vicaría provided aid and support for relatives of the disappeared and legal assistance to victims of state terror. Its Health Department organized soup kitchens and child-nutrition programs, especially in poorer urban areas that had been severely affected by Pinochet's economic reforms. Peasant organizations and unions, which had been special targets of repression, also received special support. And as military rule dragged on, the Vicaría began an extensive program of documentation and analysis. Although some lay human rights groups were also active, particularly the Chilean Human Rights Commission, in Chile as in much of the rest of Latin America, the Catholic Church could do things that were impossible for lay organizations and even other churches.

In addition to aiding victims and their families, human rights NGOs were an important source of information. In fact, the lists of disappeared people prepared by CELS and APDH provided much of the factual basis for initial UN and OAS action. Given the efforts of the juntas to hide the scope of their violence, this may have been a significant achievement.

Human rights NGOs also allowed Argentineans and Chileans a limited opportunity to struggle against, rather than simply acquiesce in, military rule and the Dirty War. (In Uruguay the system of repression was so totalitarian that no effective local human rights NGOs were able to function until the final two or three years of military rule.) Taken together, NGO activities probably played a significant role in the failure of the military governments to "normalize" their rule.

THE COLLAPSE OF MILITARY RULE

The Argentine military, ironically, finally fell from power after it lost a conventional war with Britain over control of the obscure Falkland Islands. Argentina had long protested British occupation and control of the Malvinas, as they are known in Latin America. In April 1982, the junta decided to reclaim them by force, a ploy to deflect public attention from the collapse of the economy during the global recession of the early 1980s.

But when the invasion was decisively repulsed, the Malvinas episode completed the military's humiliation rather than rescuing its reputation. Having attacked its own people, brought the economy to the brink of ruin, and then embarrassed itself and the country before the entire world, the Argentine military had little choice but to permit a return to civilian government. On October 30, 1983, Raúl Alfonsin won the national presidential election. He took office on December 10, the thirty-fifth anniversary of the adoption of the Universal Declaration of Human Rights.

In Chile, the economy also collapsed in the early 1980s. In 1982, per capita gross domestic product declined one-sixth. By March 1983, one-third of the labor force was unemployed. The minimum wage lost between one-fifth and one-half of its purchasing power. Close to half of Chile's children were malnourished, an appalling situation in a country that had previously been relatively prosperous. A wave of bankruptcies brought hard times even to the middle and upper classes.

As the junta approached its tenth anniversary in power, opposition increased in all sectors of society. Working-class residential neighborhoods began to organize. The old political parties (especially the centrist Christian Democrats, which had never been forced entirely underground) began to act, cautiously, in public. Strikes by truck drivers and copper miners in June 1983 were labor's first major challenge since the coup, followed by a successful general strike in July. Between May and November, several Days of National Protest culminated in a demonstration by close to 1 million people in Santiago.

The military, however, also found new resolve. As opposition grew, so did repression. Several deaths and over one thousand arrests accompanied the July general strike. Mass arrests increased dramatically, as did banishments, exiles, torture, and political deaths. By late 1984, the government was forced to reimpose a state of siege, and repression became more brutal. For example, two young Chileans were set on fire by the police during a protest demonstration, killing one and savagely maiming the other. Although the government claimed that the youths had accidentally set themselves aflame with a Molotov cocktail, a third victim was torched a week later, as if to remind opponents that it had been no accident.

Popular resistance, however, could not be crushed this time. In October 1988, the military tried a plebiscite to legitimate its rule. The majority of Chileans, however, rejected a new eight-year term for Pinochet. On December 14, 1989, an opposition alliance of seventeen parties, led by Patricio Aylwin, won the first free elections in Chile in nearly two decades.

The Uruguayan military was also hit hard by the economic crisis of the early 1980s. By 1984, real wages were less than one-half their 1968 levels, and more than 10 percent of the population had left the country, including one-seventh of the country's university graduates and close to one-fifth of the economically active population of the capital city of Montevideo.[17] But the military, after some initial indecision, was unwilling to adopt the Chilean strategy of increased repression in the face of growing opposition. Elections were held in 1984 and a freely elected civilian government returned to power in 1985, even without a Falklands-like blunder.

NUNCA MÁS: SETTLING ACCOUNTS WITH TORTURERS AND THE PAST

Elections, or at least the transfer of power from one elected civilian government to another (as occurred in both Argentina and Uruguay in 1989), are sometimes seen as the solution for human rights problems. But a nation that has suffered gross and systematic violations of human rights remains no less scarred than individual victims, their families, friends, and acquaintances. Furthermore, successor regimes face the problem of dealing with those responsible for human rights violations under the old order.

When the torture stops, it may not be clear how to deal with those responsible—especially when they retain political influence and control the weaponry that supported their dictatorial rule. Defining the terms of retributive justice is part of a process of national reconciliation necessary to keep the wounds inflicted under military rule from festering. The experience of the countries of the Southern Cone, however, provides some sobering lessons. Similar problems are being faced in the post–cold war world in Central and Eastern Europe, as well as in South Africa, Cambodia, and a number of other countries.

Two weeks before the election that brought a return to civilian rule, the Argentine junta issued a Law of National Reconciliation that created a blanket amnesty for all offenses connected with the "war against subversion." In his first week as president, however, Raúl Alfonsin delivered on his campaign promise that all nine members of the three military juntas that had run Argentina from 1976 to 1982 would be prosecuted.

No less significant was Alfonsin's decision to create the CONADEP, which would conduct an official investigation of the Dirty War. CONADEP's September 1984 report contained over fifty thousand pages of documentation and provided an extensive, official, public accounting of the Dirty War. The summary, published under the title *Nunca Más* (Never again)—a phrase that first attained wide political currency in the aftermath of the Holocaust—became an instant best-seller.

Where so much of the violence was clandestine, to know the nature of the crime was the essential first step to overcoming its legacies. *Nunca Más*, at minimum, finally recognized and publicly memorialized the victims, whose very existence had for so long been officially denied. Truth, however, is only a first step. Punishment or pardon usually follows, and preventing future abuses must be a high priority.

Argentina made several changes in domestic law and ratified several international human rights treaties. The military command structure was reorganized. Military spending declined from 4.3 percent of gross domestic product in 1983 to 2.3 percent in 1987. And in April 1988, a new Law of Defense defined the role of the armed forces as protecting against external aggression, effectively renouncing the national security doctrine.

Punishment was pursued through the courts. A defense of obedience to orders, however, effectively pardoned ordinary soldiers and lower-ranking officers. In a gesture to the dignity of the military, the Supreme Council of the Armed Forces was given initial jurisdiction to deal with its own through the system of military justice. But when the supreme council could find nothing illegal in any actions of the military government, the civilian Federal Court of Appeals took over the cases.

Sentences were handed down on December 9, 1985, the day before the second anniversary of the return of civilian government. Five leaders of the juntas received prison sentences, including life sentences for General Videla, the leader of the first junta, and Admiral Massera, the commander most intimately associated with the Dirty War. In addition, the court left open the possibility of further trials against more than 650 additional members of the armed forces.

Under extreme pressure from the military and its supporters, Alfonsin in December 1986 pushed through the *Ley de Punto Final*—literally, the

Law of Full Stop (period), or more loosely, the "final deadline." No new prosecutions could be filed after sixty days. The hope was that the legendary slowness of the Argentine judicial bureaucracy would leave most officers untouched. *Punto Final*, however, actually spurred monumental efforts by human rights groups and the courts. Judges even canceled their summer vacations to meet the deadline. Four hundred new indictments were registered against over one hundred officers.

On April 15, 1987, rebellious soldiers occupied several garrisons throughout the country and forced Alfonsin to push through a Law of Due Obedience, which limited prosecutions to chiefs of military areas. Even this, however, was not enough for the hard-liners. In January and December 1988 and in December 1990, new (but much less effective) revolts broke out, suggesting a precarious balance of power between hard-liners and moderates in the military and between the armed forces and the government.

Argentina's second civilian government, under President Carlos Menem, pardoned thirty-nine senior military officials in October 1989, effectively halting ongoing investigations of high leaders such as General Galtieri, the leader of the last junta. Hundreds involved in the military uprisings were also pardoned. Another eight senior officers, including General Videla, were pardoned at the end of December 1990. Although neither side was satisfied—Julio Strassera, who had prosecuted Videla, resigned from his position as Argentina's representative to the UN Commission on Human Rights,[18] while General Videla publicly indicated that even this gesture was not enough, asking instead for a full vindication of the military—over the past several years Argentine politics has increasingly left the past behind.

Uruguay's new civilian government, when it took power in 1985, faced the even more difficult task of dealing with a military that had not been humiliated on the battlefield. It is thus not surprising that President Sanguinetti chose to accept the military's self-amnesty. In December 1986, Uruguay adopted the Law of Limitations, which protected the military against prosecution for crimes committed while it ruled the country.

The reaction against *impunidad* (impunity) for the military—there had not been a single prosecution, or even an official investigation—was dramatic.[19] In February 1987, a campaign was launched to hold a national referendum. By Christmas Eve, petitions had been signed by 634,702 people, out of a total population of about 3 million. This was equivalent to obtaining nearly 50 million signatures in the United States.

In the April 16, 1989, plebiscite, however, a majority chose to let the amnesty stand. Despite heavy rain, voter turnout was over 80 percent. Fifty-three percent voted "yellow," to let the amnesty stand. Forty-one percent voted "green," to overturn it. The example of Argentina seems to have been the deciding factor—especially after public statements by highly placed members of the military suggested that they would not allow the amnesty to be overturned.

Although not an entirely free choice, Uruguayans had the opportunity to choose not to try to punish the military. Many victimized nations have not had even that much. For example, in Guatemala the military declared an amnesty just before leaving office in 1986. And to remind everyone where real power still resided, five dozen mutilated bodies appeared in various places in the country in the first three weeks of "civilian" rule. There was no plebiscite, nor even an investigation of the tens of thousands of disappearances and arbitrary executions.

Chile, following the lead of Uruguay and the lesson of Argentina, chose to forgo prosecutions, which the military made clear it would not permit. In April 1990, however, President Aylwin created the Commission for Truth and Reconciliation (CVR, the Rettig Commission). Its March 1991 report documents close to one thousand disappearances that resulted in death. (The commission's mandate did not include other violations, including tens of thousands of cases of torture.)

The outcome of such efforts, in the Southern Cone as in other countries grappling with legacies of political repression and brutality, will be determined by a complex interplay among the political will and skill of the government, its popular support, and the tolerance or intransigence of the military. These efforts do suggest, however, that even where punishment is impossible, the guilty may be denied complete impunity.

"Men are unable to forgive what they cannot punish."[20] These words of Hannah Arendt, which have often been cited by those in the Southern Cone struggling against impunity, capture the central problem with military-imposed amnesties. Pardon is an act of charity or compassion. Punishment is an act of justice (and a deterrent to injustice). New civilian regimes are often unable to punish because the guilty retain considerable political power. The pardons thus received by torturers and murders may have legal effect, but morally they are profoundly defective. This corruption of both punishment and pardon by power also makes preventing future abuses more difficult.

The task of prevention, however, is likely to be greatly aided by the truth, which can sometimes be a partial substitute for punishment or pardon. A public declaration of the crimes of the guilty may help to put the past behind and focus a country's energy and attention on preventing future abuses. At the very least, a nation unable to acknowledge its past publicly is less likely to be able to prevent new human rights violations.

The official name of Chile's Rettig Commission was thus particularly well chosen: Commission for Truth and Reconciliation. Especially where suffering has been denied, truth may permit mourning and provide a public solace that may help to make reconciliation possible. There may even be a punishment of sorts in being forced to face a public demonstration of one's crimes. South Africa's truth commission, under the leadership of Nobel Laureate Bishop Desmond Tutu, has been particularly forceful and effective in its efforts to uncover, and thus help to overcome, the horrors of the past.

Truth alone is never enough. Sometimes, though, it may make inroads against power. In any case, the task of human rights advocacy is to speak truth to power, in the name of past and present victims and in the hope of preventing future victims.

> *accuracy is essential*
> *we must not be wrong*
> *even by a single one*
> *we are despite everything*
> *the guardians of our brothers*
> *ignorance about those who have disappeared*
> *undermines the reality of the world.*[21]

Nunca Más. Never again. Never *this* horror again. Ultimately, this is the meaning of the struggle against systematic violations of human rights.

FOUR

□ □ □

The Multilateral Politics
of Human Rights

The preceding chapters have set the stage for a detailed examination of international human rights practices. The remaining chapters fall into two parts. Chapters 4 and 5 focus on the cold war era, when most multilateral human rights institutions were established and human rights became an important issue in foreign policy. Chapters 6–8 explore the changing human rights environment of the post–cold war world.

At several points I will use the concept of international regimes. An **international regime** is a set of principles, norms, rules, and decisionmaking procedures accepted by states (and other international actors) as binding within an issue area.[1] International human rights principles and norms were discussed in Chapters 1 and 2. In this chapter, we consider international and regional decisionmaking and implementation procedures in the United Nations Commission on Human Rights; the Human Rights Committee; special committees created under treaties on racial discrimination, women's rights, torture, and rights of the child; regimes on workers' rights and apartheid; regional human rights regimes in Europe, the Americas, and Africa; and the Conference on Security and Cooperation in Europe, or CSCE (now Organization for Security and Cooperation in Europe [OSCE]). Human rights in bilateral foreign policy will be addressed in Chapter 5.   ·

THE UNITED NATIONS COMMISSION ON HUMAN RIGHTS

The United Nations is the world's most prominent multilateral political forum.[2] It is not, however, a world government. It is an intergovernmental organization, a "club" whose members are sovereign states. Few UN decisions create binding international legal obligations. Even fewer can be effectively enforced. Nonetheless, when the United Nations acts on the basis of consensus, it may be said to speak for the international society of states (see Chapter 2).

The General Assembly is the center of the UN system. It sets guidelines for the organization, both through formal resolutions and through cues provided by its discussions and political dynamics. Each member has one vote in the Assembly, which must give final UN approval to all human rights treaties. On occasion, the GA has even made important drafting decisions. For example, the final compromises on the 1984 Convention Against Torture were worked out there. The GA has also been a major actor in international campaigns against racism and colonialism.

The General Assembly, however, has also been the principal site for political bias, especially during the cold war. The United Nations is a political body, used by sovereign states to further their own national interests. Because the GA is the preeminent political institution of the UN, the temptation to politicize human rights issues is especially strong there. For example, during the 1970s public human rights criticism in the GA was restricted almost exclusively to the pariah regimes of South Africa, Israel, and Chile. Although these countries richly merited international condemnation, comparable violations elsewhere were willfully ignored, for political reasons.

The narrow focus on human rights of the UN Commission on Human Rights, a permanent subsidiary body of the Economic and Social Council (ECOSOC), has somewhat reduced the problem of bias. Furthermore, in the earliest years of the UN, before the cold war set in, and in the past fifteen years, as the cold war waned and died, several states have been willing to use the UN Commission on Human Rights as a *relatively* nonpartisan forum. Therefore, the commission has been the single most important institution of the global human rights regime.

The commission initially devoted its principal efforts to working on the Universal Declaration of Human Rights and the International Human Rights Covenants. For twenty years, however, it undertook no monitoring or enforcement activities.

In 1947, the commission decided not to act on the thousands of complaints of human rights abuse that the UN was receiving annually. ECOSOC Resolution 75, passed later that year, denied the commission even the right to see those complaints. After the UN Secretariat had recorded and acknowledged their receipt, they were simply filed away. Underlying this practice was a very strong conception of sovereignty, that is, a narrow reading of the range of international human rights activities permitted by the principle of nonintervention. It also reflected the ambiguous position of intergovernmental human rights bodies.

The principal subjects of international human rights obligations, and the principal violators of human rights, are the sovereign states that are the members of the UN. They are thus unlikely to grant the organization strong enforcement powers. Furthermore, the members of the Commission on Human Rights are state representatives, not independent experts. The commission's decision not to act on human rights complaints was thus legally justifiable and politically understandable—if understandably disappointing to victims and human rights advocates.

In 1967, however, ECOSOC Resolution 1235 authorized the commission to discuss human rights violations in particular countries. Although hardly forceful action, the UN at least began to break its complicitous silence on particular human rights violations. In 1970, ECOSOC Resolution 1503 authorized the commission to investigate "communications" (complaints) that suggested "a consistent pattern of gross and reliably attested violations of human rights and fundamental freedoms." This **1503 procedure**, as it is called, often operates with considerable impartiality, in large part because the members of the commission's subcommission, where the process begins, are independent experts, not state representatives.

The 1503 procedure, however, is severely limited by being strictly confidential. Although few states fear the direct political power of the UN, its findings do have a certain authority. Domestic human rights NGOs and opposition parties may draw support from UN decisions and reports, which are also used by international NGOs and foreign governments. Confidentiality thus represents a major concession by the UN. Whether it is compensated by an increased willingness of states to cooperate with the commission in order to avoid adverse publicity is hard to assess (in part because of the procedure's confidentiality).

Confidentiality has been partially circumvented by an annual announcement by the commission chair of the countries that have been considered under the 1503 procedure that year. This "black list," which is the most that states are willing to allow, is better than no publicity. Its weakness, however, is evident.

The 1503 procedure is also very slow. Because the subcommission and the commission each meet just once a year, the 1503 procedure cannot be brought fully into play in less than two or three years after complaints are received (which may be well after serious violations began). A state can usually delay a year by pretending to cooperate, as Argentina did in 1979 and 1980. Political considerations often stretch a case out even longer. For example, genocide against Paraguayan Indians remained under scrutiny for nine years without any action. A decision on Uruguay, after seven years of scrutiny, came only after the guilty government had been removed from office.

The 1503 procedure's restriction to "situations" rather than to individual cases has the virtue of focusing attention on systematic violations where the government is obviously culpable. In addition, sufficient political support for the procedure could be obtained only by guaranteeing that states would not be subject to scrutiny for isolated violations. But because the procedure leaves individual victims without redress, it is of no value as an early warning device.

Finally, the 1503 procedure is ultimately simply weak. "Enforcement" means making publicly available the evidence that has been acquired, along with the commission's views on it. At most, the 1503 procedure provides a certain degree of semi-independent international monitoring. And only a handful of cases has even reached the stage of public disclosure.

Nonetheless, we should not ignore the value of publicizing violations and trying to shame states into better compliance with international human rights norms. Even vicious governments may care about their international reputation. And publicity often does help some of the more prominent victims of repression.

In the 1970s, human rights violations in approximately twenty countries were examined under the 1503 procedure. In the 1980s, about thirty countries were considered. This increase in 1503 cases illustrates a general growth in the range and intensity of commission activities, which were rooted in political changes that began in the late 1970s.

In the 1950s, a U.S.-dominated Western bloc controlled the commission and focused its attentions on issues of special concern to the West. In the late 1960s and 1970s, the Third World (Nonaligned Movement), with substantial Soviet bloc support, dominated the commission and focused its attention on apartheid in South Africa and issues of self-determination. During both eras, however, the dominant bloc strongly opposed general human rights–monitoring procedures.

In the late 1970s and early 1980s, some Third World countries, such as Costa Rica and Senegal, were ready to consider stronger and broader initiatives. A revitalized Western bloc, led by "middle powers" such as Canada and the Netherlands, emerged as a major force in the commission. For the first time in its history, the commission was not controlled by a single political bloc and was thus able to act in a wider range of cases, more aggressively, with greater impartiality.

The innovative breakthrough came with new "global" or "thematic" procedures. Rather than examine a range of abuses in individual countries, as in the 1503 procedure, the commission addressed particular violations globally, wherever they occurred.

In 1980, the commission created a Working Group on Disappearances to assist families and friends in determining the whereabouts of disappeared persons (see Chapter 3). After examining communications offering details of a disappearance, the working group transmits the case to the government in question. If necessary, reminders are sent, at least once a year. Over nineteen thousand cases were handled in the group's first decade of work. In roughly one case in ten, government responses established the whereabouts or fate of the individual. Special urgent-action procedures for disappearances within the three months preceding the communication—when most victims suffer torture or execution, but also when they are most likely to reappear—have resolved about one case in five.

Ironically, the first urgent inquiry handled by the commission concerned Mohamed al-Jabiri, Iraq's representative to the commission. He had been active in establishing the working group and was slated to be its first chair. But al-Jabiri apparently ran afoul of Iraqi dictator Saddam Hussein, was recalled to Baghdad, and disappeared. Theo van Boven, director of the Division of Human Rights, began diplomatic inquiries and threatened to publicize the case. About a week later, van Boven received a handwritten note from al-Jabiri saying that he had decided to retire.

It is uncertain what al-Jabiri's fate would have been without immediate UN intervention. His case does suggest, though, that aggressive international procedures can help at least a few victims. Furthermore, the working group's annual inquiries about unresolved cases, even when they are ignored, are a reminder that someone is watching and still cares.

A special rapporteur on summary or arbitrary executions was appointed in 1982. S. Amos Wako, a Kenyan national and secretary-general of the Inter-African Union of Lawyers, aggressively pursued his mandate. For example, his 1990 report noted over fifteen hundred cases in forty-eight countries. He has been succeeded in this work by Bacre W. Ndiaye of Senegal. In 1985, Peter Kooijmans of the Netherlands, the commission's outgoing chair, was named special rapporteur on torture. In addition to approaching governments with information on alleged torture in their countries (thirty-three in the first year alone), Kooijmans—who in 1993 left this position to become foreign minister of the Netherlands—developed urgent action procedures similar to those of the Working Group on Disappearances and also made official visits to several countries, including Guatemala, South Korea, Peru, Turkey, and Zaire. Other special rapporteurs have addressed religious intolerance and human rights violations by mercenaries, and a Working Group on Arbitrary Detention was created in 1991.

The commission's growing assertiveness has also been reflected in the increased use of country rapporteurs, who have investigated even relatively high-profile countries such as Guatemala, Iran, Burma, Bosnia, and Rwanda. Country rapporteurs, like their thematic counterparts, are individual experts who report to the commission, rather than acting as the voice of the commission as a whole. They thus operate with fewer diplomatic and political constraints, and their narrow mandate allows them to maintain sustained, focused pressure. They may even be able to develop a constructive exchange of views with the government.

The 1503 procedure, thematic initiatives, and country rapporteurs reflect an investigation-advocacy model of human rights implementation. They seek to acquire and disseminate authoritative information on violations, along with whatever political pressure or prestige the commission can muster, to encourage governments to improve their practices. Their basic logic relies on the desire of states to be respected by their peers and on the damage to state reputations that can be caused by publicity of systematic human rights violations.

The position of United Nations high commissioner for human rights, created at the end of 1993, generalizes this investigation-advocacy approach. The high commissioner has the global reach of the 1503 procedure, without its cumbersome procedures. Like the special rapporteurs, the high commissioner may deal directly with governments to seek improved respect for internationally recognized human rights—but with the added advantage of an explicit mandate to deal with all governments on all issues. The first high commissioner, José Ayala Lasso, who was appointed in 1994, made little progress along any of these lines. Nonetheless, the office has considerable potential. Many observers are hopeful that the new high commissioner (former president of Ireland, Mary Robinson), appointed in 1997, will be more active and effective.

The commission also undertook important new normative work in the 1980s, including the 1984 Convention Against Torture, a 1986 Declaration on the Right to Development, and the 1989 Convention on the Rights of the Child. A Second Optional Protocol to the International Covenant on Civil and Political Rights, outlawing the death penalty, was completed in 1989. In 1992, declarations were adopted on disappearances and minority rights. New initiatives have been introduced on human rights defenders, migrant workers, indigenous peoples, and human rights education. Efforts have also been made to revitalize public information and advisory services in the field of human rights, although budgetary constraints impede progress in these areas.

There are still substantial political constraints on the commission's activities. For example, during the 1990 session an almost embarrassingly mild resolution on human rights violations in China, which did not even explicitly condemn the 1989 Tiananmen massacres, was defeated (see Chapter 6).

The commission also remains painfully slow in its responses. For example, Rwanda was discussed confidentially under the 1503 procedure in 1992 and 1993. In addition, Mr. Ndiaye's thematic report on extrajudicial executions was discussed in spring 1994, just before the outbreak of the genocide. In that document, he confirmed reports of official involvement in the massacre of civilians and explicitly suggested that genocidal acts were already occurring. Nonetheless, it was not until May 25—seven weeks after the genocide began, almost a month after the secretary-general called for Security Council action, and even a week after the Security Council (belatedly) authorized a new peacekeeping force—that the commission even appointed a country rapporteur (whose report on June 28 came after the worst of the killing had concluded).

Despite such shortcomings, the Commission on Human Rights is likely to remain an active, and occasionally effective, part of the global human rights regime. And along with the newly created high commissioner, it is the primary international body with a mandate to examine human rights violations anywhere in the world.

TREATY-REPORTING SYSTEMS

An important cluster of global human rights institutions derive their authority not directly from the United Nations Charter, as the Commission on Human Rights does, but from multilateral human rights treaties. Foremost among such bodies is the Human Rights Committee, established by the International Covenant on Civil and Political Rights. More specialized bodies have been created by treaties on racial discrimination, women's rights, torture, and the rights of the child (see Table 4.1). Because the principal activity of these committees is to review reports on compliance submitted by parties to the relevant treaty, I refer to them as treaty-reporting mechanisms.

The Human Rights Committee

The Human Rights Committee is a group of eighteen independent experts elected by the parties to the International Covenant on Civil and Political Rights. Although it does not address issues of economic, social, and cultural rights—which are monitored by the separate, weaker Committee on Economic, Social, and Cultural Rights—its broad scope makes it closer to the general country-oriented procedures of the Commission on Human Rights than the commission's thematic procedures. The work of the HRC, however, focuses not on investigations but on the review of periodic reports submitted by states.

Reports are discussed in a public session, often lasting a full day, in which state representatives are questioned. Committee members often pose penetrating and critical questions. Sometimes the responses are serious and thoughtful. In such cases, the result is a genuine exchange of views that provides a real element of international monitoring.

The representative of the reporting state, however, need not answer any question, let alone answer to the satisfaction of the questioner. Many

TABLE 4.1   Major Treaty-Based Supervisory Committees

	HRC	CERD	CEDAW	CAT	CRC
Treaty in force	3/23/76	1/4/69	9/3/81	6/26/87	9/2/90
Parties (July 1995)	127	139	133	82	159
Committee members	18	18	23	10	10
Sessions per year	3	2	1	2	2
Length of session (in weeks)	3	3	2	2	2
Reporting cycle (in years)	5	4	4	4	5

HRC = Human Rights Committee (International Covenant on Civil and Political Rights).

CERD = Convention/Committee on the Elimination of All Forms of Racial Discrimination.

CEDAW = Convention/Committee on the Elimination of All Forms of Discrimination Against Women.

CAT = Convention Against Torture and Other Cruel, Inhuman, or Degrading Treatment or Punishment; Committee Against Torture.

CRC = Convention/Committee on the Rights of the Child.

reports contain little more than extracts from laws and the constitution or obviously false or evasive claims of compliance. And whatever the quality of the report, once it has been reviewed, the monitoring process typically ends until the next report is due, in five years. The committee cannot even assure timely submission of reports. Zaire presents an extreme example: its initial report, due in 1978, was not submitted until 1987. Furthermore, the entire process applies only to the parties to the covenant—although with 136 parties in mid-1996, this is becoming a much less serious problem than in the past. ·

Despite these weaknesses, the HRC can draw public attention to a country's record. This may occasionally embarrass a state into altering its practices. The need to report to an impartial international body may be a minor check on contemplated violations. The reports of some countries may even provide ideas and models for others, as may the committee's comments. And the national work of preparing a report can help to highlight areas where change is needed or possible. (The relative strengths and weaknesses of reporting systems are discussed further later in this chapter.)

The HRC may also consider complaints from individuals in states that are parties (seventy-seven in mid-1995) to the covenant's (first) optional protocol.[3] The committee may gather information, ask questions, and state its "views," that is, make a public declaration of compliance with or violation of treaty obligations. In response, several states have altered their behavior or provided redress to victims. For example, Canada has changed legislation concerning the rights of Indians living off their tribal lands, Mauritius changed legislation on women's rights, and the Netherlands has altered discriminatory social security legislation. The committee's relatively aggressive use of these powers is clear in its innovative decision to treat a state's failure to respond as an admission of culpability. (The relative strengths and weaknesses of individual petition mechanisms will be discussed at the end of this chapter.)

Racial Discrimination, Women's Rights, Torture, and Children

Regimes on racial discrimination, women's rights, torture, and the rights of the child have developed around similar treaty-reporting schemes.[4] Basic data on the relevant committees are shown in Table 4.1.

These treaties give added international prominence to the rights they address. The mandated periodic review of reports provides additional international scrutiny of state practices in these areas. And the treaties give greater range, precision, and force to the much more general formulations of the Universal Declaration and the Covenants.

For example, the torture convention states that "No exceptional circumstances whatsoever, whether a state of war or threat of war, internal political instability or any other public emergency, may be invoked as a justification of torture" (Article 2[2]). Orders from superiors are explicitly excluded as a defense. Special obligations are established for training law enforcement personnel and reviewing interrogation regulations and methods. To reduce incentives for torture, statements obtained through torture must be made inadmissible in all legal proceedings. The convention also requires that wherever the alleged torture occurred and whatever the nationality of the torturer or victim, parties must either prosecute alleged torturers or extradite them to a country that will.

Single-issue treaties and committees are typically situated at the core of a more extensive international regime. For example, the work of the Committee on the Elimination of Discrimination Against Women (CEDAW) is supplemented by the UN Commission on the Status of Women, a permanent functional commission of ECOSOC. In the case of racial discrimination, the 1960 UNESCO Convention Against Discrimination in Education and ILO Convention No. 111 Concerning Discrimination in Respect of Employment and Occupation provide supporting norms and monitoring procedures.

The torture regime includes an unusually varied array of supporting principles and institutions. The 1955 Geneva Standard Minimum Rules for the Treatment of Prisoners and the 1988 Body of Principles for the Protection of All Persons Under Any Form of Detention or Imprisonment provide supporting norms, as do regional torture conventions in Europe and the Americas. As noted earlier, the UN Commission on Human Rights has a special rapporteur on torture. The commission's Working Group on Arbitrary Detention addresses a problem often closely associated with torture. The UN Voluntary Fund for Torture Victims provides financial assistance for victims, support groups, and research on strategies to help torture victims and their families.

In addition, there has been unusually close and fruitful cooperation among states, NGOs, and intergovernmental organizations on the issue of torture. For example, both the convention and the special rapporteur owe much to the intensive lobbying and public information activities of Amnesty International over more than a decade. In a very different vein, Copenhagen is the home of an international Rehabilitation and Research Center for Torture Victims, a location that reflects the leading role of Denmark in international action against torture. Similar centers operate in Canada, Norway, and other countries.

In all the treaty-based committees, members, who are independent experts, prepare for the review of reports as they individually see fit. This often allows NGOs to have a significant, if indirect, input by providing information not included in a report. At the public session, members are free to raise any question they deem appropriate. In many instances, the result is careful scrutiny of certain areas of state practice.

Other than the personality of the members, the principal difference between committees is the time available to review reports. Most striking is the restriction of the Committee on the Elimination of Discrimination Against Women to one two-week session per year, while the Committee on the Elimination of Racial Discrimination (CERD) meets for two three-week sessions. Such a difference simply does not reflect differences in the nature of the groups' work or the pervasiveness of the problems they address. If anything, the amounts would be reversed if based on the number or severity of violations.

The other major difference between the committees concerns their authority to investigate individual communications. CEDAW and the Committee on the Rights of the Child (CRC) have no such powers. CERD is technically authorized to consider individual communications, but only fourteen states have accepted this optional provision, which is effectively moribund. The Committee Against Torture (CAT), however, has been authorized by twenty-eight states to receive individual communications. Furthermore, a substantial majority of the parties to the convention permit CAT to investigate communications concerning *situations* where torture is systematically practiced. These powers, which are similar to the UN commission's 1503 procedure, are unique for a treaty-based supervisory body.

Assessing Treaty-Reporting Systems

The weakness of treaty-reporting schemes as an "enforcement" mechanism hardly needs to be emphasized. They can, however, provide incentives for states to improve their human rights practices. Preparing a report provides a concrete periodic reminder to officials of their international legal obligations. And the review process, whatever its defects, assures that at least one international body periodically monitors the actions of those responsible for implementing internationally recognized human rights.

We should be careful, however, not to think of reporting in overly adversarial terms. Reporting procedures cannot force recalcitrant states to alter their practices. But preparing a report requires a national review of law and practice. If that review is thorough and conscientious, it can uncover areas where improvement may be needed or possible. This may be particularly valuable in liberalizing and newly democratic countries.

Reporting as an implementation technique thus functions primarily through the good intentions of states and their desires for a good international reputation. The obvious limitations of such a process simply reflect the basic problem of international action on behalf of human rights in a world of sovereign states. Each state has almost exclusive responsibility for implementing human rights in its own territory. And recalcitrant states can violate human rights with something approaching impunity.

Supervisory bodies therefore must struggle to make the most of the opportunities for influence available during the review of reports. In some cases, instead of attempting to chastise or embarrass a state, it may be more productive to try to establish a constructive dialogue. "Weaker" and less adversarial techniques may sometimes have a greater effect.

The constraints imposed by sovereignty also suggest special consideration for initiatives directed toward states with less bad, or even relatively good, records. Such states have, by their behavior, given concrete evidence of (relatively) good intentions. They are thus likely to be more open to persuasion and more concerned about their international reputation.

The result is a paradox: monitoring of human rights reports is likely to be most effective where it is in some sense least needed, that is, where human rights records are relatively good. But countries with relatively good (or less bad) records may still violate human rights. A victim of human rights violations in such a country is likely to receive little solace from knowing that there are people who are treated worse elsewhere. Any victim who is helped is a victory for international action, wherever that person resides.

One might even argue that the greatest virtue of treaty-reporting systems is their ability to address violations that are not sufficiently severe to merit scrutiny by the Commission on Human Rights, a special rapporteur, or the high commissioner. The resultant small-scale incremental progress, which is a realistic possibility in the case of any state that takes its reporting obligation seriously, is not to be sneered at—especially when we consider the typically modest impact of higher-profile investigatory or complaint procedures.

The proliferation of international human rights reporting systems, however, may be creating difficulties for even well-intentioned states. The pervasive problem of late reports reflects not merely indifference but the administrative burden of reporting, especially in small or poor states. Without the skills or resources required for a conscientious review, reporting is an empty formality, even if the government is well intentioned. Thus, the impact of reporting systems could be significantly improved by linking them to a system of technical and financial support. Although many states would not avail themselves of such help, some would. (Countries that have recently undergone a change of government would be particularly promising candidates.) But less than 1 percent of the UN budget is devoted to human rights work. And the continuing UN financial crisis makes increases highly unlikely.

Another way to ease the reporting burden would be to standardize reporting systems, which has been discussed now for a decade. The UN has also attempted to control the proliferation of single-issue regimes and their associated reports.

There has also been increased interest in alternatives to treaty-reporting systems. Creating the position of high commissioner was an attempt to generalize and strengthen semi-independent investigation-advocacy procedures. But particularly for countries and violations without a high international profile, reporting actually provides greater scrutiny. And even if stronger mechanisms were available, the periodic self-study that reporting requires is a valuable contribution that it would be a shame to lose.

WORKERS' RIGHTS AND APARTHEID

In addition to the four treaty-based regimes considered above (racial discrimination, women's rights, torture, and rights of the child), more diffuse single-issue regimes on workers' rights and apartheid have been important in the development of multilateral human rights procedures.

Workers' Rights

The first international human rights regime was the workers' rights regime developed in the International Labor Organization. Major ILO conventions (treaties) have dealt with freedom of association, the right to organize and bargain collectively, forced labor, migrant workers, and indigenous peoples, as well as a variety of issues of working conditions and workplace safety. Even nonbinding ILO recommendations provide an important international reference point for national standards.

ILO monitoring procedures, which date back to 1926, have been the model for other international human rights reporting systems. The Committee of Experts meets annually to review periodic reports submitted by states on their implementation of ratified conventions. If apparent problems are uncovered, the committee may issue a "direct request" for information or for changes in policy. Over the past two decades, more than a thousand such requests have brought changes in national policies. If the problem remains unresolved, the committee may make "observations," that is, authoritative determinations of violations of the convention in question.

The Conference Committee, which is made up of ILO delegates rather than independent experts, provides an additional level of scrutiny with greater political backing. Each year, it selects cases from the report of the Committee of Experts for further review. Government representatives are called upon to provide additional information and explanation. Special complaint procedures also exist for violations of the right to freedom of association and for discrimination in employment.

No less important than these inquisitorial or adversarial procedures is the institution of "direct contacts." Since 1969, the ILO has engaged in an extensive program of consultations and advice, often initiated by a government concerned about improving its performance with respect to a particular convention. The ILO is a leader in cooperative resolution of problems *before* they reach international monitoring bodies.

Part of the ILO's success can be attributed to its unique "tripartite" structure. Nearly all other intergovernmental organizations are made up solely of state representatives. NGOs often participate in deliberations but have no decisionmaking powers. In the ILO, however, workers' and employers' representatives from each member state are voting members of the organization. This makes it much more difficult for states to hide behind the curtain of sovereignty.

The transideological appeal of workers' rights has also been important to the ILO's success. In addition, the Committee of Experts, the ILO's central monitoring body, deals principally with technical issues such as hours of work, minimum working age, workplace safety, and identity documents for seamen. In monitoring such technical conventions, the committee develops and confirms expectations of neutrality that can help to moderate controversy when more contentious "political" issues do arise.

The ILO is, however, an international organization and is thus not entirely immune from political pressures and biases. For example, ILO criticisms of Israel for labor practices that went uncriticized in many other countries led the United States to withdraw temporarily in the late 1970s. Nonetheless, the ILO has been unusually active, effective, and impartial in its human rights work and has been a model for other international monitors.

Apartheid

The most extensive and vigorous of all international human rights regimes was also its narrowest, the regime against apartheid. For nearly half a century, South Africa was synonymous with **apartheid**, a distinctive style of unusually wide-ranging systematic racial domination. Officially abolished in 1992, apartheid was a major international human rights issue for thirty years and provides a good illustration of the strengths and weaknesses of multilateral mechanisms.

A System of Racial Domination. Racial discrimination in South Africa goes back to the initial Dutch colonization in 1652. Indigenous hunters (San, or "Bushmen") were largely killed off or pushed out, and local herding peoples (Khoikhoi, "Hottentots") were forced off their lands. Slaves began to be imported in 1658. Blacks, discriminated against in voting from the very beginning, lost the formal right to vote in 1936. They were legally excluded from many jobs after 1911.

With the electoral victory of the conservative Nationalist Party in 1948, race became the basis for regulating all aspects of life in South Africa. The Nationalist government created a totalitarian bureaucracy to enforce racism throughout South African society. The official rationale was racial and cultural preservation—separation and separate development. In practice, though, apartheid meant white privilege and domination.

The Population Registration Act of 1950, the cornerstone of apartheid, required racial registration of each person at birth. The Group Areas Act of 1950 (amended in 1957) consolidated and extended earlier laws designating land by race. The 1954 Natives Resettlement Act provided for forced removals of blacks from white-designated land.[5] Controls on the movement of nonwhites resulted in a series of pass laws and regulations that made it illegal for most blacks to be in urban areas for more than seventy-two hours without special permission. The result was the creation of black "townships," with inferior housing, education, and social services, on the outskirts of (white) cities, often two hours away from where residents worked.

Because of the absurdities of the system of restrictions on movement, the ordinary nonwhite was subject to the constant threat of prosecution. More than one-fifth of the nonwhite population could expect to be prosecuted for pass law violations within a ten-year period, a staggering level of legal intrusion on the basis of just one set of rules. And because prosecutions often led to expulsion from the area and the loss of a person's only source of income, the pass laws were an extraordinarily powerful instrument of social control.

According to 1980 official census, 48 percent of all blacks were living in white areas. And it was a good thing, for the land defined as black "Homelands" was largely barren and completely unable to support the population.[6] Getting everyone where they "belonged" would have produced mass starvation for blacks and the collapse of white standards of living and the white economy, which were built around cheap (black) labor.

Interracial marriage and sexual relations between whites and nonwhites were prohibited. The 1953 Reservation of Separate Amenities Act removed the formal legal requirement that racially segregated facilities be equal. The Native Laws Amendment Act of 1957 prohibited holding classes, church services, or any meeting by blacks in designated white areas. The euphemistically named Extension of University Education Act of 1959 effectively removed nonwhites from most existing universities and established new, and decidedly inferior, ethnic universities. And so forth.

Increasingly repressive internal-security laws were passed to prevent political opposition. By 1967, few legal safeguards remained for those suspected of political offenses. At least one hundred people died while being detained by the police or security forces, usually after having been tortured. The best-known victim was black-consciousness activist Steve Biko.

Many who were not formally detained were brought in by the authorities for questioning, often as a not-so-subtle warning. Any organization could be banned (that is, outlawed), and the printing or dissemination of any publication prohibited. South Africa also "banned" individuals, restricting their movements, limiting whom they might see (sometimes to their immediate family), and prohibiting them from speaking publicly or being quoted in the media. Most nonparliamentary opposition was thus forced underground.

This does not mean that there was no resistance. The African National Congress (ANC), the leading political group in contemporary South Africa, was founded in 1912. The 1952–1953 Pass Law Demonstrations marked the beginning of organized resistance to apartheid. But resistance took new forms after the police fired on a group of peaceful demonstrators on March 21, 1960, killing sixty-nine people and wounding about two hundred others in what has come to be known as the Sharpeville Massacre.

When the ANC and several other groups were banned, a number of leading activists of the 1950s, including Nelson Mandela, concluded that peaceful protest alone could not be successful and launched a (not very effective) sabotage campaign. When Mandela and several other leaders were convicted in 1964 and sentenced to life imprisonment, the ANC was forced into exile. The government weathered mass protests and riots in 1976 and 1977 through a combination of force, new restrictions, and minor concessions.

Peaceful opposition also continued, despite government efforts to make it illegal. South African churches became particularly important, since almost all overtly political opposition organizations were banned. The award of the Nobel Peace Prize in 1984 to Bishop Desmond Tutu symbolized this struggle. Black trade-union activity also increased and became politically important in the mid-1980s.

New and unusually violent uprisings in the townships broke out in fall 1984 and lasted for nearly two years. Torture and abuse of those detained increased dramatically, and doctors and clinics who treated torture victims became subjects of official and unofficial harassment. Official violence against those not detained also increased. Symbolic of all this was the widely seen footage of armed security force personnel popping up from their hiding place inside a passing vehicle and opening fire on unarmed children. Even more ominous was the dramatic increase in violence by police-sponsored vigilante groups.

Direct repression was accompanied by no less severe social and economic exploitation and degradation. For example, the average white under apartheid had an income more than twelve times that of the average black. Infant mortality, a widely used measure of health care, also shows a striking difference: a black child was eight to ten times more likely to die before the age of one than a white child. Other standard statistical measures revealed a similar picture.

The International Campaign Against Apartheid.   Although the United Nations addressed racial discrimination in South Africa as early as 1946, it became a priority only after the 1960 Sharpeville Massacre. In the subsequent thirty years, a flood of resolutions sought to mobilize international support for the national and international struggle against apartheid.

In 1962, the UN General Assembly called on states to break diplomatic relations and boycott all trade with South Africa. The decisions of the General Assembly, however, are only recommendations, and until the 1980s they were largely ignored by most powerful states. The Security Council, which does have the authority to impose mandatory sanctions, established only a voluntary arms embargo in December 1963.

A mandatory arms embargo was not approved until November 1977, after the murder of Steve Biko, and the ensuing riots and repression in Soweto (Johannesburg's largest black township). Both nationally and internationally, the death of the charismatic Biko, the subject of books, films, and popular songs, was a crucial turning point in South African history. Although a comprehensive, mandatory trade embargo was never established, several states did reduce or end diplomatic, cultural, and commercial relations with South Africa (see Chapter 5).

The UN developed a complex web of procedures and forums to pressure South Africa. The Special Committee on Apartheid, created in 1962, promoted a broad international campaign against apartheid. National support committees were formed, and opinion leaders in several countries were targeted. In 1975, a Trust Fund for Publicity Against Apartheid was established.

Material assistance was also provided to victims. The United Nations Educational and Training Program for Southern Africa, established in 1964, made over twenty thousand grants to South Africans studying abroad. The United Nations Trust Fund for South Africa, established in 1965, provided over $30 million in legal, educational, and humanitarian assistance to the victims of apartheid, including refugees.

The 1973 International Convention on the Suppression and Punishment of the Crime of Apartheid came into force in 1976 and had eighty-eight parties at the end of 1990 (ninety-nine in mid-1995). Although the convention attempts to establish international criminal liability, no prosecutions have occurred. Furthermore, the "Group of Three," which received reports on and made recommendations with respect to the implementation of the convention, had no discernible concrete impact.

Reiteration of antiapartheid norms and associated condemnations of South Africa became a regular feature of most international organizations. For example, the ILO paid considerable attention to questions of workers' rights in South Africa. Other specialized agencies, such as the World Health Organization, also closely scrutinized South African policies in their areas of competence. Others instead excluded South Africa, beginning with the International Telecommunications Union in 1965. The South African government in 1970 was even prevented from taking its seat in the United Nations General Assembly.

The norm of isolation was applied with particular force in sports, culminating in the 1985 International Convention Against Apartheid in Sports. South Africa was unable to participate in the Olympics from 1964 until 1992. The Special Committee on Apartheid also kept and publicized a list of sporting contacts with South Africa, in an attempt to pressure national sporting federations to join the boycott. Less systematic efforts were made to monitor, deter, and give adverse publicity to entertainment and cultural contacts.

The principal positive influence of the apartheid regime was probably the support, encouragement, and justification it provided for individuals and national and international NGOs trying to alter the foreign policies of individual states. We will see some evidence of this in the discussion of U.S. policy toward South Africa in Chapter 5. International pressure undoubtedly played some role in the process of reform that led to the 1992 decision of the white electorate to abolish a race-based social and political system in South Africa. But the fact that fundamental change in South Africa came only after thirty years of unusually strong and sustained international action underscores the ultimate limits of international human rights action in the face of truly recalcitrant violators.

REGIONAL HUMAN RIGHTS REGIMES

Single-issue regimes supplement the global human rights regime with norms and procedures covering a relatively narrow set of rights. Regional human rights regimes address a wide range of rights in smaller and more homogeneous groups of states.

Europe

A strong regional human rights regime exists for the now forty members of the Council of Europe. Article 3 of the council's statute requires members to "accept the principles of the rule of law and of the enjoyment by all persons within its jurisdiction of human rights and fundamental freedoms." This provision was treated seriously enough to prevent Spanish membership until democratic government was established after the death of fascist dictator Francisco Franco in 1975. In addition, Greece (in 1969) and Turkey (in 1981) were suspended for their human rights practices.

Whether we consider scope, depth, or impact, the European human rights regime, established under the 1950 (European) Convention for the Protection of Human Rights and Fundamental Freedoms, is unprecedented. The European Commission of Human Rights, based in Strasbourg, France, is the central organ of the regime. In recent years, it has become a sizable and extremely active agent, with a permanent secretariat in 1995 of sixty-two, supplemented by twenty-seven temporary staff.[7] Its principal function is to receive, review, and evaluate "applications" (complaints) from individuals.

In 1995, the commission opened 10,201 provisional files in response to initial inquiries or complaints. Registered applications totaled 3,481, initiating a formal review that typically begins by asking the government in question for comments and additional information. Thus, about two-thirds of initial inquiries are not pursued, usually because the applicant finds that his or her complaint is clearly not covered by the European convention. And another two-thirds or more of registered applications are found inadmissible, almost always for fairly uncontroversial technical reasons. For example, in 1995, 807 applications were declared admissible, whereas 2,082 applications (a bit more than 70 percent) were found inadmissible.

This level of work is substantially greater than in earlier decades. For example, in its first twenty-five years (1955–1979), the commission registered an average of 381 applications a year and declared an average of just 9 a year admissible. In the 1980s, the annual averages were just over 700 applications registered and 35 declared admissible. This growing workload reflects both increased post–cold war membership in the Council of Europe and a growing recognition by individuals and their attorneys of the opportunities it provides for victims of human rights violations. Nonetheless, this is still a relatively modest number of cases, which largely reflects the generally excellent human rights records of the members of the Council of Europe.

Once accepted, however, cases are pursued vigorously and impartially by the commission. In 1995, 67 cases were resolved by "friendly settlement," that is, a voluntary resolution between the petitioner and the government against which the complaint was lodged. Another 564 cases were decided on their merits. Throughout its history, the commission has decided the majority of cases against states and in favor of individual petitioners. Furthermore, although commission findings are not technically binding, they are usually accepted by states.

Even more striking is the authority of the European Court of Human Rights to take legally binding decisions, usually on cases that have been decided by the commission but where either the state in question or the commission requests a higher review. Between 1960 and 1995, the court handed down 439 decisions, 320 of which found at least one violation. Like the rest of the European system, the level of activity has increased substantially in the 1990s. In 1995 alone, decisions were handed down on 46 cases (30 of which found violations). Cases handled by the court have included such sensitive questions as public emergencies and the treatment of prisoners in Northern Ireland.

The European convention also permits complaints by one state against another. Although similar procedures in other human rights regimes have virtually never been used, they have been used a dozen times in Europe, for cases including British interrogation practices in Northern Ireland and torture in Greece and in Turkey.

The decisions of the European commission and court, and the general guidance provided by the European convention, have had a considerable impact on law and practice in a number of states. For example, detention practices have been altered in Belgium, Germany, Greece, and Italy. The treatment of aliens has been changed in the Netherlands and Switzerland. Press freedom legislation was altered in Britain. Wiretapping regulations have been changed in Switzerland. Legal aid practices have been revised in Italy and Denmark. Procedures to speed trials have been implemented in Italy, the Netherlands, and Sweden. Privacy legislation was revamped in Italy. In 1994 alone, the European convention was referred to in domestic court decisions in Austria, Belgium, the Czech Republic, Denmark, Germany, Hungary, Italy, Luxembourg, the Netherlands, Norway, Portugal, Sweden, Switzerland, Turkey, and the United Kingdom (UK).

Economic and social rights are specified in a separate European Social Charter. Despite the absence of the individual complaint and legal enforcement machinery of the commission and the court, the review of reports by a Committee of Independent Experts has produced changes in social policy in several states.

The Council of Europe system also includes a European Committee for Equality Between Women and Men, a Human Rights Documentation Center, and a Steering Committee for Human Rights (with three expert committees, dealing with the further development of human rights norms, improving procedures, and promotion, education, and information). In the 1990s, the system has added a European Commission for Democracy Through Law (Venice Commission), a European Commission Against Racism and Intolerance, and an Ad Hoc Committee for the Protection of National Minorities. There are also well-developed procedures for NGO participation.

In the post–cold war era, this system, which was originally restricted to Western bloc and neutral states, has been extended to former Soviet-bloc states. Because good human rights practices are a major condition of acceptance into "Europe," with the associated symbolic and material benefits, the efforts of the Council of Europe are likely to have a significant impact. In 1994, cooperation programs were in effect with Bulgaria, the Czech Republic, Estonia, Hungary, Latvia, Lithuania, Poland, Romania, Slovakia, Slovenia, the former Yugoslavia, Albania, Belarus, Croatia, Moldova, the Russian Federation, the former Yugoslav Republic of Macedonia, and Ukraine.

The European Parliament, a largely advisory body selected by direct popular election, has shown interest in international human rights issues. For example, it adopts an annual international human rights resolution based largely on the extensive reports of its human rights rapporteur.

There is also a human rights dimension to the activities of the European Union (EU) (previously known as the European Community [EC], whose principal component is the European Economic Community [EEC, the "Common Market"]). Economic integration in recent years has been accompanied by efforts to harmonize social policy. This has often had a positive impact on economic and social rights because policies tend to be standardized not according to the lowest common denominator but on the basis of average performers.

The EC/EU has also pursued human rights concerns in external relations. For example, a special agreement between Greece and the EEC was suspended from 1967 until 1974, at significant economic cost to Greece, in protest against military rule. Weak human rights provisions have been included in the Lomé Conventions, which since the 1970s have provided foreign aid to more than fifty countries that were former colonies of community members. In November 1991, the EC decided to include human rights conditionality in all future aid allocations. The foreign ministers of EC/EU states have issued two major declarations on human rights. Diplomatic initiatives on behalf of human rights and individual victims have become a regular practice.

A cynic might argue that the breadth and strength of the European human rights regime simply illustrate the paradox of international action on behalf of human rights: strong procedures exist where they are least needed. Because they require the permission of the states, they are likely only where states have a high interest and good records.

"Least needed," however, does not mean "unneeded." Even committed governments with good records can fall short of their best intentions. For example, Germany, Italy, and the United Kingdom have been criticized in Amnesty International reports on torture. The enforcement procedures of the European regime are available to victims when slips occur. They also provide subtle but constant pressure on states to meet the highest standards of behavior.

No less important than these adversarial remedial procedures has been the impact of the regime on national political reforms. New constitutions in Greece, Portugal, and Spain after they escaped military rule were written with the European convention in mind. The previously Communist states of Central and Eastern Europe have also reformulated their legal systems with European norms in mind. Decisions of the commission and the court have led to constitutional revisions in Sweden and the Netherlands. And, as already noted, in most countries the convention has significantly influenced legislation in many areas.

Furthermore, regional human rights standards are constantly evolving. The European Court of Human Rights applies the principle of "evolutive interpretation," by which the European convention is interpreted not according to the conditions and understandings that existed in 1950 when it was drafted but in light of the current regional practices. Especially for states that lag behind European norms, this has contributed to national changes. Examples include restrictions on corporal punishment in schools in the UK and on discrimination against unmarried mothers and children born outside of marriage in Belgium. (Recently, gender issues have been an important area for such evolving interpretations.)

The Americas

The inter-American human rights regime's procedures also revolve around a commission and a court. The Inter-American Court of Human Rights, which sits in San José, Costa Rica, may take binding enforcement action with respect to the (currently eleven) parties that have recognized its jurisdiction. Since it began operating in 1980, however, it has decided only a handful of cases. The real heart of the regime is the seven-member Inter-American Commission of Human Rights (IACHR).

Established in 1959 as a part of the Organization of American States, the authority of the inter-American commission does not rest on a separate human rights treaty (although there is a 1948 American Declaration of the Rights of Man and a 1969 American Convention on Human Rights). As with the UN Commission on Human Rights, all states that are members of the organization may in principle come under its scrutiny. And the IACHR has aggressively exploited its charge to promote and develop awareness of human rights, make recommendations, prepare studies and reports, handle individual complaints, and conduct on-site investigations throughout the Western Hemisphere.

Individual communications, however, have not been the heart of the work of the inter-American commission. Although it receives several hundred communications a year and is authorized to make findings on the merits of individual cases, the decisions of the IACHR have rarely been implemented. This reflects the very different human rights environments in the two regions.

Because of the generally excellent human rights records of its members, communications in the European regime typically deal with narrow or isolated violations that are not fundamentally threatening to the government. Even when there are serious systematic violations, as during military rule in Greece, the government involved is seen as aberrant. If the behavior persists, the country is treated as a pariah.

Most countries in the Americas, by contrast, have suffered repressive military rule within the past generation. During the entire cold war era, at any given time several OAS member states, and often a majority, were ruled by dictatorial governments. With so many cases of such high sensitivity and with governments so deeply disinclined to change, it is no surprise that the findings of the commission in individual cases have typically been ignored.

Faced with systematic violations, the inter-American commission's greatest impact has come through studies and reports on human rights situations in over twenty countries. IACHR reports, which have typically used individual communications and on-site visits to document a pattern of violations, have often been an important part of international efforts to publicize violations. The strengths and weaknesses of this process are illustrated by the inter-American commission's response to military rule in Chile (see Chapter 3).[8]

Within a week of the coup on September 11, 1973, the commission cabled Chile expressing its concern and asking for information. In October, its executive secretary, Luis Reque, visited Chile. His report advised a formal on-site visit by the inter-American commission, which took place July 22 through August 2, 1974.

During its visit, the inter-American commission interviewed government authorities, received 575 new communications, and took statements from witnesses to support previously submitted communications. Commission members also observed military tribunals, studied trial records of military and ordinary courts, and gathered information on the junta's legislation. Their visits to detention centers led to some minor changes and helped to identify facilities where torture was being practiced.

The commission's report concluded that the government of Chile was guilty of a wide range of human rights abuses, including systematic violations of the rights to life, liberty, personal security, due process, and civil liberties. In October 1974, this was hardly news. Nonetheless, the report was thorough and tough. It also provided authoritative confirmation of the charges that had been made against the Chilean junta. This made it much more difficult for sympathetic foreign governments to dismiss the complaints of exiles and human rights activists as partisan or unsubstantiated. For example, the IACHR report was a standard source of information in U.S. congressional hearings.

Over the next two years, the commission focused on individual communications. In 1975 it considered over 600 cases of torture and 160 disappearances. The government, however, was uncooperative. As noted earlier, individual communications are not well suited to handling systematic, gross violations.

The commission's second report on Chile, in 1976, applied new pressure on the Pinochet regime. Although noting a decline in some violations, it documented continuing systematic abuses and concluded that government actions and policies continued to be an impediment to the restoration of respect for human rights in Chile. This helped to undercut arguments made by and on behalf of Chile that the situation was returning to normal.

The political organs of the OAS, however, refused to follow the commission's lead. The first report on Chile provoked an innocuous resolution that did little more than ask for additional information. The OAS was so little moved that in 1975 the members overwhelmingly accepted Chile's offer to host the next session of the OAS General Assembly. Following the IACHR's second report, Chile was asked "to continue adopting and implementing the necessary procedures and measures for effectively preserving and ensuring full respect for human rights in Chile." By implying more progress than had in fact occurred, this resolution was in some ways worse than nothing. And after the third report, in March 1977, the OAS General Assembly did not even extend the formal courtesy of asking for a further study.

This icy reception underscores the limits of even aggressive and independent monitors in an organization with little concern for human rights. Nonetheless, the IACHR persisted. Its annual reports for 1977, 1978, and 1979–1980 included sections on Chile. The reports for 1980–1981 through 1982–1983, in a concession to the generally hostile organizational environment, contained no references to particular countries. But the 1983–1984 report returned to a tougher stand, with a chapter on violations in several states (including Chile).

In May 1984, in response to the worsening situation in Chile, the commission began work on a new country report, issued in 1985. A resolution criticizing Chile by name failed by a single vote in the OAS General Assembly in December 1985. And the IACHR continued to pressure the Pinochet government until it was finally removed from office.

What can we conclude from all this? A cynic can point to "the bottom line," namely, the persistence of military rule in Chile. If a state is willing to accept the costs to its reputation, which rarely exceed strained relations and reduced foreign aid, it can flout international human rights regimes.

But to expect recalcitrant states to be forced to mend their ways is wildly unrealistic. The inter-American commission, like most other multilateral human rights agencies, works primarily with the power of publicity. It can promote the regional implementation of human rights norms. It can monitor and publicize violations and try to persuade states to improve their practices. But it cannot, and is not intended to be able to, force a state to do anything. Sovereignty remains the overriding norm in the inter-American human rights regime—as in all other international human rights regimes except the European.

Nonetheless, in summarizing the commission's work on Chile, Cecilia Medina, who herself was forced into exile by the military government, has argued that

> in a situation of gross, systematic violations, the constant attention of the international community is of the highest importance; it serves as a support and encouragement for those suffering and opposing repression within the country, and at the same time prompts, and serves as a basis for, further in-

ternational action by other governmental and nongovernmental international organizations.[9]

This is particularly true when a state is subject to scrutiny in multiple intergovernmental organizations and by several national and international NGOs.[10]

Perhaps the strongest evidence for the importance of international publicity is the diplomatic effort states exert to avoid it. In the late 1970s and early 1980s, both Argentina and Chile devoted much of their diplomacy—in the United Nations, the OAS, and the United States—to avoiding public criticism.[11] If rights-abusive regimes take international condemnation seriously enough to struggle to avoid it, the work of international human rights agencies is unlikely to be entirely pointless.

We must also remember that "the bottom line" includes individuals who are helped. States often respond to international pressure by releasing or improving the treatment of prominent victims. These small victories for international action are victories nonetheless—and of immense significance to individual victims.

In rare cases, there may even be a systematic impact. For example, the 1978 IACHR report on Nicaragua increased the pressure on the dictatorial Somoza government. Furthermore, the OAS call for Somoza to resign in June 1979 shook his political confidence and seems to have hastened his departure.[12]

Reports, though, are only reports. Decisions on individual cases are only nonbinding resolutions. Real change requires additional action by states. This is an inherent shortcoming of almost all international human rights regimes.

Nonetheless, the inter-American commission has aggressively exploited its powers, to at least some effect. Its activities have improved the treatment of many thousands of victims of human rights violations. If we compare it not to Europe but to the UN commission or the single-issue regimes discussed earlier, it stands in a relatively good light. And with the end of the cold war, there seems to be a chance for organizational growth.

Elected (although not necessarily fully democratic) governments have been in office in all the mainland countries of the Western Hemisphere since 1991. And the OAS General Assembly, which in the early 1980s refused to discuss human rights abuses, has become willing to act on behalf of human rights, most notably in removing the military from power in Haiti. Of particular interest is the possibility of strengthening individual communications procedures. Although no major changes are so far apparent, this is clearly an area worth watching.

Africa, Asia, and the Middle East

A third regional human rights regime exists within the Organization of African Unity (OAU) under the 1981 African Charter on Human and Peoples' Rights—or Banjul charter, as it is often called, after the site of its adoption (Banjul, The Gambia).

The Banjul charter gives unusual emphasis to collective or peoples' rights and individual duties. The International Human Rights Covenants recognize the right of peoples to self-determination. The apartheid convention also refers to the rights of peoples to self-determination and equality. The Banjul charter, however, adds rights to development and to peace. The significance of such rights, however, is a matter of controversy.

One standard dictionary definition of a people is "the persons belonging to a place or forming a group, the subjects or citizens of a state." This is the usual sense in regional and international organizations, with the emphasis on citizens of an already established state. "People" most definitely does not mean "the persons composing a community or tribe or race or nation," another standard definition. For example, Nigerians are a people entitled to self-determination, peace, and development. Nigeria, however, contains such ethnic communities as the Yoruba, Ogoni, and Ibo, who are most definitely not considered subjects of the "peoples' rights" of the African charter. The Ibo were forcefully reincorporated into Nigeria, with the full support of the OAU, when they attempted to secede (as Biafra) in 1967.

The rights of peoples and states direct our attention to the external threats to human rights posed by foreign governments, international markets, and multinational corporations. These are important and perhaps underemphasized in international human rights discussions. Nonetheless, the great majority of human rights abuses, in Africa as elsewhere, are committed by states against their own nationals.

Peoples' rights also focus attention on the collective dimension of human rights and the connection between the collective goods of peace and development and more traditional individual human rights (which are also recognized in the African charter). But neither peace nor development, in the ordinary senses of those terms, will guarantee the enjoyment of internationally recognized human rights. For example, the citizens of the Soviet Union enjoyed peace but not human rights for four decades. In numerous countries, a small elite has obtained most of the benefits of national economic development.

The African charter's emphasis on individual duties is also problematic. A system of rights can operate effectively only if individuals attend to their reciprocal duties. Although commonplace, this is well worth repeating. Yet one may ask whether the real human rights problem in

Africa (or elsewhere) is that people have too few duties to the state and society. I would suggest instead that far too many states are all too aware of the duties of individuals but insufficiently attentive to their own duties and the rights of their citizens.

The African charter is also marred by extensive "clawback" clauses. For example, Article 6 recognizes "the right to liberty and to the security of the person" but then goes on to state that "no one may be deprived of his freedom except for reasons and conditions previously laid down by law." Because there are no restrictions on such reasons and conditions—the European convention, by contrast, explicitly restricts permissible grounds—this allows the state free rein, so long as it bothers to pass laws that suspend or abolish these (and many other) rights. Freedom of assembly may be restricted for reasons of national security or "the safety, health, ethics and rights and freedoms of others." Thus, any assembly that may offend anyone else (the ethics of others) may be banned. In good circumstances, this may not be a problem. But human rights are supposed to protect individuals above all in bad times.

Finally, the Banjul charter's implementation provisions are unusually weak. In addition to reviewing reports, the eleven-member African Commission on Human and Peoples' Rights may consider communications. But only situations, not individual cases, may be discussed. And an in-depth study of a situation requires permission from the OAU's Assembly of Heads of State and Government. This is by far the most politicized of all multilateral procedures. Furthermore, neither state reports nor the commission's review of them has been promising.

Nonetheless, the African commission does seem to approach its task with seriousness and energy. It has not merely permitted but has encouraged NGO participation. Given the relatively weak civil societies typical in Africa and the lack of a tradition of independent human rights NGOs, this may prove to be a significant contribution.

Whatever the ultimate fate of this African regional human rights regime, it is already much further advanced than those in the Arab world or in Asia and the Pacific. The Permanent Arab Commission on Human Rights established by the Arab League in 1968 has been notably inactive, except for occasional efforts to publicize human rights violations in Israeli-occupied territory. There are not even authoritative regional norms.

Taken together, Asia and the Pacific compose a large and diverse area that is not a region in any social or political sense. Thus, the lack of a regional human rights regime is not surprising. But the relatively low level of Asian ratifications of the International Human Rights Covenants (the lowest percentage of any geographical region) suggests that more than size and diversity stand in the way of even subregional human rights regimes in Asia.

But even without intergovernmental organizations, there may still be important transnational action on behalf of human rights. For example, more than one thousand NGOs are listed in Human Rights Internet's *Human Rights Directory: Asia and the Pacific*. Most of these groups operate only domestically. Nonetheless, they and their transnational colleagues play an important role, especially in countries with a relatively good human rights records. Even in extremely repressive countries, international human rights NGOs, such as the U.S.-based Human Rights Watch Asia, work hard to assure that human rights violations are not ignored by the international community.

In the Middle East as well, NGO initiatives have tried to compensate for the absence of a functioning regional regime. For example, the Arab Organization for Human Rights (AOHR), founded in 1983, issues annual reports on human rights conditions in the countries of the Arab world. In 1989—through a joint initiative of the Arab Lawyers Union, AOHR, and the Tunisian League for Human Rights, with the support of the UN Center for Human Rights—an Arab Institute for Human Rights was established in Tunis to provide information on human rights conditions and training for both government and nongovernmental personnel. There have also been efforts by Muslim individuals and NGOs to formulate Islamic human rights norms.

The general environment in the Arab world, as was noted in Chapter 1, is unusually hostile even to NGO activities. For example, AOHR operates out of Geneva, rather than an Arab country, for reasons of safety. The general hostility of governments, however, only increases the importance of the activities of national and transnational human rights NGOs. They can help to keep the idea alive and at least on the fringes of political debate. NGOs are also likely to be important in probing the limits of political tolerance and attempting to take advantage of what limited political space exists for action on behalf of internationally recognized human rights.

The Helsinki Process

A hybrid, quasi-regional human rights regime exists within the Organization for Security and Cooperation in Europe (OSCE, previously called Conference on Security and Cooperation in Europe [CSCE]), an organization made up of European countries (with the breakup of the Soviet Union and Yugoslavia, there are now fifty-four), plus the United States and Canada. The system is often referred to as the **Helsinki process**, in honor of its central normative document, the Helsinki Final Act of 1975.

CSCE was convened in 1973 to promote more stable and cooperative East-West relations. The principal Soviet objective was recognition of the territorial and ideological division of Europe. The Soviets also wanted to improve their access to Western technology and trade. During negotiations, however, they reluctantly agreed to include limited human rights provisions, under the novel notion of domestic security for citizens.

The resulting document is a marvel of diplomatic compromise. Three very different "baskets"—dealing with political and military issues (particularly the inviolability of frontiers and the principle of nonintervention), economic relations, and humanitarian relations—are held together in a delicate political balance. Our concern here will be solely with Principle VII ("Respect for human rights and fundamental freedoms, including the freedom of thought, conscience, religion or belief") and the human rights provisions of "Basket III" ("Co-operation in Humanitarian and Other Fields").

Basket III deals solely with human contacts (especially family contacts and reunification), the free flow of information, and cultural and educational cooperation. Principle VII, however, includes an agreement to "promote and encourage the effective exercise of civil, political, economic, social, cultural and other rights and freedoms." Much of the history of the Helsinki process can be seen as a struggle over the relative priorities of these provisions. The Soviet bloc states attempted to stick to the narrow focus of Basket III (and even that only reluctantly). Western states, along with human rights NGOs in both East and West, stressed the broad language of Principle VII.

Follow-up meetings in Belgrade (1977–1978), Madrid (1980–1983), and Vienna (1986–1989) provided the principal diplomatic arena for this struggle. The Belgrade and Madrid meetings deadlocked and produced little beyond harsh words. But the Vienna meeting, which ended just months before the final crumbling of the Iron Curtain, was more productive. Its concluding document included extensive new language on freedom of religion and the treatment of detainees and established new CSCE procedures for state-to-state consultations over alleged human rights violations. In addition, a separate Conference on the Human Dimension of the CSCE was established. And in Moscow in 1992, new investigatory procedures were adopted.

In hindsight, the Helsinki process can be seen as a chronicle of the gradual demise of the cold war and Soviet-style communism in the face of increasing national and international demands to implement internationally recognized human rights. The follow-up meetings provided the West with a forum for continued pressure on Soviet bloc regimes. Even more important, the Helsinki process legitimated dissident groups in the Soviet bloc.

The Final Act recognized the "right of the individual to know and act upon his rights and duties," in addition to the Basket III provisions on the free flow of information. In May 1976, eleven prominent reformers, taking the Helsinki Final Act at its word, formed the Public Group to Assist the

Implementation of the Helsinki Accords in the USSR. The purpose of the Moscow Helsinki Group, as it soon came to be known, was "to inform the governments that signed the Final Act in Helsinki, as well as the publics of those countries, of cases of direct violations of the humanitarian articles of the Final Act in the Soviet Union."[13]

In six years of work, the Moscow Helsinki Group prepared more than 150 reports on a great variety of human rights issues. These reports were an important subject of discussion at the Belgrade and Madrid follow-up meetings. The group also issued numerous statements, letters, and appeals. Local Helsinki-monitoring groups were formed in Armenia, Georgia, Lithuania, and the Ukraine. Groups such as the Working Commission to Investigate the Abuse of Psychiatry for Political Purposes and the Christian Committee to Defend Believers' Rights also cooperated more or less closely with the Moscow Helsinki Group.

Over one hundred individuals publicly joined these Soviet Helsinki groups, at great personal risk. All were harassed, and most were legally punished, often under the charge of anti-Soviet agitation and propaganda. This was a serious offense in Soviet law, and one could be found guilty even if all the facts that one was accused of disseminating were true—as was the case with the Moscow group's reports. From the very outset, members were intimidated into leaving the group or accepting an exit visa from the Soviet Union. By 1980, the group's principal activity had become monitoring the cases of their colleagues. By August 1981, only three members remained at liberty in the country. In September 1982, the Moscow Helsinki Group was forced to disband.

In Czechoslovakia, the coming of the Belgrade follow-up meeting helped to spur Charter 77, a manifesto signed in January 1977 by 242 people, including Vaclav Havel (who in 1990 became the first elected president of newly democratic Czechoslovakia). During the succeeding decade, Charter 77 became a powerful local human rights group with over thirteen hundred public adherents.

As in the Soviet Union, official harassment began immediately. In fact, a car containing Havel and two others was stopped by the security forces while they were on their way to deliver the signed document to the government and the media. Members were physically attacked, fired from jobs, blacklisted, and in some cases arrested. Telephones were cut off, apartments taken away, driving licenses and passports revoked, and individuals detained without charge to prevent them from engaging in group activities. Some were convicted of political crimes. Children and other family members of activists were harassed and discriminated against in employment, residence, and schooling.

On the one hand, the Moscow Helsinki Group and Charter 77 may be seen as failures. Of the twenty-two members of the Moscow Helsinki

Group, only Naum Meiman managed to remain active, in the country, and unpunished (although even he was forced into early retirement). Furthermore, once the more public figures had been neutralized, Soviet authorities continued to arrest and harass less prominent activists and even those only peripherally involved in the human rights movement. Persecution of Charter 77 members was less thorough and often less harsh, but still very real and costly. In other countries, the situation was even worse. The Polish Helsinki Committee was forced underground during martial law. In some countries, such as Bulgaria and Romania, monitoring groups could not even be formed.[14]

On the other hand, the immense international publicity accorded the activities of the Moscow Helsinki Group both embarrassed Soviet authorities and helped to mobilize private and public political pressure. Formal Helsinki meetings provided a well-publicized forum for airing human rights grievances. And in Czechoslovakia, Charter 77 provided much of the leadership for the Velvet Revolution of 1989.

The Helsinki process also had an impact on international human rights activities outside the Soviet bloc. For example, in the United States Helsinki Watch was founded in 1979. This then became the model for the creation of new regional watch committees, Americas Watch, Asia Watch, Africa Watch, and Middle East Watch, which now operate as divisions of an umbrella organization, Human Rights Watch.

Repressive governments can almost always ignore the pressure NGOs bring to bear. They may even choose to apply the power of the state to punish or eliminate NGOs and their members. Nonetheless, there may be international and domestic political costs to such behavior, especially if the victims are prominent.

Rarely will such costs be politically decisive. In some cases, however, we know that they have eased the burden on some victims. As we are coming to see, this is the most that usually can be realistically hoped for, at least in the short run, from international action on behalf of human rights. Whatever its shortcomings, modest amelioration of human rights conditions is better than nothing, and almost certainly worth the effort.

The revolutions of 1989 in Eastern Europe certainly cannot be attributed to either the formal Helsinki proceedings or the activities of national and international Helsinki monitors. Nonetheless, the combined pressures from above and below helped to open political space for some of the forces that ultimately overthrew Communist rule. As the Charter of Paris for a New Europe, adopted at the Paris Summit of Heads of State or Government of the CSCE in November 1990, put it: "The courage of men and women, the strength of the will of the peoples and the power of the ideas of the Helsinki Final Act have opened a new era of democracy, peace and unity in Europe."

Perhaps the greatest testimony to the value of the process is the fact that the new governments of Central and Eastern Europe seem committed to using CSCE to help to consolidate and extend their achievements. The now renamed Organization for Security and Cooperation in Europe has not dramatically expanded its powers, to the disappointment of its more enthusiastic supporters. The complaint procedures approved at the Vienna follow-up meeting, however, are of some significance. And significant new initiatives continue to emerge, such as the creation of a high commissioner for national minorities.

ASSESSING MULTILATERAL HUMAN RIGHTS MECHANISMS

Multilateral human rights institutions and procedures can be distinguished by source of authority, range of focus, and means used. Differences in each dimension have usually complementary strengths and weakness.

Some institutions, particularly the United Nations, European, and inter-American commissions, draw their authority from global and regional international organizations. Others, most notably the Human Rights Committee, are rooted in lawmaking treaties. Some procedures focus on particular rights, including the single-issue regimes and the thematic procedures of the UN commission. Other mechanisms, however, rest on a more comprehensive review of the practices of single states, such as the 1503 procedure, the country rapporteurs of the UN commission, the country reports of the inter-American commission, and the activities of the HRC.

The principal tools available within these various regimes are (1) state reports, characteristic of the treaty-based regimes; (2) investigation-advocacy procedures, such as those undertaken by the IACHR or the UN commission's thematic and country rapporteurs; and (3) individual communications (complaints), as in the European regime and the activities of the HRC under the optional protocol. The strengths and weaknesses of reporting systems were considered earlier. Here I want to focus on investigations and communications and on questions of authority and scope. Table 4.2 provides a general summary.

Human rights institutions based in international and regional organizations can draw on the prestige and influence of the broader organization. This is one of the greatest resources of the new UN high commissioner and has always been a resource of the UN Commission on Human Rights. Organization-based institutions may also benefit from internal political linkages. Because states usually have many other objectives they are pursuing within the organization, they may be constrained in resisting the organization's human rights initiatives.

TABLE 4.2 Multilateral Implementation Mechanisms

	Strengths	Weaknesses
Authority		
Organization	political support/prestige issue linkage within organization	political bias
Treaty	impartiality	no political linkages
Activities		
Country	coverage of full situation	more adversarial
Thematic	impartiality	limited coverage
Means		
Reporting	least adversarial; can address less severe violations	states set terms of discussion
Investigation	proactive advocacy	states not required to cooperate
Petition	quasi-judicial resolution, specificity of individual case	small number of cases

In addition, because these are international organizations, their decisions represent the collective activities of states, with their associated power resources. This may allow mobilizing a different kind of influence than that available to committees of independent experts. For example, the impact of IACHR activities on Chile and Argentina was increased by the support of the regional hegemony, the United States, especially during the Carter presidency.

Politicization, however, is the price often paid for the political power of multilateral organizations. For example, in the UN during the cold war, countries were singled out for scrutiny largely on the basis of their (lack of) international political support. Even though serious violations were addressed, the procedures were corrupted by the taint of political partisanship. The IACHR in the 1970s and 1980s also illustrates the problems that can arise if the broader organization is substantially less interested in human rights.

Committees of independent experts have been relatively nonpartisan. Even during the cold war, the Human Rights Committee, for example, was far less politicized than even the UN commission, let alone the General Assembly. Given the heavy reliance on publicity and persuasion, a reputation for integrity and fairness can be a powerful tool.

Combining these two lines of argument suggests that an international human rights institution can maximize its impact if it is backed by a broader organization while avoiding the taint of politicization. This assessment is confirmed by the record of the UN, inter-American, and European commissions. The inter-American commission was far more aggressive, and effective, than the highly politicized OAS General Assembly. Even the UN commission has been able to draw on the combination of a reputation for relative impartiality and the prestige of the broader organization. This has, for example, at least improved access for special rapporteurs in unusually closed countries such as Iran and Burma. Likewise, the widespread voluntary compliance with the decisions of the European commission rests on a combination of the Council of Europe's prestige and influence and the commission's own unparalleled reputation for neutrality. This line of argument also suggests that the office of UN high commissioner has considerable potential in the hands of an aggressive yet impartial individual.

I noted earlier that single-issue and country-specific initiatives have largely complementary strengths and weaknesses. Because thematic or single-issue mechanisms avoid singling out individual countries, even when they do address particular state practices, the inquiry is likely to be less threatening. But in countries facing systematic violations across the spectrum of internationally recognized human rights, anything short of a countrywide approach may appear timid or even futile.

Yet even where systematic violations persist, incremental improvements in particular areas resulting from single-issue mechanisms may still be valuable. Furthermore, countrywide initiatives often produce only the same sort of incremental improvements in limited areas, such as the release of prominent political prisoners or the modification of particular laws, decrees, or administrative practices.

In examining particular implementation mechanisms, we again see a picture of complementary strengths and weaknesses. Earlier in the chapter, I assessed reporting systems in some detail. Their reliance on state initiative in preparing the reports and their use of independent committees of experts make them the least adversarial of all procedures. This is at once their greatest strength and their greatest weakness.

It is tempting to look upon the individual petition systems available in Europe and the HRC as an ideal. From an individual victim's point of view, the near-universal compliance with the decisions of the European commission and court are undoubtedly preferable to the uncertainties of reporting and investigatory-diplomatic methods. But as the general failure of the inter-American complaint procedure suggests, it is not so much the use of individual petitions that is crucial as the commitment of states to abide by the resulting quasi-judicial proceedings.

This is underscored by the voluntary nature of the optional protocol, which limits the HRC to considering complaints from citizens in less than half the countries of the world. The optional protocol thus presents a striking example of the typical trade-off between the scope and the strength of international procedures. Much the same lesson is apparent in the European regional regime, where the strongest of all international procedures apply only to a relatively small group of states with generally excellent human rights records.

The other obvious drawback of individual complaint mechanisms is the small number of cases they can address. The European commission and the HRC together have taken decisions on under four thousand complaints.

But focusing on individual cases gives these procedures a valuable specificity and concreteness. Because violations are personalized and detailed evidence of individual violations is provided, it is more difficult for states to deny responsibility.

Individual petitions, like the other kinds of procedures, occupy a special niche. They are particularly desirable where violations are either narrow or sporadic. But widespread adherence to individual complaint mechanisms is more an effect than a cause of high levels of implementation of internationally recognized human rights.

Investigation and reporting mechanisms will continue to be needed for a very long time. I am even tempted to argue that they are the heart of multilateral human rights activity. In a world still organized around sovereign states, the international contribution to implementing human rights rests on persuasive diplomacy, which itself rests considerably on the power of shame that lies at the heart of investigatory and reporting mechanisms.

If this is true, the key to change in state practices probably lies not in any one type of forum or activity but in the mobilization of multiple, complementary channels of influence. This would seem to be the lesson of the international campaign against apartheid. In the Southern Cone as well, the combination of pressure from the UN, the OAS, and national and international human rights NGOs, along with the foreign policies of individual states, seems to have had a cumulative delegitimizing impact.

Having considered in this chapter the multilateral dimension, and to a much lesser extent the NGO dimension, it is now time to turn to bilateral foreign policy.

FIVE

□ □ □

Human Rights
and Foreign Policy

The preceding chapter dealt with the multilateral politics of international human rights. This chapter considers national foreign policy, the bilateral politics of international human rights. The first four sections are devoted to the United States, with special emphasis on the 1970s and 1980s, when human rights matured as an issue in international politics. The policies of some other Western countries are discussed in much less detail in the final two sections.

CENTRAL ISSUES IN U.S. INTERNATIONAL
HUMAN RIGHTS POLICY

Chapter 1 provided a brief overview of major events in postwar international human rights. For the United States, we can distinguish five phases.

- 1945–1948: initial enthusiasm, culminating in the adoption of the Universal Declaration of Human Rights
- 1949–1973: human rights concerns subordinated to anticommunism and cold war rivalry with the Soviet Union
- 1974–1980: emergence of human rights as a prominent element in the public diplomacy of the United States, first in the Congress and then during the Carter presidency
- 1981–1988: the (ultimately unsuccessful) Reagan attempt to subordinate human rights to the (new) cold war
- 1989–present: post–cold war spread and deepening of human rights concerns[1]

This chapter concentrates on the first four periods. Post–cold war developments will be considered in Chapters 6–8. Because Chapter 1 has already provided a brief chronological overview, my approach here will be thematic and topical.

Anticommunism and American Exceptionalism

U.S. foreign policy from 1945 through the end of the 1980s was dominated by anticommunism. Even during the "liberal" Democratic presidencies of Truman, Kennedy, Johnson, and Carter, fear of communism was an overriding concern. The Korean War began under Truman. U.S. advisers and then troops were committed to Vietnam under Kennedy and Johnson. Carter's Central American policy was strongly shaped by the desire to avoid "another Cuba." Individual presidents certainly disagreed on strategy and tactics, but anticommunism had the highest foreign policy priority in every administration from Truman through Reagan. As a result, the United States usually supported avowedly anticommunist governments. Whether this was good foreign policy or bad, its human rights consequences were disastrous.

Totalitarian, Soviet-style communism, which today persists only in isolated enclaves such as China, North Korea, and Cuba, systematically violates most internationally recognized civil and political rights. But the fact that anticommunist regimes were often guilty of serious, and sometimes no less severe, violations did not stop the United States from regularly equating anticommunism with the pursuit of "freedom" and human rights. In country after country—Bolivia, Chile, Guatemala, Haiti, Iran, Liberia, Pakistan, Paraguay, Somalia, South Africa, Sudan, South Vietnam, South Korea, and Zaire, to name just a few—the United States supported repressive military dictatorships and narrow civilian oligarchies (along with U.S. economic and geopolitical interests) in the name of democracy and human rights.

This confusion of anticommunism with human rights has been strengthened by what students of domestic politics in the United States call **American exceptionalism,** the belief that the United States is different from (and generally superior to) most other countries, in large part because of its domestic commitment to individual rights. The isolationist variant of American exceptionalism, expressed with particular clarity in George Washington's Farewell Address, has seen the country as a beacon of hope for an oppressed world—but only an example, not an active participant in the struggle for freedom overseas. No less powerful, however, has been interventionist exceptionalism, which stresses an active American mission to spread its values though direct foreign policy action, even military force.

This interventionist strand has often led to identifying the international interests of the United States with democracy and human rights. During the cold war, the logic typically ran roughly this way: communism is opposed to human rights. The United States favors human rights. Therefore, American action against communism is equivalent to action on behalf of human rights.

Even where it has not led to intervention, American exceptionalism has often been associated with a narrow and self-serving definition of human rights. Americans typically act as if human rights problems exist only in places that must be reached by crossing large bodies of salt water. Other countries have human rights problems. The United States, however, is said to suffer from, for example, police brutality or a health care crisis, which are spoken of as if they are qualitatively different from torture or denial of the right to health care. Although strictly speaking beyond the scope of this book, which is about international human rights, this systematic reluctance of Americans to look at themselves through the lens of internationally recognized human rights cannot be ignored.[2]

This is particularly true because the interaction of exceptionalism and anticommunism has contributed to an American tendency to denigrate economic and social rights. Only civil and political rights (plus certain elements of the right to property) are constitutionally guaranteed in the United States. Because most Americans think first of constitutional rights when they hear the term human rights, there has been a strong tendency to view economic and social rights as at best much less important (see Chapter 2). For example, homelessness or lack of access to medical care is rarely presented as a human rights problem. The fact that Communist regimes emphasized economic and social rights created a sort of guilt by association.

During the cold war, this regularly led Americans to misinterpret events in the Third World. U.S. foreign policy reacted suspiciously to action on behalf of economic and social rights (other than the right to private property), especially when it involved redistributing wealth. By labeling economic and social reformers "Communists" and "subversives," right-wing rulers could generally retain U.S. support for systematic repression to protect their own wealth, power, and privilege, often under an American banner of "democracy."

Beyond the devastating human rights consequences, such policies frequently prevented the achievement of professed U.S. goals. For example, repressive military dictatorships often eliminated not only the far Left but also the political moderates that the United States claimed to support. There is more than a touch of irony in the fact that in all of Central America in the 1980s, only in "Marxist" Nicaragua (and disarmed Costa Rica) did a democratic opposition acquire power through peaceful electoral means.

The incoherence of American policy is especially clear in U.S. attitudes toward elections. Although Americans in general have a deep, even exaggerated, faith in elections, U.S. foreign policy consistently ignored restrictions on political participation, corruption, intimidation of voters, or outright fraud by client regimes. The United States regularly, and rightly, criticized one-party elections in Communist countries. But the mere fact of voting in "friendly" (anticommunist) countries was usually accepted as evidence of the ruling regime's democratic character. And when the United States disapproved of governments brought to power through free and fair elections, it was not above using force to remove them. Sponsorship of the 1954 military coup in Guatemala, subversion in Chile in the early 1970s, and continued support for the Nicaraguan contras after the 1984 election are striking examples.

Such inconsistencies were "reconciled" by an appeal to anticommunism. Elections that brought (alleged) Communists to power were bad and had to be overturned. When force or fraud brought anticommunists to power, that was an acceptable price to pay to keep Communists out of power and on the run. And the United States, the leader of the "Free World," was the self-appointed judge of "democratic" credentials.

The Problem of Trade-Offs

The preceding discussion has focused entirely on the international human rights dimension of U.S. foreign policy. One might accept this description but argue that the policy was nonetheless entirely justified. An argument that the struggle against communism (or the military and political power of the Soviet Union) was an appropriate overriding priority for U.S. foreign policy during the cold war raises the issue of the proper place of human rights in foreign policy.

In a world of sovereign states, foreign policy is principally concerned with the pursuit of the national interest, as each country sees it. The national interest may include respect for human rights in other countries, either as an intrinsic value or for instrumental reasons (such as the belief that rights-protective regimes are more likely to be dependable friends in international relations). But in no country can the national interest be reduced to international human rights.

The obvious question, then, is *what* place human rights occupy. The best way to tell is to look at what happens when there is a conflict of objectives. Talk about human rights is cheap—often not entirely without cost, but usually relatively cheap. The decisive tests are the costs a country is willing to bear in pursuing human rights concerns and the competing objectives it is willing to sacrifice or subordinate.

A well-designed foreign policy chooses means by comparing their cost to the value of the goal being pursued. The three principal means used by the United States (and other countries) on behalf of international human rights have been **quiet diplomacy** (private discussions with foreign governments), public statements, and granting or withholding foreign aid. This consistent use of only weak instruments of foreign policy is clear evidence of the low value placed on human rights.

Consider, for example, the Reagan administration's insistence on quiet diplomacy as the principal, and usually the sole, appropriate means to pursue human rights goals in foreign policy—at least with "friendly" (anticommunist) governments. Governments rarely engage in the sorts of human rights violations that provoke serious diplomatic concern unless they feel that something very important is at stake. Therefore, it is implausible to imagine that quiet diplomacy alone, without at least the threat of more forceful public or punitive action, will produce anything more than symbolic gestures.[3]

Even symbolic gestures may improve the lot of individual victims. Quiet diplomacy, under both Carter and Reagan, helped free hundreds of political prisoners, and it ameliorated the conditions of detention of many more. But never did it significantly improve a country's general human rights situation.

The strongest means typically used to back international human rights policies has been the conditioning of aid on human rights practices. Although Congress has required that bilateral economic assistance, bilateral security assistance, and U.S. participation in multilateral financial institutions take into account the human rights records of potential recipients, this had little systematic impact during the cold war. Aid decisions were altered in some individual cases, but there is no strong, clear general linkage between U.S. economic (let alone security) assistance and the human rights practices of recipient states.[4]

The United States, like most other states, has been willing to pay very little to achieve its international human rights objectives. The Carter, Reagan, and Bush administrations—and the Clinton administration as well—took various concrete steps ranging from private diplomatic expressions of concern to the suspension of foreign aid. Rarely, though, has the United States been willing to use stronger means or to accept significant costs to its other interests. During the cold war, human rights were consistently subordinated to even minor security, political, economic, or ideological objectives.

Human rights have had a place in U.S. foreign policy since the mid-1970s. That place, however, has been peripheral, especially during the cold war. We can see this clearly by considering the cases of Central America, the Southern Cone, and South Africa. Although this focuses our attention primarily on human rights policies of right-wing American allies, these were in fact the three most intensely debated areas of U.S. bilateral international human rights policy in the 1970s and 1980s.

CENTRAL AMERICA AND U.S. HUMAN RIGHTS POLICY

Central America is the geographical area that lies between North America (Canada, the United States, and Mexico) and South America. It became a major international human rights concern in the 1980s largely because of U.S. support for the conservative government of El Salvador and parallel U.S. efforts to overthrow the leftist government of Nicaragua.

Human Rights in El Salvador and Nicaragua

El Salvador. Salvadoran independence from Spain in the 1820s was in many ways less significant than the economic reforms in the second half of the nineteenth century that transferred one-third of the country's land to a small coffee oligarchy. For the following half century, protests by dispossessed peasants were ruthlessly suppressed, culminating in the systematic killing of at least ten thousand people and as many as thirty thousand in the *matanza* (massacre) of 1932.

After World War II, the Salvadoran economy grew, but the benefits of growth were distributed extremely unequally. In the mid-1970s, more than two-thirds of the children under five suffered from malnutrition. Three-fourths of rural families (which made up about two-thirds of the total population) were landless. Less than 40 percent had access to piped water. Half lacked the income necessary for a minimum healthy diet. Urban poverty was only somewhat less extreme.[5] Not only was distributing the benefits of growth to the mass of the population largely ignored, but the ruling oligarchy regularly used force against those seeking a more egalitarian society.

Elections were held regularly, but the official military-backed party used patronage, threats, and when necessary, blatant fraud to assure victory for its candidates. As disillusionment grew, "popular organizations" emerged that engaged in direct nonviolent action—sit-ins, strikes, demonstrations, civil disobedience. A few opponents also turned to armed insurrection, but in the mid-1970s they were of negligible political significance.

The security forces and their paramilitary supporters responded to peaceful protest and guerrilla activity alike with violence. The government of General Carlos Humberto Romero, installed after the fraudulent elections of 1977, imposed total press censorship, outlawed not only strikes but also public meetings of all sorts, and suspended judicial due process. Death squads, which worked closely with both the party and the Salvadoran national security agency, became a regular part of the Romero regime's repressive apparatus.

In an attempt to head off civil war, reformist junior officers staged a coup in October 1979. In January 1980, however, all the civilian members of the cabinet resigned because of the government's inability to control the security forces. For example, military sharpshooters opened fire from the top of the National Palace on a peaceful demonstration commemorating the *matanza* of 1932, killing between twenty and fifty people. A second junta collapsed in March, again because the military refused to allow civilian political control. This was vividly illustrated by the assassination on March 24, 1980, of Archbishop Oscar Arnulfo Romero. As opposition continued to grow, the government declared a state of siege.

Although the intensification of repression led all other civilian political parties to refuse to participate, the conservative wing of the Christian Democrats, led by José Napoleon Duarte, joined the third junta. Political deaths jumped from under two thousand in 1979 to twelve thousand in 1980. In November 1980, six leaders of the Democratic Revolutionary Front (FDR), a party made up principally of Social Democrats and the left wing of the (centrist) Christian Democrats, were dragged from a meeting and brutally murdered. After this, most of the remaining leaders of the nonviolent opposition went underground or into exile. Duarte, however, remained in the fourth junta, which instituted a reign of terror. Americas Watch estimated that out of a total population of less than 5 million, there were over thirty thousand government-sponsored murders in 1980–1983 alone (roughly equivalent to killing 1.25 million Americans).

Duarte's election as president in 1984 (largely as a result of U.S. pressure) helped to reduce the level of violence. The human rights situation, however, remained dismal. The government estimated that death squads were killing "only" about thirty people a month in 1985.[6] Torture continued. The number of political prisoners even increased, apparently because of the decline in political murders.

El Salvador thus settled into a sad routine of reduced, but still widespread and systematic, human rights abuses. At the end of the decade, most civil and political rights remained regularly violated. A bad economic situation was, at best, about the same (and that only because of massive U.S. aid). The guerrillas, whose strength grew along with the repression in the early and mid-1980s, continued to operate, but with no real success. Peaceful political opposition, and economic organization by workers and peasants, remained dangerous.

The electoral transfer of power between civilian governments in March 1989 was a notable event in Salvadoran political history. But under Alfredo Cristiani's right-wing National Republican Alliance (ARENA) government, political space in El Salvador actually contracted in 1989. At least seventy human rights activists were arrested, labor activists came under increased attack, the offices of COMADRES (Committee of Mothers of Political Prisoners, Disappeared, and Assassinated in El Salvador) were bombed, and six Jesuit priests and two lay women were murdered by the military.

A UN-mediated end to the civil war was agreed to at the end of 1991, and UN monitors arrived in 1992. This has stopped the fighting and initiated efforts at structural political reform (especially greater civilian control over the armed forces). Although serious human rights issues remain, they now involve little direct state violence against the people. But throughout the 1980s, when it was a principal subject of U.S. human rights policy, El Salvador was either a brutal military dictatorship or a somewhat less brutal military-civilian oligarchy.

Nicaragua. Nicaragua's early political history was not much different from that of El Salvador.[7] In 1936, however, Anastasio Somoza García seized power and initiated what was to be more than forty years of authoritarian family rule. When Somoza was assassinated in 1956, power passed first to his son Luis Somoza Debayle and then to his younger son, Anastasio Somoza Debayle, who ruled until overthrown in 1979.

The Somozas retained the forms of democracy, but elections were rigged and civil and political rights were regularly violated. (Large-scale systematic killings, though, were not part of their repertoire.) Economic and social rights were also systematically infringed, both through the predatory accumulation of immense personal wealth by the Somozas and their cronies and through disregard of social services. For example, in the early 1970s, the Nicaraguan government spent three times as much on defense as on health care while its neighbors typically spent about equal amounts on each.

Massive corruption in the cleanup and recovery effort following the 1972 earthquake in the capital city of Managua, which left perhaps ten thousand dead and hundreds of thousands homeless, exacerbated and highlighted the endemic problems of inequality. Two years later, Somoza was reelected in a contest that even by Nicaraguan standards was farcical. In January 1978, the pace of disaffection accelerated after the assassination of Pedro Joaquin Chamorro, the leader of the moderate opposition. Even the business community turned against Somoza, under whom it had profited, organizing a general strike to protest Chamorro's death. Eighteen months later, Somoza was forced into exile.

Somoza was swept from power by a mass popular revolt incorporating many different social and political groups. Its military forces were led by the Sandinista National Liberation Front (FSLN), established in 1961 as a radical breakaway from the Soviet-oriented Nicaraguan Socialist Party. But during his final two years in power, Somoza was opposed even by Nicaragua's traditional and conservative Catholic Church and by the United States, the Somozas' traditional patron.

The revolution, although widely supported, had immense human and economic costs. About one-fifth of Nicaragua's population of roughly 2.5

million became refugees. Casualties included 40,000–50,000 people killed, 150,000 wounded, and perhaps 40,000 orphaned. The war also disrupted agricultural production and most other sectors of the economy. Real gross domestic product fell by one-fourth in 1979 and by another one-fifth in 1980. Direct economic losses from the revolution were about $2 billion, or roughly Nicaragua's entire annual gross domestic product.

Human rights conditions generally improved in revolutionary Nicaragua. The Sandinista government increased spending on social programs, especially health care, and redirected spending for education toward mass literacy. Personal and legal rights were fairly widely respected. Internationally recognized civil liberties were extensively implemented for the first time in Nicaraguan history. Mass political participation was actively fostered, and the 1984 election was generally considered by outside observers to have been relatively open and fairly run.

The government itself admitted serious human rights violations during the forced relocation of Indian populations on the Atlantic Coast. Restrictions on freedom of the press, freedom of association, and due process were imposed. Sandinista mass popular organizations and the government-controlled media received preferential treatment. Nonetheless, political opponents operated under fewer constraints, and with far less fear of retaliation, than most of Somoza's opponents had. Human rights NGOs such as Americas Watch consistently judged the human rights situation to be significantly better than in neighboring El Salvador and Guatemala.

This record, although acceptable only in relative terms, was noteworthy because the Sandinista government was under intense attack from U.S.-financed "contras" (a shortened form of the Spanish for counterrevolutionaries). The contras originated in the Nicaraguan Democratic Forces, a group of former Somoza national guardsmen led by Colonel Enrique Bermúdez. In 1981, the U.S. Central Intelligence Agency (CIA) began financial and logistical support, which by 1983 involved $100 million provided to a force that had grown to more than ten thousand guerrillas.

Contra strategy emphasized terrorism, including attacks on farms, schools, and health clinics, indiscriminate attacks on civilian economic targets, kidnappings, and assassinations. Nonetheless, the rights to life and security of the person were surprisingly consistently respected by the Nicaraguan government. In sharp contrast, U.S.-supported governments in neighboring Guatemala and El Salvador typically justified state terrorism by the need to combat guerrilla violence.

With the winding down of the contra war in 1988 and 1989, respect for civil and political rights again improved. Peaceful political opposition was generally tolerated during the 1989–1990 election campaign. And in national elections in February 1990, the Sandinistas were voted out of power. This was particularly noteworthy because it involved not merely a change in government, as in neighboring El Salvador and Guatemala, but a change in social and political philosophy.

The new government of President Violetta Chamorro tried to set aside ideological and political disputes in the name of national reunification. Her government achieved a solid record on civil and political rights and seems to have restored the economy to a relatively solid foundation, following the devastation of the revolution and the contra war. But economic and social rights, especially for the poor, have generally stagnated or suffered. The October 1996 presidential election saw the second defeat of Sandinista leader Daniel Ortega, this time by Arnoldo Aleman. Although this second transfer of power by electoral means is certainly an encouraging sign, the vicious and polarizing campaign waged by both candidates is not. In addition, Aleman seems more concerned with recovering property nationalized during the revolution than with improving economic and social rights for the average Nicaraguan.

U.S. Policy in Central America

In the early twentieth century, U.S. policy in Central America was directed toward establishing military, economic, and political hegemony. Central America was strategically significant for its proximity to the United States, the Panama Canal, and Caribbean sea-lanes. U.S. pressure and intervention were also regularly used to further the interests of U.S. banks and corporations. By the 1920s, Central America had become a special U.S. sphere of influence, "our backyard," as it was still often put in the 1980s.

Since World War II, however, the role of economic concerns in U.S. policy has declined dramatically. In 1954, the U.S.-backed overthrow of the freely elected government of Jacobo Arbenz in Guatemala did reflect the interests of the United Fruit Company, which had special influence in both the State Department and the CIA. Even then, though, anticommunism was probably a stronger motivating force. By the 1980s, when Central America reemerged as a central issue in U.S. foreign policy, economic interests were largely irrelevant. For example, U.S. exports to Nicaragua averaged just under $200 million per year for 1976 to 1978. U.S. direct foreign investment was a mere $60 million.

Human rights concerns, however, did not replace economic interests. "Human rights is a residual category in United States policy toward Latin America; it (along with economic development) is what policy emphasizes when there is no security problem on the horizon."[8] During the cold war, U.S. policy was instead driven by the fear that domestic instability might increase support for local Communists and their Soviet (and Cuban) backers. U.S. policy in Central America thus oscillated between neglect during periods of domestic calm and intervention at times of domestic instability. In both modes, though, U.S. policy usually supported the military and traditional civilian elites, to the detriment of the rights of most Central Americans.

Consider Nicaragua. In 1912, U.S. troops prevented a liberal political revolution, then remained until 1933, except for eighteen months between 1925 and 1927. Furthermore, the United States was the leading force behind the creation of the National Guard, the principal base of Somoza power. Economic interests and strategic concerns over a potential second canal through Nicaragua explain the initial U.S. involvement. But after World War II, the Somozas' support of U.S. cold war policies became their major asset. The (probably apocryphal) assessment of the senior Somoza attributed to Franklin D. Roosevelt aptly summarized the relationship: "He's a son of a bitch, but he's *our* son of a bitch." Even when the United States was not actively backing the Somozas, its toleration of their dictatorial rule was widely, and with some justice, seen as tacit support.

U.S. policy in Guatemala and El Salvador was similar. Following the overthrow of Arbenz in 1954, the United States supported a series of vicious Guatemalan military governments. In El Salvador, although dictatorship was established with little American involvement, the United States supported a series of military-dominated governments.

The postwar U.S. record on economic and social rights in Central America was more mixed. The Alliance for Progress, a major foreign aid initiative for Latin America launched in 1961, brought substantial increases in U.S. aid to Central America. This seems to have contributed to rapid economic growth in the 1960s and early 1970s. U.S. aid also helped to improve life expectancy and literacy. The benefits of growth, however, were distributed so unequally that the gap between rich and poor widened in the 1960s and 1970s. And in El Salvador, Guatemala, and Nicaragua alike, U.S.-backed governments regularly used their power against political parties, trade unions, peasant organizations, and most other groups that tried to foster more rapid reforms or structural changes in society or the economy.

There were signs of U.S. uneasiness. For example, after martial law was imposed in Nicaragua in 1974, the Ford administration moved to distance itself from Somoza (although not so far as to support any alternative). Nonetheless, the logic of anticommunism dominated U.S. policy in Central America in the first three decades after World War II.

The Carter administration entered office in 1977 intent on giving human rights at least equal place in its policy. In Central America, the administration took both concrete and symbolic action. Early in 1977, Guatemala's military government announced that it would not accept U.S. aid if it was contingent on public U.S. reporting of Guatemalan human rights practices. Neither Congress nor Carter, however, was willing to leave it at that. Military assistance credits to Guatemala were banned in 1978, and the U.S. refused to support multilateral loans to Guatemala in 1979 and 1980. The United States also carried out an active program of public diplomacy, including a well-publicized visit by Assistant Secretary of State William Bowdler. In summer 1977, the administration announced that continued military aid to Nicaragua would be contingent on human rights improvements.

Although notable, such changes were also limited. For example, although new military aid to Guatemala was cut off, already committed ("pipeline") aid was continued. And Carter never seriously pressed for major structural reforms. For example, when Somoza lifted censorship regulations and the state of siege, the United States largely dropped the issue of human rights.

When Nicaragua did emerge as a major concern of U.S. foreign policy, in fall 1978, internal turmoil rather than human rights was the major American concern. Carter's goal was to remove Somoza without yielding power to the Sandinistas, who were seen as too closely tied to Cuba and the Soviet Union. The desire to avoid "another Cuba" dominated policy.

The United States tried to strengthen the political center, but it was suffering under political and financial retaliation by Somoza, and the assassination of Pedro Joaquin Chamorro had deprived it of its most respected and effective leader. After four frustrating months of U.S. mediation, Somoza simply refused to leave. Carter responded with wide-ranging sanctions. Military and economic aid was terminated, the Peace Corps was withdrawn, and the size of the U.S. Embassy in Managua was reduced by more than one-half. But when these sanctions failed to convince Somoza to step down, there was little that could be done short of the use of force—which Carter refused to consider, for reasons of principle and policy alike.

In June 1979, when the Sandinistas (FSLN) launched their "final offensive," the United States again tried to promote a centrist "third force." The pace of events, however, combined with the moderate opposition's lack of organization and foresight, proved fatal. When Somoza left in July, power passed to a provisional coalition government dominated by its most astute and best-organized faction, the FSLN.

The Carter administration attempted to set aside its suspicions. Food and medical supplies were sent almost immediately. When Carter left office in January 1981, eighteen months after Somoza's fall, the United States had provided $118 million in aid to Nicaragua. This was more than the United States gave to any other Central American country in the same period and was the largest amount provided to Nicaragua by any Western government. In addition, the United States supported $262 million in World Bank and Inter-American Development Bank loans.

In El Salvador, because of human rights concerns, the United States backed the October 1979 coup led by reformist military officers. But when most of the civilians in the junta resigned in January 1980 to protest the government's inability to control the military or halt human rights violations, the Carter administration remained supportive (although it still did not restore military aid). Even after Colonel Majano, the leader of the reformist faction in the military, was forced out of the junta in December 1980, the United States continued to characterize the Salvadoran government as reformist, despite massive and mounting violations of civil and political rights and lack of progress on land reform and other economic and social rights.

It is also important to note that even Carter's limited efforts on behalf of human rights met with substantial domestic opposition. For example, in June 1979 more than one hundred members of Congress signed a full-page ad in support of Somoza that ran in the *New York Times* under the headline "Congress Asks: Please, Mr. President, Not Another Cuba!" The Carter administration itself also included skeptics among its high officials, most prominently National Security Adviser Zbigniew Brzezinski. As these elements increasingly came to dominate policymaking, the Carter administration began moving the United States toward what would become Reagan's new approach.

Reagan's approach to Central America (like the rest of the world) started from radical anticommunism. Although Soviet power prevented efforts to "roll back" communism in Central and Eastern Europe, the Third World did present opportunities. Central America (along with Afghanistan) became a test case for Reagan's new global political strategy. By summer 1981, the CIA was working with the contra military opposition in Nicaragua. On March 14, 1982, the war began when two bridges were destroyed by former members of the National Guard who had been trained by the CIA.

The "Kirkpatrick Doctrine" provided a rationale for this new approach. In an influential article that helped to earn her the position of U.S. ambassador to the UN, Jeane Kirkpatrick argued that Carter had failed to understand that the most serious threats to human rights were posed not by authoritarian dictatorships but by totalitarian Communists. Furthermore, because many authoritarian dictatorships were U.S. allies, Carter's policy hurt U.S. friends while giving insufficient attention to communism, the most serious threat to human rights.[9] As one conservative group summed up the Carter approach, "Faced with the choice of an occasionally deplorable ally and a consistently deplorable enemy, since 1977 the United States has aided its adversary and alienated its ally."[10] For the Reagan administration, global strategic rivalry with the Soviet Union *was* a struggle for human rights, whatever the actual human rights practices of the governments in question.

Many in Congress, however, had a more complex vision of Central America, and they were supported by a wide range of liberal interest groups. The Reagan administration thus faced constant, but only sporadically successful, resistance to its requests for aid to the contras. Aid was suspended in July 1983. But "humanitarian" assistance resumed in June 1985, and military aid was approved the following summer. Not until February 1988, during Reagan's last year of office, was military aid again stopped.

The Reagan administration blocked multilateral loans to Nicaragua, cut the import of Nicaraguan sugar by 90 percent in 1983, and imposed a complete trade embargo in May 1985. The United States orchestrated a massive assault on Nicaragua, using the full range of resources short of the direct use of U.S. troops—but including illegally mining Nicaraguan harbors in 1984. Funds were even illegally diverted to the contras, and those responsible lied under oath to Congress.

This campaign of military and economic aggression had devastating consequences. As many as 40,000 people were killed, and at least 250,000 displaced. Food production declined by at least one-fourth. Advances in health care and social services were reversed by terrorist attacks on clinics, schools, and social service offices. By 1988, the Nicaraguan economy had been destroyed, with hyperinflation raging at 31,000 percent per year.

All of this must be contrasted with strong U.S. support for the government of El Salvador. The human rights situation in El Salvador in the late 1970s and early 1980s was far worse than in Nicaragua under either Somoza or the Sandinistas. Salvadoran security forces regularly used indiscriminate violence against civilians. Clandestine paramilitary death squads, with links to the security forces and right-wing political parties, operated with impunity, kidnapping and killing politicians, labor leaders, peasant activists, intellectuals, church activists, and other civilians believed to sympathize with the guerrillas.[11] And in addition to the tens of thousands of Salvadorans killed, Americans were also victims. In December 1980, four American churchwomen were abducted, raped, and murdered. In March 1981, two officials of the American Institute for Free Labor Development were assassinated in the San Salvador Sheraton Hotel. Yet massive aid continued—about $500 million a year in 1984 and 1985 (compared to less than $100 million in 1979 and 1980 combined), totaling almost $4 billion for the decade.

To release American aid, Congress required the president to certify that the government of El Salvador was respecting internationally recognized human rights and had gained control over the armed forces. The first such certification came in January 1982, after a year in which the Salvadoran government and its paramilitary allies had murdered well over ten thousand civilians. After four such cynical certifications, President Reagan vetoed new legislation requiring further certifications.

The human rights situation in neighboring Nicaragua was hardly ideal. For example, the 1984–1985 Americas Watch annual report noted "prior censorship of the press, political jailings, the denial of due process of law by special tribunals, the mistreatment of prisoners by incommunicado detention, and forced relocation."[12] But torture and extrajudicial executions, which were commonplace in El Salvador, were rare in Nicaragua. Nonetheless, the United States helped to launch and aggressively supported a guerrilla war of terrorism against Nicaragua. As Americas Watch put it, "So consistent is this double standard that it can be fairly said [that] the Reagan administration has no true human rights policy."[13]

The Kirkpatrick Doctrine did suggest that the cause of human rights would be ultimately furthered by the success of a geopolitical struggle against the Soviet Union and its clients. Human rights as an independent and immediate concern, however, had virtually no place in the Reagan administration's Central America policy. Criticisms of the human rights practices of leftist regimes and the defense of the human rights practices of "friendly" governments were simply a continuation of the struggle with the Soviet Union by other means.

The gap between the Carter and Reagan policies toward Central America, however, was not as wide as their rhetoric suggested. Carter spoke of human rights as the "heart" of U.S. foreign policy, but in practice they were only a secondary goal. And Reagan's attempts to relegate human rights to the bottom of the list of U.S. foreign policy objectives were at least partially defeated by Congress. Carter did significantly elevate the place of human rights in U.S. policy toward Central America. But they never reached the top. Reagan did force human rights back down the list. But they never reached the bottom.[14]

The Bush administration's Central America policy, both in word and in deed, lay between its predecessors. Bush generally supported the Salvadoran and Guatemalan governments, despite their lack of control over the military. For example, he strongly opposed congressional efforts to cut military aid to El Salvador after the November 1989 murder of six Jesuits. In January 1991, Bush even restored the aid Congress had cut in half just two months earlier, despite the continuing abuses and the absence of a single successful prosecution of anyone for these (or any other) human rights violations.

But Bush did act to prevent further deterioration in the situation. For example, he suspended military aid to Guatemala in late 1990 after an upsurge in political violence. Vice President Dan Quayle was sent to El Salvador twice in 1989 to express the administration's concerns. Bush supported the implementation of the UN-mediated end to El Salvador's civil war. And in Nicaragua, he pursued a somewhat less belligerent strategy of opposition to the Sandinistas.

The Clinton administration has been generally supportive of human rights in the region. This would appear to be Clinton's inclination. But given the low priority of human rights in his foreign policy, the most important factor has probably been the implementation of the peace agreement in El Salvador, with continuing American support, and a similar United Nations initiative in Guatemala in 1994. And Clinton, like his predecessors, has given almost no serious attention to issues of economic, social, and cultural rights.

THE UNITED STATES AND THE SOUTHERN CONE

As we saw in Chapter 3, Argentina, Chile, and Uruguay suffered under brutal military regimes in the 1970s and 1980s. What Argentineans call the Dirty War was a concerted campaign of violence directed against the political Left, trade unions, intellectuals, mainstream autonomous social organizations, and dissidents of all sorts, as well as ordinary, apolitical citizens who were forced into or became accidentally enmeshed in the politics of torture and disappearances.

The United States played a significant supporting role in the rise to power of the Chilean military. The Nixon administration saw the 1970 election of Salvador Allende, an avowed Marxist, as an intolerable intrusion of communism in Latin America, despite Allende's fair and free election, strong democratic socialist background, and independence from Soviet and Cuban influence. Henry Kissinger, national security adviser and later secretary of state, crafted a campaign of economic sabotage. In addition, U.S. support encouraged dissident military officers (although the 1973 coup was largely a local Chilean initiative). Although the United States played only a small role in the rise of military rule in Uruguay and Argentina, U.S. diplomacy supported all three new military regimes.

Congress tried to distance the United States from the junta in Chile, limiting economic aid and banning new military assistance. Kissinger, however, did his best to circumvent Congress. For example, in 1976 he publicly reprimanded the U.S. ambassador to Chile for even raising the issue of human rights in private discussions. Even when human rights initiatives were undertaken, as in Argentina in 1976, they were low-key, private, and accompanied by public support for the military.

The Carter administration sharply reversed U.S. policy. President Carter, Secretary of State Cyrus Vance, and Assistant Secretary of State for Human Rights Patricia Derian all drew public attention to human rights violations in the Southern Cone. No head of a Southern Cone military regime was invited for a state visit to Washington. By contrast, human rights activists and major figures in the political opposition were received at the State Department and had access to local U.S. embassies.

A month after entering office, Carter reduced military aid to Argentina and Uruguay by two-thirds. In fact, during Carter's term all military aid to Southern Cone countries was halted (although Congress deserves much of the credit for this). The Carter administration voted against or abstained on twenty-three loans by international development banks to Argentina, eleven to Uruguay, and five to Chile (although the fact that all these loans were ultimately approved suggests that the votes were largely symbolic). The United States also supported UN and OAS activities directed against Argentina, Uruguay, and especially Chile.

These policies led to the release of several political prisoners, including prominent opposition journalist Jacobo Timerman and human rights activist (and future Nobel Peace Prize recipient) Adolfo Pérez Esquivel. Conditions of detention were eased for many others. The Carter administration also claimed credit for reductions in disappearances and political prisoners, although a much more important factor was probably the success of earlier efforts at terror and repression.

The Carter policies, however, did not end military rule. Relations with Chile, Uruguay, and especially Argentina were strained. One may debate whether the achievements were great enough or the costs sufficiently low to justify the policy. It is clear, though, that the Carter approach to the Southern Cone represented a major shift in U.S. policy. And unlike Central America, this new approach was sustained through the full four years of the Carter presidency.

In 1981, the Reagan administration abruptly returned to the policies of Nixon, Kissinger, and Ford. In fact, Argentina and Chile were principal examples in Jeane Kirkpatrick's criticism of the Carter administration for foolishly sacrificing more important U.S. interests to the quixotic pursuit of human rights.

Although Congress had explicitly prohibited economic or military aid to Chile, the Reagan administration did everything it could to foster cordial relations with the Pinochet government. In August 1981, Ambassador Kirkpatrick paid a formal visit to Chile and called for the full normalization of U.S.-Chilean relations. At the UN Commission on Human Rights, the United States voted against continuing the special rapporteur on Chile. Joint military exercises were reinstituted. Loans from the Inter-American Development Bank to Chile jumped from zero in 1980 to over $180 million in 1981 and 1982. In 1983 alone, Chile received more than three times the total of multilateral loans it had obtained during the entire Carter administration.

For Argentina, the Reagan administration obtained repeal of the 1978 Humphrey-Kennedy amendment that had banned U.S. military sales and security assistance. General Viola, the leader of Argentina's second junta, was one of the first foreign leaders invited by Reagan for a state visit, in March 1981. U.S. representatives to international financial institutions were instructed to cease abstaining on loan applications, despite a clear legal requirement that they do so. Ambassador Kirkpatrick did not even reply to a letter from the Mothers of the Plaza de Mayo asking for a meeting during her 1981 visit to Buenos Aires.

These signals of renewed U.S. support led directly to new human rights violations. Immediately after Kirkpatrick's visit, Chile expelled several political leaders, including centrist Christian Democrats, and arrested and tortured a number of human rights activists. The United States issued no public response. In Argentina, seven leading Argentine human rights activists were detained incommunicado immediately prior to General Viola's visit to Washington, to keep them from saying anything that might cloud Viola's reception. The Reagan administration made private efforts to obtain their release, but there was no public protest, and General Viola received a warm welcome at the White House.

Although the Reagan administration did engage in quiet diplomacy on behalf of individual victims in the Southern Cone, human rights violations were treated as a matter for private discussions between friends. The overriding priority was to maintain close relations. Other interests were considered far more important than pervasive human rights abuses.

Even after Argentina's Falklands disaster, which proved to be the prelude to the return of civilian rule, the Reagan administration did not publicly raise human rights concerns. The new civilian government was embraced in Washington. But the United States had nothing to do with its creation. In Uruguay as well, civilian rule returned despite, rather than because of, U.S. policy.

In Chile, the Reagan administration did speak out against the intensified repression that led to the reimposition of martial law in 1984. Assistant Secretary of State Elliott Abrams, previously a vocal supporter of the Chilean junta, publicly criticized the Pinochet government. The United States also abstained on some multilateral loans to Chile in February and March 1985. But soon after the state of siege was formally lifted in June 1985, the United States supported Chilean requests for $345 million in multilateral loans, even though the human rights situation had not significantly improved. And in December 1985, the United States cast the decisive vote in the OAS General Assembly that removed reference to Chile from a resolution on human rights violations. Even after Pinochet lost the 1988 plebiscite for another eight-year term as president, U.S. criticism of military rule remained low-key. As elsewhere in the region, democracy returned to Chile largely in spite of U.S. policy.

U.S. POLICY TOWARD SOUTH AFRICA

The human rights situation in South Africa was discussed in Chapter 4. Here we will be concerned with the response of the United States. Before the Sharpeville Massacre in 1960 and the ensuing state of emergency, the

United States treated apartheid as an internal South African matter. The turmoil following Sharpeville, however, raised the specter of revolution and mobilized American fear of communism. The United States thus began to treat apartheid as a matter of international concern. The Eisenhower administration even agreed to put apartheid permanently on the agenda of the UN Security Council.

The new Kennedy administration initiated a policy review in 1961 (which dragged on until 1964). Kennedy also imposed a selective arms embargo even before the Security Council called for a voluntary embargo at the end of 1963. As the crisis receded, however, so did U.S. attention. Sanctions remained in effect, but they were modest and had no discernible impact.

When Henry Kissinger took over as national security adviser to President Nixon in 1969, he instituted a series of policy reviews for all areas of the world. The resulting document on South Africa, National Security Memorandum 39 (NSM 39), proposed closer association with South Africa in order to put the United States in a better position to press for reform. Relations were not fully normalized. For example, the arms embargo was loosened but not eliminated. The goal was to combine negative sanctions with more positive inducements to change and to use areas of mutual interest, such as regional security, as a wedge to open South Africa to U.S. pressure on apartheid.

This approach, however, had no more impact than the Kennedy-Johnson strategy of dissociation had. Part of the problem was weak and inconsistent implementation. For example, false certifications of the nonmilitary nature of certain arms were accepted. A 1978 U.S. Department of Justice study found that 178 of South Africa's 578 military aircraft had been purchased from the United States during the embargo.[15] Furthermore, U.S. concessions were tied to no particular demands on South Africa. In other words, there was no real *policy* on South Africa. NSM 39 was adopted, but never seriously implemented.

There were also major conceptual flaws in both the Kennedy-Johnson and the Nixon-Kissinger approaches. The United States asked for changes that the South African government refused even to consider. Although willing to ease some elements of "petty apartheid" (for example, by desegregating some public facilities in large cities), the government was unwilling to end racial separation. Democratic majority rule was not even open for discussion. The negative sanctions and positive inducements the United States was willing to use fell far short of what would have been necessary to make the white government change its mind.

The other conceptual error in U.S. policy was an excessive reliance on economic change and private enterprise. Liberals and conservatives alike believed that South Africa's atavistic racial policies would inevitably be eroded by the modernization that accompanied economic development. Trade and investment thus appeared as instruments for change rather than as support for apartheid. In practice, however, reforms required by economic necessity were prevented from spilling over into social and political changes. South Africa's immense bureaucracy, which intervened with totalitarian thoroughness in all aspects of life, largely prevented unplanned changes in the fundamental character of apartheid from going unnoticed or unchecked.

After the Portuguese coup in April 1974, which led to the rapid decolonization of Angola and Mozambique, even these modest U.S. efforts were largely abandoned in favor of a focus on "regional security," that is, containing expanding Soviet influence. South Africa now appeared as a pro-Western regional power. Kissinger even met Prime Minister Vorster twice in 1976, the first official meeting at this level in thirty years.

The Soweto riots of 1976 returned apartheid to the center of international attention. Soon afterward, the election of Jimmy Carter changed the U.S. approach. The arms embargo was restored to its pre-Nixon status. Outstanding Export-Import Bank credits to South Africa were cut in half. South Africa's October 1977 clampdown on nonviolent opposition even led to U.S. support in the Security Council for a mandatory arms embargo.

These actions, however, were largely symbolic. Furthermore, there were tensions within the Carter administration. National Security Adviser Zbigniew Brzezinski favored a policy that, like Kissinger's, emphasized regional security. As Brzezinski's influence grew in the second half of Carter's term, U.S. policy took on an increasingly cold war tone, stressing the Cuban presence in Angola and the Soviet naval threat in the South Atlantic and the Indian Ocean. Even more than in Central America, the end of the Carter administration prepared the way for Reagan.

Reagan's policy of "constructive engagement" returned to the Nixon-era strategy of pursuing closer relations in order to increase U.S. leverage. Assistant Secretary of State Chester Crocker, the principal architect of the policy, had been a staff member on Kissinger's National Security Council. In the 1980s, he tried to turn the idea behind NSM 39 into an effective policy.

Despite international calls for new sanctions, the United States eased many that were already in place. New Export-Import Bank credits were approved. Efforts to discourage private bank loans were halted. In 1982, the Reagan administration supported a $1 billion International Monetary Fund (IMF) credit to South Africa, the largest ever made through the fund's Compensatory Financing Facility. Restrictions on the sale of aircraft, computers, and nuclear-related equipment with dual military and civilian uses were eased. In fact, the United States became South Africa's largest trading partner. Total private investment and loans rose to $10 billion.

The justification for constructive engagement was a belief that the government of P. W. Botha was pragmatic and committed to managing an ongoing transition from apartheid. The U.S. role, therefore, was to foster change through enlightened private enterprise and support for moderate forces of social change, such as trade unions and education. But there was an immense gap between policy and practice. The United States actually devoted almost no resources to education or trade unions. The reforms introduced by U.S. corporations helped a small number of employees but had no systematic impact on apartheid.

As in the early 1970s, the United States did not insist on any concrete human rights improvements in return for closer relations. And South African intentions continued to be misjudged. The Botha government was willing to modernize apartheid. It was not willing to eliminate it.

Events in South Africa, however, again forced a reevaluation of U.S. policy. Violence erupted in August 1984 in protest over elections held under the new Constitution of 1983, which completely excluded blacks from direct political participation. When repression once more tightened rather than eased, constructive engagement lost any remaining credibility.

The decisive changes in U.S. policy came from Congress. Progress on a bipartisan compromise sanctions bill forced Reagan to issue an executive order in September 1985 imposing limited economic sanctions. As late as July 1986, however, Reagan still argued that "we and our allies cannot dictate to the government of a sovereign nation—nor should we try." Critics scoffed, noting that Reagan had for years been funding a war against Nicaragua and had imposed sanctions against Cuba, Libya, Nicaragua, and Poland. Soon afterward, Congress overrode a presidential veto of a new sanctions bill.

Such strong congressional action was the work of a bipartisan coalition. In November 1984, Republican Senators Richard Lugar, chair of the Foreign Relations Committee, and Nancy Kassebaum, chair of the African Affairs Subcommittee, who were early supporters of constructive engagement, called on the president to review the administration's South Africa policy. The following month, thirty-five conservative members of the House, including Newt Gingrich, also called for abandoning constructive engagement, citing it as an embarrassing political liability—a view shared by most congressional Democrats.

These changes mirrored changes in the electorate that had been prepared by extensive NGO work. Activity on South Africa by U.S. NGOs goes back to at least 1912, when the National Association for the Advancement of Colored People (NAACP) was involved in the initial formation of South Africa's African National Congress. The American Committee on Africa was formed in 1953 in response to the pass law demonstrations. In the late 1970s and 1980s, groups like TransAfrica focused their efforts on apartheid. Other NGOs, such as the American Friends Service Committee, the Interfaith Council on Corporate Responsibility, and the Lawyers' Committee for Civil Rights Under Law, made South Africa a major priority. In addition, churches, state and local governments, colleges and universities, student organizations, unions, and black organizations divested assets in corporations that did business in South Africa.

These activities brought home to a local audience the concerns and activities of the international antiapartheid regime (see Chapter 4). Some of these U.S. NGO activities were even coordinated with divestment campaigns in other countries, with international antiapartheid groups such as the International Defense and Aid Fund, and with other international NGOs such as the World Council of Churches and the Lutheran World Fund. They were also facilitated by Bishop Desmond Tutu's Nobel Peace Prize and his well-publicized visit to the United States at the end of 1984.

It is important not to overestimate U.S. efforts or their impact. Reagan's 1985 executive order was so limited and full of loopholes that Bishop Tutu described it as "not even a flea bite." The 1986 sanctions were also limited and partial. Nonetheless, South Africa was losing access to international capital (although in the short run more from lender fear caused by the 1984–1986 township riots than from sanctions). And the loss of U.S. support, even if the Reagan administration never actively opposed the white government, created concern among many of South Africa's less-conservative leaders and citizens, particularly in light of the growing internal crisis.

Apartheid ultimately collapsed because of the inability of the white government to keep opposition repressed. Nonetheless, changes in U.S. policy, particularly in the context of the global antiapartheid campaign, made a small contribution to the final demise of apartheid. And even if American sanctions were primarily symbolic—as was the support provided by constructive engagement—it was a very different sort of symbolism than had been typical of U.S. policy in the preceding years.

OTHER WESTERN APPROACHES TO INTERNATIONAL HUMAN RIGHTS

Although the United States led the way in the 1970s in introducing human rights into bilateral diplomacy, other countries also incorporated human rights into their foreign policies. Particularly notable have been the efforts of the **like-minded countries,** a dozen smaller Western countries that since the mid-1970s have attempted to act together in international diplomacy as intermediaries between the larger Western countries, with which they are formally or informally aligned, and the countries of the

Third World, for whose aspirations they have considerable sympathy. Norway and the Netherlands in particular have emphasized human rights in their foreign policy and issued White Papers in 1977 and 1979.

Even more than in the United States, foreign aid has been a central instrument in the international human rights policies of the like-minded countries. Development assistance tends to be an important element of their foreign policies and a matter of consensus among the major political parties. In the Netherlands, there is even a separate minister for development cooperation within the Foreign Ministry.[16] By contrast, in the United States foreign aid is a relatively peripheral part of foreign policy yet is a subject of considerable political controversy.

Their approach to linking human rights and development assistance also differs. The United States tends to base initial foreign aid decisions on political and humanitarian factors, modifying allocations at a later stage in light of human rights concerns. The like-minded countries, which lack the resources to engage in a massive, global foreign aid program, target their development assistance at a small set of countries—variously called "core," "program," or "priority" countries—with which they seek to develop relatively intensive, long-term aid relations. The Dutch and Norwegians in particular have emphasized both civil and political and economic, social, and cultural rights in selecting program countries.

In Norway, selection criteria since 1972 have included a strong preference for countries in which "the authorities of the country concerned [are] following a development-oriented and socially just policy in the best interests of all sections of the community." The Norwegian Storting (parliament) in 1976 reiterated its desire to cooperate with countries pursuing a "socially just policy" and committed to implementing the economic, social, and cultural rights laid out in the Universal Declaration and the Covenants. And in 1984, a center-right coalition government, using language more characteristic of left-wing liberals in the United States, declared that "development assistance is an extension to the international level of the efforts to create social justice, characteristic of the Norwegian welfare state" and that "all have the right to have their basic needs for food, water, clothing, education, and housing satisfied."[17] Social justice is given roughly equal priority with civil and political rights largely across the Norwegian political spectrum.

As early as 1973, the Dutch officially emphasized a "close relationship between peace, a just distribution of wealth, international legal order and respect for human rights."[18] Since the late 1970s, the Dutch have also stressed a desire to cooperate with countries that emphasize civil and political as well as economic, social, and cultural rights in their domestic politics and development strategies. In practice, the selection of priority countries only partially meets these noble statements of intent.[19]

Nonetheless, the overall human rights records of recipients of Dutch aid compare favorably with international averages and with the pattern of American aid.

Even more striking than the selection of priority countries has been the relatively rapid response of the like-minded countries to changes in human rights conditions. For example, Norway broke its aid relationship with Uganda in 1972, the year that Idi Amin overthrew the government of Milton Obote and embarked on a dictatorial career that made him one of the most notorious human rights violators of the decade. The Netherlands dropped Uganda from its list of program countries in 1974. The United States, by contrast, was Uganda's largest trading partner until October 1978, less than a year before Amin was overthrown.

Sweden stopped all assistance to Chile shortly after Pinochet's coup and was a significant international supporter of the work of the Vicaría. Canada was also a vocal critic of military rule in the Southern Cone. In the 1980s, as ethnic violence escalated in Sri Lanka, a country with which Norway had developed close ties in the 1970s, the Norwegians dramatically downgraded their relationship. Canada, the Netherlands, and the Nordic countries all increased their aid to Nicaragua in the 1980s, reflecting a radically different understanding of human rights than the Reagan administration.

The Dutch response to the deteriorating human rights situation in their former colony of Suriname is especially revealing. They strongly condemned the 1980 military coup. Following the execution of fifteen opposition figures in 1982, the Netherlands not only suspended all aid but refused to provide new aid for the remainder of the decade. And the Dutch led the effort to apply international pressure on Suriname, for example, by regularly raising the issue in annual UN discussions of human rights violations. The contrast to U.S. behavior toward its Caribbean Basin clients in Guatemala and El Salvador, who were guilty of much more severe human rights violations, is striking.

The Dutch even carried human rights into relations with Indonesia, a country of far greater importance. Although severe Indonesian abuses in the 1960s were not a major concern of Dutch foreign policy, "from 1977 on, the Dutch Government tried to raise informally the human rights issue" in aid consortium meetings.[20] In 1990, in response to new political executions, 27 million guilders in aid was withdrawn. When additional executions were announced, the Dutch took the issue to the Council of Ministers of the EC. Throughout 1991, Minister for Development Cooperation Jan Pronk continued public criticisms of Indonesia. Following the Dili massacre in November 1991, which brought ongoing human rights problems in Indonesian-occupied East Timor into the international spotlight, another 27 million guilders in aid was suspended. The Indonesian response was to terminate its aid relationship with the Netherlands in 1992.

These actions were not easy. The Dutch, as a former colonial power, were especially sensitive to Indonesian charges of paternalism. Substantial commercial interests also cut against acting on human rights concerns. Nonetheless, the government of the Netherlands took relatively forceful public actions that had real costs for their relations with Indonesia. And they did so despite the failure of other Western countries or Japan, Indonesia's largest source of aid, to follow their lead. The Dutch acted because they felt it was the right thing to do and because it was demanded by the precedents established by their previous actions and policy statements.

The like-minded countries also adopted an approach to South Africa very different from that of the United States in the 1970s and 1980s. Starting in 1969, Sweden and Norway provided both political support and development assistance funds to the ANC during its exile from South Africa. The Dutch adopted a similar policy in 1973. And in the 1980s, these efforts were expanded by the Nordic countries and the Netherlands alike into broad, high-priority programs for the whole region of Southern Africa. These countries also played a leading role in the international movement for sanctions against South Africa.

We should be careful not to romanticize the policies of the like-minded countries. Considerations other than human rights are central, sometimes even overriding, in their foreign policies. For example, Dutch aid sanctions against Indonesia did not extend to trade or other economic relations. Canada has also pursued close relations with Indonesia for commercial reasons. Economic interests in South Africa seriously delayed Canada's decision to adopt sanctions and led Norway to exclude shipping from its initial sanctions. Nonetheless, the overall international human rights record of the like-minded countries is clearly superior to that of the United States, both in avoiding associations with severe violators and in responding to abuses in countries with which they have special relations.[21]

EXPLAINING DIFFERENCES IN INTERNATIONAL HUMAN RIGHTS POLICIES

Jan Egeland, in comparing Norwegian and U.S. international human rights policies, argued that "small and big nations are differently disposed to undertaking coherent rights-oriented foreign policies." In fact, Egeland argued that the relatively meager international human rights accomplishments of the United States are "because of, rather than in spite of, her superpower status."[22] Small countries are not so much "better," in this analysis, as less constrained than large states. "The frequency and intensity of the conflict between self-interest and [international human rights] norms seems, in short, proportional to a nation's economic and military power, as well as to its foreign policy ambitions."[23] Large states have multiple interests and responsibilities that preclude the consistent pursuit of human rights objectives. Small states rarely have to choose between human rights and other foreign policy goals.

This explanation focuses on the structure of the international system. Large states are also more likely to pursue bilateral policies because they are more likely to have the power to achieve their aims by unilateral action. Small states, by contrast, tend to prefer international organizations because multilateral processes allow them greater opportunities to exert international influence. Such structural explanations would also seem to be supported by the fact that larger powers such as Britain, France, Japan, and to a lesser extent Germany, have international human rights policies closer to those of the United States than to Norway or the Netherlands.

But size alone cannot explain even the differences that are influenced by relative power. For example, despite declining American power, the United States remains reluctant to operate through multilateral channels (unless it can control the organization). As the power of Germany and Japan grows, they continue to rely heavily on multilateral organizations. Britain has tended to pursue a much more unilateral foreign policy than France, Germany, or Japan. Among small states, Sweden, Austria, and especially Switzerland have emphasized a neutral foreign policy. Canada, Belgium, and the Netherlands have had a strong Western orientation in their foreign policies. Size or power at most inclines states in certain directions.

Furthermore, we should not overlook factors that have little or nothing to do with size. Why did the United States emphasize international human rights in the 1970s while other large powers did not, and Japan still does not? Why did Britain and France intervene in their spheres of influence so much less frequently than the United States? Why are human rights as a foreign policy issue so much more controversial in the United States than in most other Western countries? Such questions can be answered only if we take history, political culture, and institutions into account.

Throughout the cold war era, the United States viewed the world in East-West terms, reducing all foreign policy issues to U.S.-Soviet rivalry. Although part of this can be attributed to the size and power of the United States, the cold war was not just any kind of bipolar political rivalry between hegemonic states. It was a rivalry that placed immense emphasis on ideology. It was usually simply assumed that radical reformers and their programs were Soviet backed, inspired, or influenced. Without the ideological element, many actual or attempted political changes in the Third World would not have seemed a threat to the United States and thus would not have led to a conflict with human rights objectives. Ideology, however, has nothing to do with size. Many small states, especially in Latin America, were at least as anticommunist as the United States. Conversely, it is historically rare for a large state to define its interests in ideological terms.

Consider also the tendency of the like-minded states to view international conflicts more in North-South than East-West terms. During the cold war, these countries saw the principal lines of international cleavage as dividing rich and poor, not liberal democratic and Communist. For example, in 1982, Mark MacGuigan, the Canadian secretary of state for external affairs, argued that "instability in Central America . . . is not a product of East-West rivalry. It is a product of poverty, the unfair distribution of wealth, and social injustice. Instability feeds poverty and injustice. East-West rivalries flow in its wake."[24] The Dutch and the Nordic countries share this view.

Some part of this might be related to size. For example, it is not surprising that countries like Canada, which fears being overwhelmed by the United States, or the Netherlands, which borders on powerful Germany and France, are more sympathetic to a perspective that sees differences in power as no less important than differences in ideology. But size alone cannot explain the difference in ideological perspective.

We can see this even in Egeland's own analysis. In explaining the "strong moral impact" on Norwegian policy, he stressed four factors: (1) no legacy of imperialism and intervention, (2) a good domestic human rights record, (3) a high level of foreign aid and support for changes in the world economy to favor Third World countries, and (4) consistent support for decolonization and national liberation movements.[25] The first of these four factors is related to size—although Belgium, Portugal, and the Netherlands did have significant colonial holdings; German, Austrian, Russian, and American colonial holdings were small; and the Netherlands rapidly overcame its imperial legacy. The other three factors, however, have little or nothing to do with size.

Size explains almost nothing about internal human rights records, as comparison of pairs of similarly sized countries such as the United States and the Soviet Union, China and India, Japan and Indonesia, Argentina and Holland, and Costa Rica and Guatemala vividly illustrates. If small size were really central, we would expect unusually good human rights records in Latin America and Africa, when in fact the opposite if anything has been the case. Nor does size have much to do with levels of foreign aid. The United States chooses to be niggardly, while Norway and the Netherlands (and Japan) choose to be generous.[26] And the United States has had a better record on supporting decolonization than small states such as Portugal and Spain or second-tier powers such as Britain and France.

Much the same can be said of the role of consensus in Norwegian international human rights and foreign policy, another factor Egeland emphasizes. Foreign policy consensus is hardly characteristic of small states, as the varying policies of dozens of Third World countries indicate. In the Nordic countries, foreign policy consensus is a function of a parliamentary system, in which there is no sharp division between executive and legislative branches, a strong reliance on a professional foreign and civil service (in contrast to the extensive use of political appointees in the U.S. bureaucracy), and a political tradition that assures direct representation and special consideration for all major social groups.[27] Conversely, although multiple interests and the large size of the U.S. bureaucracy do create more arenas for foreign policy conflict, the lack of consensus is at least as much a function of a presidential system and the turnover of the leadership of most bureaucratic agencies with every election.

Size tells us little or nothing about whether or why a country will choose to emphasize human rights in its foreign policy. Certainly it is not size that explains why Norway and the Netherlands in the 1970s embarked on unusually active international human rights policies while Austria, Belgium, and Greece did not. Likewise, size cannot explain either the active (if inconsistent) international human rights policy of the United States or the lack of an active international human rights policy in Japan, let alone China.

How a country defines its interests is constrained by its power and its position in the international system. But interests are not fixed by power or position. Most impediments to strong international human rights policies lie in the relatively free decisions of states to give higher weight to other foreign policy objectives. Most of the factors that contribute to aggressive efforts to pursue international human rights in a country's foreign policy have much more to do with its national political culture and contingent political facts (e.g., the election of Carter) than with its international political position. To take a simple but telling example: on a per capita basis, Dutch membership in Amnesty International exceeds American membership in the National Rifle Association, one of the largest and most powerful interest groups in the United States.

National political culture is especially important in explaining the striking differences between the attitudes of the United States and the like-minded countries toward economic and social rights. American foreign aid has been used almost exclusively in the pursuit of civil and political rights objectives. Humanitarian objectives such as nutrition, literacy, and health care have been pursued, but they simply are not conceived in human rights terms. In the United States, foreign aid and human rights are seen as two fundamentally separate issues that have been tactically linked. The like-minded countries, by contrast, see development assistance as central to their international human rights policies. They also emphasize the intrinsic importance of economic, social, and cultural rights and their interdependence with civil and political rights.

Size, power, and the structure of the international system are of secondary significance. States have considerable latitude in formulating international human rights policies. Differences between the United States and the like-minded countries are largely matters of choice, of differing understandings of and priorities attached to internationally recognized human rights. Countries such as Norway and the Netherlands place a relatively high value on international human rights not because they are small and weak but because they choose to, because international human rights matter that much to them.

SIX

□ □ □

Responding to Tiananmen

The year 1989 was a decisive turning point in world history and in the international struggle for human rights. The remarkably quick and bloodless collapse of the Soviet empire, symbolized most dramatically by the opening of the Berlin Wall and by Czechoslovakia's Velvet Revolution, ushered in a new historical era. Combined with the steady progress of democratization in Latin America and accelerating liberalization in Africa and Asia, these changes suggest that it is not entirely wishful thinking to talk of a new world order, especially in human rights.

Understandable satisfaction with change, however, should not blind us to no less striking continuities, especially in *international* human rights policies. This first of three chapters on post–cold war human rights politics examines international responses to one of the most prominent recent setbacks, China's Tiananmen massacre—ironically, in June 1989, the cusp of the cold war and post–cold war eras.

CHINA'S DEMOCRACY MOVEMENT

Students have been the heart of China's democracy movement since its symbolic beginning on May 4, 1919, when three thousand students took to Tiananmen Square to protest concessions to Japan at the end of World War I. For over a thousand years, China's governing elite was composed of Confucian scholar-bureaucrats recruited through a national system of competitive examinations. Beyond their ordinary duties, these officials had an extraordinary right, even obligation, of political remonstrance: in difficult times, they were expected to call on the emperor to live up to the standards of good government that justified his rule.

The emperor's authority was seen to rest on a Mandate of Heaven. Remonstrances recalled to the emperor the duties to his people that accompanied the heavenly grant of power. This provided limited checks and balances in a political system without formal separation of powers. Remonstrances allowed the people, through intellectuals acting as their representatives, to press for reform when they were no longer able to tolerate injustice but were unwilling to resort to riots and rebellions (a recurrent feature of Chinese politics, especially in hard economic times). Widespread protests by intellectuals have long been a recognized sign of political crisis in China. Student protests thus have unusually heavy cultural weight in China.

Human rights problems in contemporary China are rooted in the creation of the People's Republic of China on October 1, 1949, when Mao Zedong and his Communist Party installed a classic Leninist party-state totalitarian regime. Under Communist rule, all aspects of life have been controlled by a centralized bureaucracy that enforces rigid conformity with ideological directives. Most internationally recognized civil and political rights are regularly and systematically violated. Remarkable progress has been made in some areas of economic and social rights, especially by abolishing feudal land tenure and social relations. But tens of millions of people died in state-created famines in the 1950s. And in the 1990s, housing, health care, and social services have become problematic for the bottom one-fourth of the population.

The most frightening systematic human rights violations in contemporary China, however, came during the Great Proletarian Cultural Revolution. On July 28, 1966, all universities and schools were closed. In August, the Chinese Communist Party (CCP) called upon the masses to form cultural revolutionary groups to attack "rightist" elements that had taken a "capitalist road." "Red Guards" spread an arbitrary reign of political intimidation and terror, dispensing "socialist justice" for offenses as minor as a casual critical comment, insufficient revolutionary fervor, or simply because a friend or relative's former job had branded that person a "class enemy."

Many millions of people were accused—and thus almost automatically found guilty—of ideological offenses. At minimum, this meant demeaning forced "reeducation." Most also lost jobs, school places, and housing. Literally millions suffered forced internal exile or imprisonment, usually accompanied by violent physical abuse during detention. An unknown number of people were executed.

Repression in contemporary China, however, has been punctuated with interludes of political opening. The best known followed a speech in May 1956 by Mao that called for letting a hundred flowers bloom—instead of the single path previously enforced by the CCP. But the party soon returned to its old ways, imprisoning many of the Hundred Flowers intellectuals.

Serious public stirrings of a new democracy movement began in April 1976 with national demonstrations in memory of Zhou Enlai, one of the leaders of the Chinese revolution and through much of the Mao era the second most powerful man in China. Although these demonstrations were violently repressed, Mao's own death in September 1976 touched off an intense power struggle. The result was a new political opening at the end of 1978.

In Beijing, public political debate took place in "big-character" posters on what came to be known as Democracy Wall. Particularly noteworthy was Wei Jingsheng's call for a "fifth modernization"—democracy—to complete the officially proclaimed modernizations in industry, science and technology, agriculture, and defense. Wei called on China to think of progress as involving more than just power and prosperity, to recognize important human and political dimensions beyond economic and military development. But the Democracy Wall movement, like the Hundred Flowers opening, was short lived. Wei and other leading dissidents were sentenced to long prison terms in 1979.

In the 1980s, under the leadership of Deng Xiaoping, China did embark on sustained economic liberalization. A cheap and disciplined workforce made China a rapidly growing presence in world markets. Markets were also given an expanding role in domestic production and pricing decisions. A thriving industrial economy developed on China's south coast, and the government used its control over agricultural marketing to pay farmers more for their produce. Average farm incomes doubled during the decade.

But political reforms continued to be resisted. In December 1986, demonstrations at over 150 campuses in more than twenty cities called for better living conditions, a free press, and democracy. In mid-January 1987, the authorities cracked down. Fang Lizhi, who was emerging as one of China's leading dissidents, was removed as vice rector of the University of Science and Technology in Hubei. And the CCP purged its leading advocate of reform, General Secretary Hu Yaobang. The ensuing campaign against "bourgeois liberalization," however, was mild and notably unsuccessful. Debate over democracy, although restricted to private discussions, continued through 1988.

In a country unusually attuned to historical symbolism, China's democracy movement easily anticipated the approach of 1989, a most portentous year: the two hundredth anniversary of the French Revolution, the seventieth anniversary of the May 4 movement, the fortieth anniversary of the Chinese Revolution, and the tenth anniversary of the repression of the Democracy Wall movement.

Fang Lizhi kicked off new protests in February 1989 with a letter calling for the release of Wei Jingsheng and other political prisoners. This in effect reopened the arguments of the Democracy Wall movement. Following the death of Hu Yaobang on April 15, 1989, students defied the government and held their own unofficial memorial, as they had with Zhou Enlai in 1976. Beginning with ten thousand students, their numbers grew to over one hundred thousand on April 22, the day of the official funeral. This was the start of the Tiananmen democracy movement.

A statement drafted by Fang in December 1988, on the fortieth anniversary of the Universal Declaration of Human Rights, received wide endorsement as the movement developed. Its five proposals indicate the general tenor of demands.

1. Lift the ban on nonofficial publications ... The government should not intervene as long as those publications do not advocate violence or spread pornography ...
2. Guarantee the right of freedom of association ... With a prerequisite of nonviolence, people, through organizations and parties not in power, have the right to openly criticize the policies of the party in office.
3. Direct elections of county and district leaders ...
4. Release all political prisoners ... Delete the words "crime of counter-revolution" from the code of criminal law. Declare that it is forbidden to charge anyone for reasons of ideology or politics.
5. Separation of party and government.[1]

In spring 1989, China's democracy movement was developing into a theoretically coherent call for political opening, focusing on freedom of speech and association. Practically, it was taking to the streets. And in a symbolic gesture, recalling Qing dynasty (1644–1922) remonstrances, student leaders knelt on the steps of the Great Hall of the People and asked Premier Li Peng to come out to talk. When he refused, they launched a massive boycott of classes on April 24.

The official response was complete rejection of all student demands. A private speech by Deng Xiaoping on April 25 set the tone: "This is not an ordinary student movement but a turmoil. We must take a clear-cut stance, carry out effective measures, and counteract quickly to stop this agitation. ... This entire episode is a planned, conspiratorial activity."[2] On April 26, the official *People's Daily* published an editorial entitled "We Must Oppose the Turmoil with a Clear-Cut Stance."

The protesters, however, seemed to be inspired rather than intimidated. Although the government would carry out its implied threats in less than six weeks, the surprising resolve of the students provided breathing room. On May 4, over one hundred thousand students marched to Tiananmen Square. New petitions called for even greater reforms. And on May 13, three thousand students began a hunger strike.

The hunger strike coincided with the visit of Mikhail Gorbachev, the first by a Soviet leader since 1959. For the government, Gorbachev's visit symbolized the end of the Sino-Soviet rift and China's new position in the world. To the students, however, Gorbachev symbolized dramatic reform from within. More broadly, the hunger strike, held in front of Mao's mausoleum, in the shadows of the monument to the martyrs of the Communist revolution, was a gesture of self-sacrifice. It recalled, for example, Qu Yuan, a fourth-century functionary who, when his advice was rejected, committed suicide, demonstrating both loyalty and his inability to accept the emperor's decision.

Popular support continued to grow. By May 17, as a thousand hunger strikers were hospitalized, over 1 million protesters and onlookers jammed the streets in and around Tiananmen Square. Smaller demonstrations were being held in over twenty cities. And the CCP was losing its monopoly over civil society.

Totalitarian states seek to maintain control not through direct force but by monopolizing public and private associations, preventing citizens from acting collectively outside of state control. By late spring, increasingly sophisticated and effective autonomous student organizations began to emerge. Press reports on Tiananmen were largely ignoring official controls. The students were also receiving growing support from workers, businessmen, bureaucrats, and even some soldiers.

China's rulers faced a decisive choice: accept structural political changes or crack down, with violence if necessary. In fall 1989, Communist leaders in Eastern Europe did not have the heart or the stomach to shoot their own people. In late spring 1989, China's leaders did.

On May 20, 1989, martial law was declared in Beijing. Troops were summoned to remove the protesters. Demonstrators, however, still numbered over 1 million. And the troops were slowed by mass passive resistance: "The people of [Beijing] took to the streets and erected makeshift barricades. They surrounded the army convoys, sometimes to let the air out of tires or stall engines but more often to argue with or cajole the troops, urging them not to enforce the martial-law restrictions and not to turn their guns on their fellow Chinese."[3]

With absolute party rule at stake, Deng called in new, hardened, and loyal troops. The students, sensing crisis, reduced their numbers in the square. But they did not go quietly. On May 29–30, a statue of the Goddess of Democracy was erected.[4] Defiant declarations and interviews continued. And an estimated one hundred thousand people attended what proved to be the final demonstrations on June 2–3.

The army's attack—as shocking as it was inescapable—came on June 3. The government admits killing three hundred unarmed protesters and bystanders. Outside estimates put the number at three times that figure, plus another three hundred killed in Chengdu. In the ensuing repression, thousands were arrested. Thousands more fled underground or overseas. At least dozens were executed. And hopes for human rights and democracy in China lay bulldozed beneath the treads of the tanks of the "People's Liberation Army."

INTERNATIONAL RESPONSES TO TIANANMEN

The international response was swift, strong, and coordinated. On June 5, the United States imposed an arms embargo, suspended high-level official contacts, and froze new aid. The European Community adopted similar sanctions on June 27, one day after the World Bank froze $780 million in loans to China. Japan suspended its new five-year aid program, valued at ¥810 billion (roughly $6 or $7 billion, depending on exchange rate fluctuations). The Group of Seven (G7) annual economic summit in Paris in July also condemned the massacre.

China's political costs are extremely difficult to (even know how to) measure. Its economic costs, however, were demonstrably significant. New commitments of bilateral foreign aid dropped from $3.4 billion in 1988 to $1.5 billion in 1989 and to $0.7 billion in 1990. Assuming a 20 percent annual increase in aid commitments without the disruption of Tiananmen (well below the average 50 percent annual growth for the period 1985–1988), China lost about $11 billion over four years in bilateral aid alone.[5]

Despite numerous small violations, sanctions were widely observed until July 1990, when Japan announced the end of its aid moratorium. Most other countries then began to relax their sanctions more or less rapidly. A series of visits by foreign ministers to Beijing in spring 1991 marked China's emergence from diplomatic isolation. The renewal of China's economic boom in late 1991 substantially increased the incentives to abandon sanctions. By 1993, most countries other than the United States had returned to business as usual—which included criticism of Chinese human rights practices (especially the treatment of dissidents) but not sanctions. Official bilateral aid committed in 1992 exceeded the previous record year of 1988. We can get a good sense of the politics involved by looking at the actions of the two principal bilateral actors, Japan and the United States, and the multilateral response at the United Nations.

Japan[6]

Japan opposed more than guarded statements of disapproval, imposing sanctions only under pressure from its allies (especially the United States). This position reflected strong economic interests, regional security concerns, and a genuine belief that isolating China was an inappropriate and unproductive strategy.

Within the limits set by U.S. pressure, Japan consistently advocated what amounted to Reagan-style quiet diplomacy and constructive engagement (see Chapter 5). On June 5, the day that U.S. sanctions were announced, Japan merely indicated that it was monitoring the situation, regretted the loss of life, and hoped for a quick end to the turmoil. On June 7, the Chinese ambassador was given a note indicating that Japan had no desire to interfere in China's internal affairs (which was China's description not only of sanctions but even of public criticism). Japanese lobbying before and during the Paris G7 summit succeeded in avoiding new collective sanctions. And after Paris, Japan worked to end international sanctions as quickly as possible, and in the interim to blunt their impact.

In September 1989, a Diet (parliament) delegation led by Foreign Minister Ito Masayoshi met with Deng Xiaoping and other top Chinese leaders. In December, Japan renewed cultural exchanges and donated a symbolic $3.5 million to modernize a hospital and a television station. Requests for political asylum were denied. Japanese authorities allowed Chinese embassy and consular officials to harass and intimidate Chinese students in Japan. Students were sent home against their will, despite official pledges made in June and July 1989 to extend lapsed student visas. And the resumption of foreign aid, along with a major new five-year $8 billion agreement at the end of 1990 to exchange oil and coal for technology and equipment, helped to buffer China from continuing Western sanctions.[7]

Much money was to be made in China, and both Japanese firms and their government wanted to make sure that Japan got at least its fair share. But economic engagement was also part of a broader strategy of tying China into cooperative bilateral and regional relationships to maximize regional stability, Japan's overriding geopolitical goal. Japan is deeply committed to the power of cooperative diplomatic engagement and the long-run transforming power of economic development, a topic addressed later in the chapter. As an Asian regional power, Japan also had security interests (e.g., in Korea and the South China Sea) that could be compromised by Chinese hostility. The Japanese response to Tiananmen thus was a consistent part of a clear general strategy.

Peter Van Ness has aptly described Japan's policy as "nominal conditionality."[8] Without allowing Chinese brutality to pass unnoticed, Japanese officials tried to minimize its impact on their relations with China and focused their diplomatic effort on doing the least they possibly could to harm or even offend China.

The United States

The United States represents the other end of the spectrum of international responses. Americans were captivated by the Tiananmen protesters. Popular shock and disgust at the massacre produced an unusually strong and long-lasting reaction. As the rest of the world returned to business as usual with China, the United States maintained, and even considered expanding, its sanctions. But divided government—a Republican president who preferred engagement and a Democratic Congress that preferred sanctions—led to considerable inconsistency.

In July 1989, four aircraft were delivered to China with navigation systems covered by the arms embargo. Secretary of State James Baker met with Chinese Foreign Minister Qian Qichen in Paris to discuss Cambodia, despite the embargo on high-level contacts. National Security Adviser Brent Scowcroft and Thomas Eagleburger, the number two official at the State Department, made a secret visit to Beijing. And Secretary Baker's speech at the annual meeting of the Association of Southeast Asian Nations (ASEAN) did not even mention China.

December 1989 was another month of multiple American concessions. Scowcroft and Eagleburger made a second visit to Beijing. Three communications satellites were sold. And President George Bush vetoed a bill to extend the expired visas of Chinese students.

Bush did criticize China, both publicly and privately. In December 1990, he devoted the bulk of his discussions with Foreign Minister Qian to human rights. In April 1991, Bush met with the Dalai Lama, thus raising the sensitive issue of human rights in Tibet.[9] There was even limited administration support for material sanctions. For example, Bush accepted November 1989 legislation that called for suspending new World Bank loans to China. In April 1991, the sale of U.S. parts for a Chinese communications satellite was blocked.

Conversely, Congress did not consistently demand stronger sanctions. Despite early tough talk, sanctions legislation did not receive a final vote in 1989 or 1990. Nonetheless, Congress, with support from and prodding by NGOs, was the driving force behind U.S. pressure on China. Representative Nancy Pelosi and Senate Majority leader George Mitchell led an extended campaign against administration policy that came closest to success in March 1992, when Bush was forced to veto legislation that linked human rights to an extension of China's most-favored-nation (MFN) trading privileges in American markets.

Candidate Bill Clinton criticized Bush's position during the 1992 campaign. As president, on May 28, 1993, he issued an executive order listing seven human rights criteria (including a general provision on observance of the Universal Declaration of Human Rights) that China would be required to meet if he were to recommend extending MFN privileges again in 1994. China now faced a credible threat of reduced access to the American market.

But delinkage of trade and human rights began almost immediately. A memorandum by Assistant Secretary of State Winston Lord in mid-July 1993 called for a new strategy of "comprehensive engagement." This became administration policy in September. As National Security Adviser Anthony Lake put it, "the successor to a doctrine of containment must be a strategy of enlargement—enlargement of the world's free community of market democracies."[10] Top officials from the Departments of State, Defense, Treasury, and Agriculture visited China. And in November 1993, Clinton met with Chinese president Jiang Zemin at the Seattle summit of leaders from the Asia-Pacific Economic Cooperation forum. The United States was clearly preparing for China's return to full status in the international community.

Meanwhile, with George Bush no longer there to do the work (and take the heat), opponents of human rights conditions on MFN status began to organize. Business mobilized its considerable lobbying skills and power. A bipartisan group in Congress argued that blunt, blanket sanctions like withholding MFN privileges were not an appropriate tool—a view shared by former President Carter and former Secretary of State Vance. As one administration official put it, the MFN designation was "an atomic bomb. And nobody drops a bomb. What we need is to get usable tools."[11] A growing number of people were also becoming convinced that rapid social change in China was making broad trade sanctions obsolete, even counterproductive. For example, Massachusetts Senator John Kerry returned from a trip to China in early 1994 a convert to ending linkage.

Aggressive Chinese diplomacy also had an impact. Protests and threats were effectively mixed with cooperative gestures. Strategically timed releases of prisoners were a standard tactic. China also made concessions on secondary human rights issues, such as prison labor, and on unrelated issues. For example, China signed the Nuclear Nonproliferation Treaty in 1992. Understandings were reached with both the Bush and Clinton administrations on transferring missiles and missile technology. Discussions were opened on piracy of music and software.

Few were surprised, then, when on May 26, 1994, Clinton announced that despite China's failure to meet the conditions of the 1993 executive order, MFN status would be extended, unconditionally. "In the end, economics won the day. It wasn't really even close."[12] China's energy market alone was estimated to be worth as much as $150 billion over the coming decade. By the end of the century, $30 billion was to be spent for telephone modernization. Aircraft purchases over two decades were projected to be $40 billion. These were staggering opportunities for profits and jobs.

Trade and investment had never been included in American sanctions (except for military and "dual use" products). Nonetheless, there was concern that continued human rights friction would harm the competitive position of American firms. For example, German Chancellor Helmut Kohl returned from a visit to China in November 1993 with nearly $3 billion in new contracts. And China did prove generous after linkage was buried. A business delegation led by Secretary of Commerce Ron Brown returned in September 1994 with over $5 billion in contracts. The following February, a visit by Energy Secretary Hazel O'Leary netted $2 billion in new contracts.

But there was more to the decision than simple greed. The collapse of allied support left the United States with little choice. Trade sanctions are vulnerable to "free riding" and "defection," that is, some parties not abiding by sanctions to take advantage of those who do. With limited defections (e.g., Japan in 1990) sanctions may still affect the target, and the costs will remain spread across several cooperating parties. But by 1994, when everyone else had already defected, the United States, not China, was most likely to be harmed by sanctions.

Cooperation on security issues also counterbalanced China's human rights record. We have already noted the civil war in Cambodia, missile technology, and nonproliferation. China also acquiesced in the UN attack on Iraq after its invasion of Kuwait.

For all its limitations, the most striking feature of the U.S. response to Tiananmen was its sustained strength, especially given China's economic and military power. Only against South Africa in the 1980s has the United States ever pursued a comparably strong set of human rights initiatives. And never before (or since) has the United States been willing to accept such high political and economic costs on behalf of human rights.

Some of this can be attributed to the particular details of the case. But part of the explanation lies in the maturing of human rights as an international issue, and the improved post–cold war environment for international human rights.

The United Nations

China's power largely insulated it from multilateral criticism. The massacre was never the subject of a UN General Assembly resolution. Even a mild resolution in the Commission on Human Rights was defeated in 1990. But the commission's subcommission did adopt a resolution in August 1989. And Geneva became the site of intensive diplomatic struggle.[13]

The subcommission is the only United Nations human rights body made up of (ostensibly, and often in fact) independent experts, rather than instructed government delegates. It was thus the place where China was most vulnerable to multilateral criticism—especially because the subcommission's scheduled annual meeting was in August, when the issue was fresh. Although they had little time to prepare, Chinese diplomats met unprecedented Western and Third World cooperation with intensive lobbying. "At times it seemed as if every table in the delegates' lounge had been commandeered by the Chinese mission, and there appeared to be no way in which a member of the Sub-Commission in need of a tea-break could escape."[14]

The focus of all this activity was a resolution that read, in its entirety:

> The Sub-Commission on Prevention of Discrimination and Protection of Minorities,
> Concerned about the events which took place recently in China and about their consequences in the field of human rights,
> 1. Requests the Secretary-General to transmit to the Commission on Human Rights information provided by the Government of China and by other reliable sources;
> 2. Makes an appeal for clemency, in particular in favor of persons deprived of their liberty as a result of the above-mentioned events.

Timid as this resolution may seem, Chinese Ambassador Fan Guoxiang responded that it "constituted interference in China's internal affairs . . . [was] incompatible with the purposes and principles of the Charter of the United Nations, and contravened the rules that regulated international relations."[15] And China descended on the Commission on Human Rights the following February with an entourage of forty diplomats committed to preventing even such a mild reference to these "events."

Such exertion by a potential target of multilateral human rights criticism is perhaps the strongest evidence that it is not all just hot air and pointless words. If a government that calls up the army to shoot unarmed students is this concerned about oblique criticism by a relatively obscure UN body, shame and reputation cannot be entirely negligible considerations.

But in multilateral no less than national politics, power usually triumphs in a struggle with justice. The resolution considered by the Commission on Human Rights, although as mild as that of the subcommission six months earlier, was defeated 17–15, with 11 abstentions. Even the subcommission was not immune to politics. At its August 1990 meeting, a resolution on Tibet was never introduced in return for Chinese agreement not to oppose a resolution on Iraq.[16]

In August 1991, the subcommission did narrowly adopt a resolution on human rights in Tibet.[17] This, though, was the final victory for China's critics in Geneva. At the 1992 commission session, a resolution on Tibet was defeated 27–15 (with 10 abstentions). China managed to escape even a vote in the 1992 subcommission. At the 1993 commission meeting, the resolution on China was defeated 22-17-12. And at the August 1993 subcommission meeting, a resolution on Tibet was defeated 17-6-2.

The case of China may even illustrate a weakening of the Commission on Human Rights, a return to the 1980s after the immediate post–cold war euphoria wore off. The expansion of the commission to fifty-three members in 1992 has reduced the influence of the Western and other powers that have pushed for stronger action and has led to the development of a more unified Third World bloc that is skeptical of forceful human rights initiatives. In the subcommission as well, the case of China seems to show growing politicization and decreased initiative.

ASSESSING THE IMPACT OF INTERNATIONAL ACTION

The "bottom line" is that China's Communist dictators seem even more firmly entrenched today than they were in 1989. Despite looser controls on speech and publication, pleas for political reform remain rare and dangerous. For example, Tiananmen activist Wang Dan was sentenced in November 1996 to eleven years in prison for continuing to call for democracy. But other elements must be included in a full accounting.

Numerous individual prisoners were released, both in response to general pressure (for example, 573 detainees were released when martial law was lifted in January 1990) and in exchange for particular concessions. For example, in early May 1990, prior to Bush's first MFN decision, China released two hundred detainees. In January 1994, in response to Clinton's moves toward engagement, some prominent Tibetan prisoners were freed. Several thousand lives, perhaps even tens of thousands, were improved because foreign governments were willing to exert political influence and expend political and financial resources on behalf of human rights. International pressure also seems to have been a modest deterrent to new acts of repression, some executions, and mistreatment of some prisoners.

China was also punished for its behavior. Several billion dollars were lost, and China's economic boom was delayed by a year or two. Furthermore, as was just mentioned, the Chinese acted as if they were stung by international criticisms.

Chinese concessions on security and economic issues were further costs. They were also a benefit to the United States, Japan, and Europe. Although human rights advocates may be reluctant to trumpet such indirect, nonrights benefits of international human rights policies, they cannot be ignored in a broader foreign policy assessment. Rights-abusive governments may be forced to make side payments to third parties even where direct benefits for victims cannot be obtained.

In passing, we should also note that sanctions were not cost free to the sanctioning states. Bilateral foreign aid is usually sufficiently "tied" to donor-country suppliers to produce substantial sales (and thus jobs). Suspending military sales even more clearly forgoes profits and jobs (which are usually well paid and, especially in the United States, often located in politically significant places). After Tiananmen, sanctioning countries did more than just talk. They accepted modest domestic economic costs to pursue international human rights objectives. And even talk created frictions that had costs for the pursuit of other objectives in relations with China. Human rights remained a serious irritant in Sino-American relations through 1996.

We should also consider the potential moral and political costs of inaction. One's own commitment to human rights requires some sort of action, even if there is scant chance to punish or transform the target state. To fail to act in the case of gross violations would be shameful. Furthermore, considerations of consistency may also require action that one knows is likely to be largely symbolic. And even symbolic action has symbolic value. Rarely is it entirely futile.

Finally, I want to suggest that international action subtly but significantly transformed China's normative political environment, both nationally and internationally. Consider the changes in the regime's counteroffensive after Tiananmen.

China initially used "the big lie." For example, one Chinese diplomat claimed that "not a single person had been killed by the army or run over by military vehicles."[18] But even the Chinese leadership seems not to have expected many to accept this account.

Appeals to sovereignty were therefore central. For example, the first issue of *Beijing Review* published after the massacre described the U.S. response as "flagrant accusations against China regarding something which is exclusively China's affair."[19] But in 1989, few other countries saw talk about human rights as an interference in a country's internal affairs.

A more subtle Chinese argument allowed talk, but only talk. "The two countries may exchange criticisms on issues of human rights . . . but it is not advisable for one to use human rights as a tool to hurt the other."[20] All foreign policy, however, manipulates negative and positive incentives, harms and benefits, to alter the behavior of others. And by the late 1980s, diplomatic protests and military and economic sanctions had become an accepted, even an expected, means for expressing human rights disapproval. China was thus forced to back away from extreme claims of sovereign prerogative.

As a result of post-Tiananmen diplomacy, "China [came] to accept human rights as a legitimate part of the international agenda."[21] Chinese defenses thus increasingly emphasized arguments of cultural relativism. For example, China's 1991 Human Rights White Paper claimed that human rights were indeed being realized in China, particularly subsistence rights, the most important rights of all. The substance of such arguments will be addressed in the final section of this chapter. Here I am interested only in the politics.

Although clearly intended as cynical manipulation of the language of human rights, this change in rhetoric has had subtle positive consequences. A decade ago, the very term "human rights" was dangerous. Even Chinese scholars of international law writing in English rarely touched on human rights. Today, however, the term is relatively widely used.

Although there are still severe limits on how human rights issues are addressed, those boundaries are not fixed. And arguing over the proper human rights strategy rather than the very use of international human rights norms is significant progress. The Chinese have been dragged beyond denial and forced to engage the international human rights regime—with consequences that are hard to predict.

Human rights have an internal logic that may escape state control, as Soviet bloc countries discovered with the Helsinki process. China now operates in a realm of national and international discourse in which human rights are legitimate grounds for argument and action. The result is implicit recognition of a new kind of accountability. That recognition is extremely limited, and has been even more reluctantly tendered. But this conceptual opening may prove to be the principal contribution of international responses to the Tiananmen massacre.

CONSTRUCTIVE ENGAGEMENT REVISITED

Europe and the United States initially adopted a "classic" strategy of punishment, shame, and isolation. They came around, however, to Japan's strategy of engagement. Is there more to be said for constructive engagement in the 1990s than its failure in South Africa in the 1980s would suggest?

Engagement has a broad foreign policy justification. Because countries have multiple, cross-cutting policy objectives, it would be self-defeating for them to let any one objective preempt efforts to pursue other objectives. Human rights is but one important issue in Sino-American relations. Therefore, human rights concerns must be integrated with interests such as trade and security into a general bilateral strategy. Comprehensive engagement attempts to maximize linkages and increase overall influence and achievements.

Engagement, however, also has a human rights justification, which will be our focus here. Markets, it is argued, lead those whom they make prosperous to demand civil and political rights. Economic "freedom" leads to calls for political freedom that repressive governments cannot ultimately resist. Therefore, fostering economic development contributes to fundamental political change. Manipulating selfish economic interests thus becomes a way to realize civil and political rights. Economic support that appears to help stabilize repression actually undermines it.

This argument seems suspiciously convenient and a bit too clever. Reliance on automatic mechanisms, even if successful, fails to respond to the psychological and moral need to do what one can, here and now, to resist (and if possible punish) gross and systematic violators of human rights. It also consigns those who face a moderately efficient state, unusually ruthless oppressors, or a highly underdeveloped economy to decades of suffering. It sounds distressingly like an economic analogue to the Kirkpatrick Doctrine's support for right-wing dictators.

But public criticisms and sanctions have almost never caused structural political change. And in countries such as South Korea, prosperity does seem to have supported demands for political opening. Engagement thus deserves a hearing. There must, however, be active engagement in the human rights struggle of living people today—*constructive* engagement, rather than passive waiting.

Consider an analogy with peace. Democracies, understood as regimes that respect internationally recognized political rights, almost never fight wars with other democracies. Therefore, if markets produce civil and political rights, they will also produce peace. But no one would seriously suggest handing national security policy over to the Department of Commerce and the International Monetary Fund. While waiting for peace, immediate, concrete security interests and objectives must be addressed. Likewise, we cannot sit back and wait for markets to produce human rights—if we take human rights seriously as a foreign policy objective.

Long-term economic engagement may be a significant background force for human rights. But if engagement is to be a defensible human rights strategy, both sides must be at least minimally engaged in an active, ongoing process of change. For example, target governments must be expected to produce at least the symbolic gestures and incremental changes that public strategies of pressure regularly yield. This requires foreign states to retain and periodically use the reactive and punitive tactics of the 1970s and 1980s.

Likewise, if business involvement is justified in part because it helps human rights, we can legitimately ask for concrete evidence of that help. At the very least we can ask that firms avoid actively denying human rights—for example, that they try to avoid actively participating in state efforts to suppress free trade unions. During the MFN debate, however, American business opposed even voluntary codes of conduct for firms operating in China. Resisting even such modest measures of responsibility and accountability raises suspicions that profits, not human rights, lay behind the appeal for a return to business as usual in China.

Consider also a recent full-page ad by a major U.S. company under the title "Staying the Course Benefits Others."[22] The company argued that in the future as in the past, "rather than cut and run from trouble spots, we will work to change them." And this company explicitly pointed to civil and political rights. "Particularly in countries where attention is focused on civil and political reforms . . . great global companies can be a positive force for change." As Calman J. Cohen of the Business Coalition for U.S.-China Trade put it during the 1994 MFN debate, trade is "part of the solution—not part of the problem."[23]

The ad's first example is Indonesia. The "bloodshed and months of turmoil" mentioned were in fact one of the most massive episodes of state terrorism anywhere in the world in the 1960s. But the "change" the company touts is new jobs and the transfer of skills and technology. This does not even address, let alone contribute to ending, systematic violations of civil and political rights. And the same government that murdered several hundred thousand Indonesians—estimates range up to a million—remains in power today, more than three decades later.

The ad also points to Nigeria, which suffered under a succession of military dictatorships over three decades and which became a prominent international concern when human rights and environmental activist Ken Saro-Wiwa was executed in 1995. Again, though, the "change" produced is jobs. Although these jobs are a significant benefit to the fifteen hundred Nigerian employees and their families, there is no connection between employment and civil and political reforms.

Multinational corporations that provide good jobs to local workers and are aware of the social consequences of their activities are indeed desirable. But the issue in engagement arguments is the link between the pursuit of profits and political change. Treating workers well is irrelevant—especially for firms that see human rights almost entirely as a matter of civil and political, not economic and social, rights. If the best advocates of engagement can point to are regimes that have for decades successfully resisted structural political change, the strategy would seem to be completely bankrupt.

My point is not to criticize business in general, let alone particular firms. Quite the contrary, taking business seriously as a human rights agent may open exciting avenues for thinking about implementing human rights. In reminding us that the transnational sector includes not just NGOs but also multinational corporations (MNCs), this perspective suggests largely unexplored responsibilities and opportunities. The question is whether business is committed to active constructive engagement or merely passive waiting and hoping.

If businesses are simply pursuing profits, let them argue for the single-minded pursuit of gain. Debate then would focus on when, where, or even whether firms should pursue human rights objectives. But if they claim to be making a human rights contribution, it is fair to ask for the evidence.

Similar challenges must be posed to advocates of foreign policy engagement. "Engagement" may easily degenerate into inaction against, or even collusion with, human rights violators. In engaging others, we must not become disengaged from our own values and day-to-day efforts to realize them. Even where we cannot remove murderers from power, we must speak out against them and do what we can to make them pay for their crimes.

POSTSCRIPT: ASIAN VALUES

As I noted earlier, China claimed to be pursuing a distinctive and defensible human rights strategy emphasizing economic and social rights. This sort of argument has become associated with broader cultural relativist arguments based on "Asian values." Although often little more than devices by which repressive regimes try to cover their abuses, appeals to Asian values do tap a widespread concern. Human rights are based on autonomous individuals. Traditional Asian values, however, emphasize harmony and deference within a group, not individual assertion.

I readily grant the existence of cultural differences between East and West. In fact, I went out of my way earlier to indicate ways in which historical and cultural context shaped the development, expression, and reception of China's democracy movement. Cultural facts, however, are only a starting point for moral argument. Traditional practices require political and moral, not antiquarian, justifications. That things used to be done this way ought to earn a hearing for any cultural practice. But it is a powerful reason to continue only for morally indifferent legal and political practices (e.g., the attire of judges).

Many relativist arguments mistakenly assume that culture is static and of timeless value. How relevant, though, are practices evolved in small, static, agricultural communities in anonymous urban societies with immense social and demographic mobility? How similar are authoritarian leaders of intrusive modern states and traditional leaders? How are traditional social sanctions changed when they are coercively enforced by modern states? What has become of local autonomy, so much a part of traditional social and political relations, in the face of economic and political integration?

Most relativist arguments reflect a belief that because Asians did things a certain way in the past, they have no desire to do them differently today. "Popular pressures against East and Southeast Asian governments may not be so much for 'human rights' or 'democracy' but for good government: effective, efficient, and honest administrations able to provide security and basic needs with good opportunities for an improved standard of living."[24] Even if most ordinary Asians have traditionally expected (or hoped for) no more from their governments, I am skeptical that this remains true today.

Consider the pressures for democratization throughout the region, which have been relatively successful in South Korea and Taiwan but resisted by governments in, for example, China, Burma, and Indonesia. These examples suggest that good government is the minimum Asians are willing to accept, not what they aspire to. And even good government, especially in the long run, seems unlikely in the absence of human rights.

Civil and political rights provide clear and powerful mechanisms to ascertain whether rulers' claims about popular preferences are true. For all their shortcomings—which I emphasize in Chapter 8—open and fair elections do provide a relatively reliable gauge of popular political preferences.

Furthermore, even if a country "enjoys" an efficient and relatively benevolent and incorruptible despot or ruling elite—for example, Lee Kwan Yew's relatively "soft" and clean authoritarianism made a small and resource-poor Singapore into an Asian "tiger"—maintaining that over time without civil and political rights seems unlikely, especially with the immense amounts of wealth made available by economic growth. Closed politics is a recipe for colossal corruption, as most countries in the region illustrate. There is an internal self-correcting logic to human rights that is absent in traditional mechanisms (at least when they operate in modern states rather than small and relatively static communities).

If such benefits of human rights could be purchased only at the cost of cultural suicide, the choice might boil down to that of the lesser evil. But international human rights norms no more ask Asians to give up their culture than John Locke or Thomas Paine asked the English, Americans, or French to give up theirs. In fact, they leave considerable space for distinctively Asian implementations.

In Chapter 2, I called this general position weak cultural relativism. Strong relativism, which I reject, allows significant variations from the list of rights specified in the Universal Declaration. Weak relativism holds that tradition is no excuse for violating internationally recognized human rights specified at the level of generality of torture, free speech, and health care. But that leaves much room for historical, cultural, and even idiosyncratic variations in implementing these rights.

For example, Article 5 of the Universal Declaration of Human Rights states, "No one shall be subjected to torture or to cruel, inhuman, or degrading treatment or punishment." A weak relativist position holds that because countries may not legitimately pick and choose among internationally recognized human rights, they must respect the prohibition on torture. No matter how deep the tradition of inquisitorial or punitive torture, locals should not be forced to continue to endure it, and outsiders should be free to condemn it.

The general prohibition of cruel and unusual punishment, however, leaves much room for legitimate variation. Consider the controversial punishment of Michael Fay in Singapore in 1994. For all the hoopla, caning someone who vandalized hundreds of thousands of dollars of private property is obviously permissible. It is probably less cruel than imprisonment in most of the world's jails. And a country like the United States, which executes children and warehouses criminals in unsafe and demeaning prisons, has no cause for indignation. What is universal is the overarching right, not the details of its implementation in any one country, no matter how highly that country thinks of itself.

Variations, however, are limited to the (relatively narrow) band specified by the core content of the right in question. Crucifying, drawing and quartering, or disemboweling a criminal are obvious examples of practices that today are by any reasonable standard inhumane. Amputation, no matter how "humanely" carried out, almost certainly exceeds the limits. Execution is a matter of intense controversy.

Should we be concerned about "imposing" such limits? Not, I would suggest, when we are talking at this high level of generality. And not when the "imposition" involves persuasion and modest forms of coercion such as reductions in aid. Invading a country that tortures convicts probably exceeds the moral bounds of proportionality and would undoubtedly violate the international legal prohibition of intervention. But it would be entirely proper for states and NGOs to raise the issue diplomatically and even forcefully pursue it in public.

Pornography is a subject often raised by proponents of strong relativism. But free speech simply does not require licensing pornography. Most, and perhaps all, states limit some graphic sexual depictions, most notably those involving children. Most also restrict the depiction of certain acts and control the display of pornographic material.

Speech is no less appropriately limited by public morals than by public safety—although the meanings of these terms are themselves controversial, as are questions of how to strike a balance. Drawing the lines is always an appropriate matter for local controversy. Only in extreme cases, though, would it be an appropriate matter of international human rights concern. The effort of some Taliban members in Afghanistan to prohibit all pictures showing unveiled women is perhaps such a case. But even here, the central issues concern discrimination against women and wholesale restrictions of free expression, not pornography.

To take a very different example, the Asian preference for consensual decisionmaking is likely to have an impact on party politics. Consider de facto one-party rule in postwar Japan. If peaceful political activity by opposition parties is unhindered and elections are carried out fairly and under more or less impartial rules, the choice of voters cannot be legitimately challenged by outsiders.

Gender equality, which touches everyday life for most people, is an un-usually sensitive issue. International norms do require that all human rights be available equally to men and women. Therefore, to deny women the right to run for political office is to violate their human rights. They remain free, however, not to run. And voters are at liberty to treat sex as a relevant consideration in casting their ballots. Article 22 of the Universal Declaration recognizes the right of everyone to work and to free choice of employment. Therefore, women cannot be legitimately prevented from working outside the home. They are free, however, to choose not to.

I realize that discussion of free choice is somewhat forced. Women (everywhere) are under immense pressure to conform to traditional role models. But that is precisely why the right to choose is so crucial. Tradi-tional roles must be protected by the state neither more nor less than non-traditional roles.

"Free" choice is rarely without costs in any domain. Human rights fo-cus on assuring that the state is not directly or indirectly responsible for those costs. At the very least, acts that would be prohibited were they done by men to men must be treated as especially heinous offenses when they are done to women for acting "uppity." And no group can be al-lowed to use the apparatus of the state to impose rules and roles on any other group that they do not impose on themselves.

Human rights empower those individuals and groups that will bear the consequences to decide, within certain limits, how they will lead their lives. Differences across time and place are thus not merely justifiable, they are to be expected. For example, we would anticipate that Asian chil-dren would give greater weight to the views and interests of their families than North American children. Confrontational political tactics are likely to be less common (and less successful). There is likely to be less social tolerance of deviant behavior of all types.

These examples, however, illustrate individuals exercising the same human rights in different ways, not a different conception of human rights. And they do not suggest the legitimacy of prohibiting "Western" exercises of these rights. To prevent children who meet requirements such as minimum age and genetic distance from marrying their chosen partner is to deny the human right to marry and found a family. Families are free to ostracize rebellious children. The state, however, has no business en-forcing family preferences on adult children.

A human rights approach rests on the idea that people are probably best suited, and in any case entitled, to choose the good life for them-selves. If Asians value family over self, they will exercise personal rights with family consequences in mind. If they value harmony and order over liberty, they will exercise their civil liberties in a harmonious and orderly fashion. Such choices must be respected. But only so long as they remain matters of choice.

Cultural traditions are socially created legacies. Some are good, others bad. Many are morally indifferent. Some have become irrelevant. Traditions change with time. And in most cases, no group, either inside or outside that society, is entitled to impose on others its views of which traditions are (or deserved to be) living and which are dead.

The choices and opportunities guaranteed by human rights make people (co)creators of their traditions rather than passive subjects to them. If people accept traditions, they will reproduce them as valued parts of their life. If not, so much the worse for tradition—and those who would impose it on others. The necessity of massive state coercion is the clearest evidence that we are dealing with "traditions" that do not have the respect of local people and do not deserve ours.

SEVEN

□ □ □

War and Genocide in the Former Yugoslavia

In the two remaining chapters, we will consider three post–cold war "case studies" that are linked by conflicts between collective values and individual human rights. This chapter presents a geographical case study, the international response to the unusually brutal civil wars in the former Yugoslavia, especially in Bosnia-Herzegovina, which introduced **ethnic cleansing** to the world's vocabulary. Chapter 8 presents thematic studies of democracy and markets.

BACKGROUND TO THE CONFLICT

Yugoslavia was created at the end of World War I, an assemblage of the previously independent states of Serbia and Montenegro; the former Austro-Hungarian territories of Slovenia, Istria, Dalmatia, Croatia-Slavonia, Vojvodina, and Bosnia-Herzegovina; and Macedonia, taken from the Ottoman Empire's last European holdings. Although the dominant Serbs actively discriminated against other ethnic groups, until the late 1980s, different groups lived together more or less harmoniously (except under Nazi occupation during World War II, when Serbs were targets of genocide by the Ustasha, a local fascist group operating a puppet regime in Croatia).

After World War II, the Communists, the strongest force in the "partisan" resistance to Nazi rule, reorganized Yugoslavia under the leadership of Josip Broz Tito. In a country in which every ethnic group is a minority,[1] a federal political system granted substantial power to six republics (Serbia, Croatia, Slovenia, Bosnia-Herzegovina, Macedonia, and Montenegro) and to the two autonomous regions within Serbia (Kosovo and Vojvodina). Ethnic separatism or claims of superiority were discouraged and even suppressed.

For three decades, the system worked tolerably well (except for discrimination against ethnic Albanians in Kosovo). But Tito's death in 1980 removed the final arbiter from a system with immense potential for squabbling and deadlock. At the same time, the accumulated inefficiencies of decades of control by nine separate Communist bureaucracies (six republics, two autonomous regions, and the federal government) ended the economic growth that had greased the system. By the mid-1980s, Yugoslavia faced a political and economic crisis well beyond the management capabilities of its ruling Communist functionaries, whose visions were largely restricted to maintaining their local bases of power.

Crisis began to become catastrophe, however, only in 1987, when Slobodan Milosevic in the Serbian republic seized on Serbian nationalism to consolidate his rapid rise to power. Milosevic skillfully manipulated memories of Ustasha brutality, fostering hatred of Croats. He also invoked the quasi-mythic grandeur of Serbia's fourteenth-century Nemanjid dynasty. He aimed to paint Muslims (who made up about one-sixth of the country's population) as enemies, for it was the Turks who had defeated medieval Serbia. And he revived and manipulated the Serbian Orthodox Church as a device to further mobilize hostility toward Croats, most of whom are Roman Catholics and Muslims.

Using tactics made famous by Hitler, Milosevic and his front group, the Committee for the Protection of Kosovo Serbs and Montenegrins, organized over one hundred mass protest demonstrations with average turnouts of over fifty thousand people. By February 1989, the last vestiges of regional autonomy in Vojvodina and Kosovo were eliminated, and Milosevic allies had been installed in Montenegro, leaving him in firm control of half the country.

Kosovo, whose population was 90 percent ethnic Albanian, was particularly severely repressed. When mass demonstrations did not force the regional government to resign, Milosevic declared it abolished. Serbo-Croatian was imposed as the official language, Albanian-language media were banned, and six thousand teachers were fired when Albanian-language secondary schooling was prohibited. In Milosevic's new nationalist myth, this was simply liberating Serbs from the remnants of the "Turkish yoke." In July 1991, he even confiscated six thousand hectares of land for distribution to Serbian colonists.

The other republics, especially Slovenia and Croatia, were alarmed by this protofascist Serbian imperialism. Legally and politically, they had the power to block Milosevic at the national level. But his increasing reliance on extralegal means—for example, in fall 1990, arms shipments for the Yugoslav National Army (JNA) "inexplicably" began appearing in Knin, Croatia's principal Serbian city—led to growing fear.

On December 23, 1990, Slovenes overwhelmingly voted for independence, which the government announced it would declare if a new federal political formula could not be agreed upon within six months. When

Slovenia and Croatia declared independence on June 25, 1991, Yugoslavia was already dead, the victim of irreconcilable conflict between Serbian demands for centralization and Slovene and Croatian insistence on maintaining a loose federal system.

WAR AND GENOCIDE

Serbian tanks rolled into Slovenia on June 26, 1991. A cease-fire negotiated in early July by the European Community required Slovenia to suspend its declaration of independence. It seemed likely, though, that Slovenia, which was ethnically homogeneous, prosperous, and did not share a border with Serbia, would eventually be able to go its own way—although not at its own pace or necessarily even on its own terms.

The conflict thus shifted to Croatia, where violence had been escalating since the ethnically Serb region of Krajina declared autonomy in March 1991 and asked for union with Serbia. Both Croats and Serbs manipulated memories of discrimination and atrocities and prepared to inflict new ones. For example, in May 1991, sixteen people died in ethnic violence in the Serb-dominated town of Borovo Selo. Croatian authorities obtained a guarantee of safety for their investigators. "But when the Croatian police entered the village, white flags in hand, the Serbs opened fire on them, killing 13 police and wounding 21. Some Croatian police were mutilated by Serbs: their eyes were gouged out, their throats slit, and their genitals cut off."[2]

In the last four months of 1991, Serbs and Croats fought a brutal war that targeted "opposition" civilians no less than opposing armies. The fifteenth cease-fire, reached on January 2, 1992, and supported by fourteen thousand peacekeepers of the United Nations Protection Force in the former Yugoslavia (UNPROFOR), lasted about a year. Serbian separatists, however, controlled one-third of Croatia's territory, which remained under (sporadically violent) dispute until a successful Croatian offensive in summer 1995.

The stalemate in Croatia turned attention to an even more brutal conflict in Bosnia-Herzegovina (hereafter, Bosnia, for convenience). Bosnia was in many ways a microcosm of Yugoslavia. Like the country as a whole, Bosnia was a republic of minorities. In the 1991 census, 44 percent identified themselves as "ethnic Muslims," 32 percent as Serbs, 17 percent as Croats, and 7 percent as "Yugoslavs" or other. In fact, Bosnia was the only Yugoslav republic without an ethnic majority.

Through the late 1980s, Bosnia was a place of considerable ethnic tolerance, especially in the capital of Sarajevo. But when war did come, it hit with unprecedented ferocity. And Bosnia's Muslims were particularly vulnerable because they lacked the support of neighboring co-nationals.

Separatist Serbs gained control of two-thirds of the territory of Bosnia-Herzegovina. They perfected and popularized the strategy of ethnic cleansing, introduced by Croatian Serbs the preceding year. The goal was to rid "Serbian" territory of Muslim (and Croat) residents through systematic terror and sporadic mass murder.

Serbian military action was directed as much at innocent civilians as at opposing soldiers. Lacking the bureaucratic resources of Hitler or Stalin in the 1930s and 1940s or the Khmer Rouge in Cambodia in the 1970s, Serbian genocide was more disorderly but only slightly less effective. Relief supplies were blocked. Villages and cities were shelled from a distance and shot up and burned at close range. Captured men were routinely tortured or murdered, often en masse. Women, children, and the elderly were sometimes shot, often physically abused, but more typically "merely" forced to flee. And Serbian soldiers systematically, on orders from superiors, raped young Muslim women, to degrade them and shame their families.

THE INTERNATIONAL RESPONSE

Although often, and in many ways fairly, criticized for doing too little, too late, the international community did not sit by and idly watch the genocide, as had been its practice during the cold war. The UN Security Council "experiment[ed] with about every available form of coercion short of war."[3] An arms embargo was imposed on all parties. Serbia was suspended by the CSCE and placed under a comprehensive UN economic embargo. Peacekeepers were sent to protect civilians and facilitate the delivery of humanitarian assistance. Intensive multilateral diplomatic efforts sought to bring an end to the conflict. A special war crimes tribunal was established.

When a peace agreement in Bosnia was finally signed in December 1995, there were fifty thousand UN peacekeepers in the former Yugoslavia, at an annual cost of about $2 billion. Three thousand humanitarian workers were in the field. The United Nations high commissioner for refugees alone was spending $500 million a year on humanitarian assistance.

Nonetheless, out of a prewar population of 23 million, 250,000 people died and 2.5 million were left homeless. The outcome in the former Yugoslavia thus illustrates the persisting limits of even expanded international human rights activity.

Initial responses reflected geopolitical concerns. The principal goal of the West, especially the United States, was to keep Yugoslavia intact. The Bush administration was willing to allow immense suffering to prevent

Yugoslavia from becoming a precedent for an even more catastrophic breakup of the Soviet Union, which had not yet dissolved. Thus, even newly democratic and westward-looking Slovenia was pressured into formally remaining within the increasingly imaginary federal Yugoslavia. Although such fears may now seem exaggerated, at the time they were not unreasonable, and they seem to have been sincerely felt.

When the war entered its Bosnian phase, however, the Soviet Union had already broken up. The EC had already recognized the independence of Croatia and Slovenia. Under German pressure, the United States came around in April 1992. Geopolitical concerns continued to intrude. For example, politics within NATO and the problem of defining the post–cold war place of Russia complicated diplomatic and peacekeeping activities. Nonetheless, for the remainder of the conflict the United States, Europe, Russia, and the United Nations maintained sustained efforts in human rights, humanitarian assistance, peacekeeping, and diplomacy that were without parallel during the cold war.

Multilateral Human Rights Agencies

In August 1992, at the first special session in its forty-five year history, the UN Commission on Human Rights appointed Tadeusz Mazowiecki, former prime minister of Poland, as special rapporteur. He visited Bosnia on August 21–26, accompanied by Louis Joinet (France), chair of the Working Group on Arbitrary Detention, and Bacre W. Ndiaye (Senegal), special rapporteur on extrajudicial, summary, or arbitrary executions. His report of August 28 confirmed "massive and grave violations of human rights" throughout Bosnia-Herzegovina. A second mission in October concluded that "the Muslim population are the principal victims and are virtually threatened with extermination." A second special session of the commission, held November 30 and December 1, 1992, condemned Serbia, the JNA, and leaders of Serb controlled areas. Never before had the commission responded with anything even close to such speed.

The Security Council also acted quickly and with resolve, beginning with an embargo on arms to all parties in the former Yugoslavia. At the end of May 1992, the council imposed trade sanctions on Serbia, to pressure Milosevic to end his support of the Bosnian Serbs. In August 1992, it condemned the violations of humanitarian law. In October, it established a War Crimes Commission. And in February 1993, the Security Council created a war crimes tribunal for the former Yugoslavia, which by 1996 was actively prosecuting (mostly but not only Serbian) war criminals.

The Conference on Security and Cooperation in Europe (see Chapter 4) also became rapidly engaged with Bosnia. In July 1992, Serbia's membership was suspended and in September a rapporteur mission was appointed under the new Moscow Human Dimension mechanism. The report by Hans Cornell (Sweden), Helmut Turk (Austria), and Gro Hillestad Thune (Norway), endorsed by the CSCE ministers' meeting in Stockholm in December 1992, created further momentum for a war crimes tribunal.

These initiatives responded to, rather than stopped, the genocide. But as we have seen, the international community has never even seriously discussed giving coercive enforcement powers to multilateral human rights institutions. They must rely primarily on international public opinion, which, at least in the short run, has little effect on shameless butchers like the Bosnian Serbs.

The UN Commission on Human Rights and the CSCE did everything in their power. And the war crimes tribunal, the first since Nuremberg, was a major innovation. The problem lies in the refusal of states to confer greater power on multilateral human rights institutions. And the consistency of this refusal suggests that for all the talk, states consider this "problem" preferable to the "solution" of transferring authority to an international agency that might force them to act more strongly.

Humanitarian Assistance

The task of humanitarian assistance is not to stop wars but to cope with some of their most pressing human consequences. Humanitarian workers are not meant to prevent violence but to ease the burden on civilian victims. But even these limited tasks undercut the Serbian strategies of ethnic cleansing in the countryside and strangling Sarajevo. The Bosnian Serbs therefore saw humanitarian assistance as intensely political—which it was, given their strategy—and consistently used all means in their power, including force, to stop international relief from reaching its targets. Muslim and Croat forces also prevented aid deliveries, although much more irregularly.

Forcing recalcitrant parties to permit delivery of humanitarian assistance, however, must remain a task for other actors if the integrity and safety of humanitarian operations are to be assured. And for reasons of both cost and sovereignty, the international community has only rarely used force to protect the flow of aid. Somalia was the exception, not the rule.

Within the limits set by the international community and in comparison with comparable cases, the international humanitarian response in Bosnia was swift, sustained, and relatively effective. The United Nations used strong diplomatic pressure and (limited) force to deliver aid to more than 2 million people. UNPROFOR provided intelligence, occasional armed convoys, and most important, a visible and watching presence that reduced attacks on civilians. And all the external parties pressed both the Bosnian Serbs and the Milosevic government to allow humanitarian aid to flow.

I do not mean to minimize the horrible suffering in Bosnia. More than one-third of Bosnia's people were forced to flee their homes. Most Bosnian Muslims who did not flee were forced to endure extended Serbian sieges. The more than two hundred thousand deaths in Croatia and Bosnia-Herzegovina, an already staggering absolute number, were proportionally equivalent to the deaths of about 5 million Americans.

Nonetheless, to have achieved more, the group of nations attempting to give assistance would have had to issue a credible threat to enter the conflict as an active military participant on the side of Bosnia's Muslims. Not even a bluff was offered. The failure lay not in humanitarian inaction or ineptitude but in a conscious political decision by foreign states to rely solely on diplomacy, humanitarian assistance, and sanctions short of the punitive use of force.

Peacekeeping

UNPROFOR was a **peacekeeping** force. Its aim was not to repulse or punish an aggressor. That is a job for collective security enforcement, as in the Gulf War of 1991. Peacekeeping involves interposing neutral forces *with the permission of the belligerents* in order to monitor or maintain a truce or settlement. Peacekeepers are lightly armed and authorized to use force only to protect themselves when attacked.

UNPROFOR's mandate was not to stop the war, let alone to bring about the victory of one side, but to limit the extent and severity of the fighting. The international community condemned ethnic cleansing. It was willing to prosecute those responsible once the fighting ended. But the international community refused to commit itself to end the conflict through force rather than diplomacy. Genocide was not stopped in Bosnia because outside powers were unwilling to fight a war to stop it.

But the classic peacekeeping model of the "thin blue line" of UN troops interposed between armies after the fighting has ended simply did not fit the situation in Bosnia. The task of UNPROFOR was less to prevent war (soldiers shooting soldiers) than to prevent war crimes (soldiers massacring civilians). To the Serbs, UNPROFOR represented a hostile external world frustrating their objectives, which they were well on their way to achieving when the UN intervened. They thus focused their efforts on subverting UNPROFOR and completing the ethnic cleansing of "their" country. This was a near-certain recipe for disaster.

The compromised mission of UNPROFOR came to be embodied in the institution of United Nations Protected Areas (UNPAs) or "safe areas." First established in 1992 in Croatia, they were extended to Bosnia in 1993. UN strategy increasingly came to focus on excluding the Bosnian Serbs from UNPAs in Srebenica, Goradze, Tuzla, Zepa, and Bihac (as well as Sarajevo, which had been under siege since March 1992). These enclaves were a humanitarian refuge for victims of the fighting. They were temporary frontiers across which "peace" was to be kept. And they represented an implicit refusal of the international community to bow in full to ethnic cleansing.

The Serbs showed some tolerance for the first of these objectives, but they rejected the second and third. Therefore, the enclaves were under constant pressure and sporadic attack. And in late spring and summer 1995, the delicate and unsatisfying set of compromises embodied in UNPAs collapsed.

Serbs resumed heavy shelling of Sarajevo at the end of May 1995, provoking retaliatory NATO air strikes near Pale. The Serbs counterretaliated by shelling the safe areas. For example, 65 children were killed in a single artillery barrage on the center of Tuzla. In addition, 325 UN peacekeepers were taken hostage. When NATO sent in 12,500 new troops armed not merely for self-defense but with significant air- and ground-fighting capabilities, the Serbs responded by transforming the "safe areas" into killing zones.

In July 1995, Srebenica was overrun, as an appalled and ashamed UN contingent could only stand by and watch. Adult men were separated from the rest of the refugees, who were sent fleeing. Of a total "protected" population of about 40,000, some 7,000 were slaughtered and buried in mass graves. People were now dying not in spite of the "best efforts" of the international community but in significant measure as an unintended but very real consequence of those efforts.

Finally, the West, and particularly the United States, had had enough. NATO air strikes increased in number and severity. Political pressure built up to end the arms embargo, which had helped the Serbs (who received Serbian and JNA weapons) and harmed the Muslims (who had access only to modest quantities of primarily small arms smuggled in with difficulty). Coupled with the Croatian victories in Krajina and under some pressure from Milosevic (who was being increasingly squeezed by the West), the Bosnian Serbs were forced to the negotiating table.

In November 1995, a marathon three-week session at Wright Patterson Air Force Base in Dayton, Ohio, backed by immense U.S. pressure, produced a peace agreement that was signed on December 14, 1995. Throughout 1996, a 60,000-person multilateral implementation force (IFOR) supervised the military disengagement. Fragile political institutions for an ostensibly unified confederal Bosnia-Herzegovina were created. And American and other peacekeepers—who were finally able to play something more like a classic peacekeeping role—agreed to remain until mid-1998 with a 30,000-person Stabilization Force (SFOR).

NEW PATTERNS AND PRECEDENTS

Bosnia is often presented as an example of failure. From a simple before-after humanitarian point of view, it is hard to dispute this assessment. People died and suffered in great numbers because the international community waited three and a half years to meet Serb force with force. Earlier military engagement would have risked high human and financial costs. Nonetheless, much of the suffering of Bosnia's civilians could have been prevented. Decisive military commitments strongly backed when first challenged might even have reduced the total human, financial, and political costs.

But Bosnia and its people were, quite literally, kept alive. Sarajevo did not fall, averting an even greater disaster. The arms embargo prevented an even larger bloodbath (especially if one attributes part of the relatively good record of the Bosnian Muslims to their lack of opportunities to exact revenge). More than 2 million people were kept alive by humanitarian assistance. UN peacekeepers sent to the border of Macedonia in December 1992 stopped the fighting from moving east and south. And the international response, for all its inadequacies, was more than had previously been done in comparable cases.

It would be naive to assume that future cases will automatically receive an international response at least as vigorous. Precedents are less matters of past fact than present and future interpretation. Certainly there are multiple and conflicting lessons that might be drawn. But combined with other high-profile missions in the 1990s, Bosnia does reveal a limited but significant systematic transformation in international responses to genocide and humanitarian crisis.

Perhaps most notable is the intermingling of human rights, peacekeeping, and humanitarian assistance activities. During the cold war, they had been kept tightly segregated. This reflected both the politicized nature of UN human rights discussions, which might corrupt the neutrality of peacekeepers and humanitarian workers, and the desire of most states to avoid creating a precedent for direct UN multilateral action on behalf of internationally recognized human rights. A link between human rights and international peace and security has always been a central part of United Nations doctrine. In the post–cold war era, it has become a part of UN practice.

In addition to Bosnia and Croatia, UN peacekeeping operations in Namibia, El Salvador, Cambodia, Mozambique, Guatemala, Haiti, Rwanda, Somalia, and Northern Iraq have had human rights components. Peacekeepers have monitored the activities of the police and security forces, verified the discharge of human rights undertakings in agreements ending civil wars, supervised elections, assisted and protected new civilian institutions, encouraged authorities to adopt international human rights instruments and comply with their international human rights obligations, and provided human rights education. Peacekeepers in El Salvador, Haiti, Guatemala, and Rwanda have even had explicit mandates to investigate human rights violations.

We should neither underestimate the reality and importance of the change represented by these operations nor overgeneralize from them. Because most of them arose in the context of ending internationalized civil wars, they do not provide an obvious precedent for UN action in the absence of a peace and security mandate. In addition, most rested on either the consent of the authorities of the state in question or the near complete collapse of civil authority. Only in Iraq, a very special case, and in Haiti, a questionable precedent because of American regional hegemony, was there a substantially coercive element directed against an established, functioning government.

Furthermore, willingness to act in response to genocide, as in Bosnia and Rwanda, or in response to the collapse of civil order, as in Somalia, does not obviously translate into willingness to take similar action in the face of human rights violations short of genocide. As we saw in some detail in Chapters 3 and 6, recalcitrant states can ordinarily continue to engage in gross and persistent systematic violations of internationally recognized human rights perhaps not indefinitely, but certainly for a very long time. Multilateral mechanisms for dealing with human rights violations, as we saw in Chapter 4, remain weak. As long as a state has either the internal capacity to prevent massive political violence or the international power to block peacekeeping initiatives (which are established on an ad hoc basis through highly political mechanisms) gross human rights violators are still left largely to their own devices.

Even a recalcitrant genocidal government that maintains considerable control over much of its country would seem to be able to flout international pressures and avoid coercive humanitarian intervention. For example, in Sudan's genocidal civil war, which has dragged on and off for four decades, both sides, and especially the government in Khartoum, have resorted to the brutal targeting of civilians and the use of military force to prevent aid from reaching dying civilians. Both multilateral aid agencies and NGOs have pressed the limits of sovereignty by providing humanitarian relief in the absence of government permission, sometimes even when faced with opposition by the government in Khartoum. But sovereignty continues to prevent more forceful international action. Like China, Sudan illustrates that governments that remain capable of controlling much of their territory can bring up international human rights action far short of the use of force.

Nonetheless, for the first time in history we have a clear and fairly consistent stream of coercive international action on behalf of internationally recognized human rights. In earlier eras, the international community would almost certainly have found an excuse to stay out of Somalia, Bosnia, and Rwanda. And the willingness of new civilian governments in El Salvador and Guatemala to accept an active UN role in their internal political affairs reflects a major change in political attitudes in at least some countries. Furthermore, few of these cases are tainted by the sort of crude self-interest that corrupted unilateral humanitarian interventions during the cold war era.

China and Sudan illustrate the gaps that remain inescapable in an international system that is based on power and sees human rights violations, so long as they can be contained to a state's own people and territory, as ultimately a matter of sovereignty. But cases such as Bosnia do show that for the first time in history the international community is willing to try to stop genocide and punish it, not because that contributes to achieving other political objectives but simply because of their (moral) interest in human rights.

NATIONALISM AND HUMAN RIGHTS

The case of the former Yugoslavia illustrates the reemergence of a new threat to human rights: exclusive group loyalties and ethnicity, or more broadly, nationalism. Nationalism helped bring down Communist rule in Yugoslavia, as in much of the rest of Central and Eastern Europe. But in Croatia and Serbia, it has replaced relatively tolerant Communists with only somewhat less repressive and much more intolerant former Communists. And the former Yugoslavia illustrates the deeper threat to human rights posed by nationalism when a sense of national difference progresses to a sense of national superiority or ethnic privilege.

Nationalism is a special problem in Central and Eastern Europe because it was suppressed during Communist rule. We now see some previously dominant groups, such as Serbs, becoming even more aggressively overbearing. Previously dominant Russians now fear nationalist retribution in many of the other former Soviet republics. Some previously subordinate groups, such as Slovaks and Croats, seem more concerned with addressing old ethnic grievances than with establishing a new democratic order. Many other minorities remain subordinated, with their interests still ignored (e.g., ethnic Hungarians in Slovakia) or actively under attack (e.g., ethnic Turks in Bulgaria). Still others, such as Ossetians in Moldova and Georgia, have simply seen new ethnic oppressors replace the old.

The human rights problems raised by nationalism are at least as severe in Sub-Saharan Africa, where many countries have ethnically diverse populations with strong senses of group identity and loyalty. For example, recent elections in Kenya, Zimbabwe, and many other countries have been concerned with ethnic rivalry as much as anything else. In Sub-Saharan Africa, too, political repression has often helped to contain ethnic conflict. And liberalization and democratization are certain to release pent-up ethnic discontents. For example, ethnic-religious riots in the states of Katsina and Bauchi in Nigeria in April 1991 killed as many as one thousand people, and new riots broke out in Kaduna in May 1992. This may not justify military rule, but it does cause one to pause when condemning tolerant dictators.

Especially under conditions of economic scarcity, where an expanding supply of goods and services cannot be used to help to defuse intergroup rivalries, there is a relatively high probability that group competition will lead to ethnic conflict, sometimes even violence. Economic growth allows grievances to be addressed by directing new resources to disadvantaged groups. But in times of scarcity, which has been the norm for over a decade in most of Africa, politics tends to turn into a potentially volatile zero-sum contest over an inadequate pie.

Separatism has been a solution of sorts in parts of the former Soviet Union and Yugoslavia. But "Balkanization," the breakup of larger political units into small, fragile, and hostile nationalist states, presents serious economic, political, and human rights problems. And in much of Africa, the problems of political transition and economic development are severe enough without opening up the possibility of years, even decades, of tumults that may lead to nothing more than nationalist repression or the creation of new and even more feeble states.

Nonetheless, separatist demands for self-determination do seem well worth taking seriously even where dominant nationalities are not oppressive. Both internally, and especially internationally, there is a genuine dilemma. Resolving competing ethnic claims is difficult enough for those whose rights and interests are directly at stake. It is virtually impossible for outsiders. How should foreign actors balance the competing demands of national self-determination, other human rights, and economic and political viability, as well as their own national interests in that area? What right do they have to become involved at all?

Human rights issues are inherently problematic in a world structured around sovereign states. Questions of self-determination are the most problematic of all because they are about defining the very units that are entitled to participate in international relations. From a moral point of view, self-determination is no less problematic, raising the question of determining the community within which human rights are to be pursued and protected. It is unclear whether foreign actors have a right to do anything at all beyond encouraging the peaceful resolution of disputes and attempting to moderate the severity of conflicts that lead to violence—

which is pretty much how the international community responded in the former Yugoslavia.

Nationalism was an important factor in the collapse of oppressive rule in the Soviet bloc. But the short- and medium-term human rights implications of nationalism today are largely negative. And foreign actors are in a particularly weak position to deal with these new threats to human rights. This is perhaps one of the clearest possible examples of even progress bringing with it new problems.

EIGHT

□ □ □

International Human Rights in a Post–Cold War World

The international reactions to the Tiananmen massacre and the events in the former Yugoslavia discussed in the preceding chapters illustrate the central theme of this broader chapter on the post–cold war world: new challenges and opportunities, but substantial continuity amid all the change. I begin with general theoretical discussions of the impact of the end of the cold war and the character of power and interdependence in the contemporary world. The next two sections deal with issues that have become closely associated with human rights in recent years: democracy and markets. The final section offers some concluding comments on improving international human rights policies. I will focus throughout primarily on U.S. foreign policy, not (I hope) out of arrogance or insularity, but because I am an American writing for a primarily American audience.

IDEOLOGY AND INTERVENTION

Both bipolarity and East-West ideological rivalry, defining features of the cold war international order, have (for very different reasons) disappeared. This is undoubtedly beneficial for international human rights.

In the cold war era, both superpowers regularly intervened militarily to reverse impending or ongoing human rights improvements. Both also regularly supported domestic forces of oppression in other countries in order to maintain or develop political influence. Marcos in the Philippines, Duvalier in Haiti, Park in South Korea, the shah in Iran, Stroessner in Paraguay, Pinochet in Chile, and Mobutu in Zaire were but a few of the dictatorial beneficiaries of U.S. support. The Soviet record was at least as appalling. In addition to the well-known examples of Central and Eastern

149

Europe and Afghanistan, the Soviets backed the Mengistu regime in Ethiopia, arguably the most brutal Third World regime of the late 1970s and early 1980s. During the cold war the greatest contribution that either superpower could have made to human rights in dozens of countries would have been to get out.

Economic decline and internal political change have largely eliminated Russian incentives and capabilities for such involvements. U.S. capabilities persist, but the end of the cold war has eliminated the principal American justification.

Since 1945, almost all U.S. antihumanitarian interventions—that is, interventions that harm human rights—have contained a substantial element of anticommunism. Few could have been sold to Congress and the public without it. During the cold war, most unsavory dictators could obtain, or at least maintain, U.S. support by playing on anticommunism. Because this is no longer true, the post–cold war international environment for human rights has undoubtedly improved.

Strategic and economic rationales persist for support of or engagement with dictators, as we saw in the discussion of China. New justifications may emerge. But without the overarching appeal to anticommunism, it will be much more difficult for American governments to muster domestic support for repressive foreign regimes. And without anticommunism to distort or constrain American humanitarian impulses, there are real opportunities for beneficial change.

Consider military tolerance, under some U.S. pressure, of civilian governments and negotiations with the guerrillas in Guatemala and El Salvador. Although the human rights situation remains far from good, the end of almost unconditional cold war American support has forced the military to curtail most of its most blatant human rights violations. Haiti, where intensive and sustained pressure on the military forced the return of the elected Aristide government, also illustrates major progress in U.S. policy toward authoritarian regimes.

We should not underestimate the remaining problem. U.S. intervention to pursue narrow national interests, especially in the Western Hemisphere, long predates the cold war. But with ideology no longer distorting American perceptions, it is becoming increasingly clear that relatively few countries are of real strategic significance. Economic interests, other than oil, have played a relatively minor role in U.S. foreign policy toward the Third World over the past two decades. And other rationales are more limited in scope, less emotional in appeal, and thus substantially less threatening to human rights.

The post–cold war reduction in foreign support for repression is a significant advance in the international struggle for human rights. But there is no automatic translation into policies of support for newly democratic countries that would lead to comparable further progress in the next several years. Because the United States has generally stopped actively harming or cooperating with those who cause harm does not imply that it is likely to begin actively aiding victims, let alone that it is willing to use aggressive preventive diplomacy to prevent harm.

The psychological and political dynamics of positive policies of human rights support are quite different. Slogans such as "U.S. out of _____ [fill in the blank]" point to collusion with abusive regimes and thus to clear responsibility for human rights violations. They also propose the relatively simple, clear, and low-cost response of breaking relations: "Just say no!" Active policies of support for victims are far more complex and costly, as are policies to prevent, deter, reduce, or punish abuses. The discussion of constructive engagement in Chapter 6 suggests that instead of such active engagement, we are seeing the emergence of a U.S. strategy of largely passive support for international human rights.

SOVEREIGNTY, POWER, AND INTERDEPENDENCE

A similar picture of limited progress is apparent if we turn from cold war ideological rivalry to the underlying international balance of power. Russia remains capable of immense destruction. The United States has become the world's only military superpower. Both countries, however, confront a world in which military power is not readily translated into other forms of power.

In the past, states with high power on one dimension (e.g., military power) used that power to increase their holdings in other dimensions of power (most notably, economic power). Today, however, military power and economic power have become unlinked. The former Soviet Union is the most vivid example of the incapacity to use force to create prosperity. Conversely, Japan and Germany have emerged as major international (and especially regional) political actors, their strength based on their immense economic power despite their (relatively) paltry military power.

"Power" is no longer a simple, undifferentiated capacity, even as a first-order approximation. Today's Great Powers are powers in very different senses of the term. And some states, such as Saudi Arabia, are significant powers in some international issues but negligible actors in most others.

International political processes and outcomes thus vary dramatically from issue to issue. This may help to loosen the traditional dominance of security concerns, which could free space for human rights initiatives. But it also means that we cannot automatically generalize across issue areas. In particular, growing recognition of the need for international economic cooperation does not automatically translate into increased international human rights cooperation.

Some developed countries are increasingly willing to relinquish significant elements of economic sovereignty. We see this both in formal multilateral organizations (most notably, the European Union) and in less formal modes of international cooperation, such as the coordination
symbolized by the annual economic summits. Many Third World and formerly Communist states are increasingly relinquishing economic sovereignty through IMF-imposed structural adjustment packages—although
often out of dire necessity rather than genuine desire.

More complex and less state-centric patterns of order and cooperation,
based on new and relatively deep conceptions of international interdependence, are also emerging in some noneconomic issue areas. A striking
example is the rapid progress in regulating ozone-depleting emissions. In
security relations, however, interdependence has not penetrated very far
into U.S. policy. Even President Bush's triumphant Desert Storm vision of
the new world order, as he was at pains to note, did "not mean surrender-
ing our national sovereignty."[1]

A state-centric, sovereignty-based conception of international order
dominates international human rights as well. Most states still jealously
guard their sovereign human rights prerogatives. For example, the multilateral human rights institutions discussed above are much weaker than
the IMF or World Trade Organization (WTO). Even in Europe, the regional human rights system pales in comparison to the redefinition of the
range of state sovereignty achieved through regional economic institutions. And while economic and monetary union is deepening EU restrictions on its member states, there has been no parallel institutional growth
of the European human rights regime.

The persisting strength of sovereignty in the field of human rights rests
in part on the inherent sensitivity of human rights issues. Even rare or isolated violations can be sufficiently embarrassing to deter some states from
accepting strong international procedures. Another part of the explanation
for the continuing attachment to sovereignty is a qualitative difference between the material interdependence that underlies international economic
cooperation and the moral interdependence that underlies international
cooperation in human rights. Moral interdependence is neither less real
nor less important than material interdependence. It does, however, typically produce national and international political processes and relations
that make international cooperation more difficult to achieve.

Economic interdependence has a relatively tangible impact on daily
life. The incentives to cooperate are immediate and concrete and thus are
more readily recognized and more easily included in foreign policy. With
material interdependence, each side has at least some unilateral power to
prevent enjoying the benefits of cooperation. For example, trading part-
ners unilaterally control goods that the other partner desires. This greatly

facilitates self-help retaliation against violations of international norms by an injured party, an important consideration in the absence of effective multilateral enforcement mechanisms.

The moral interdependence underlying human rights, by contrast, is not a tangible part of the daily life of most ordinary citizens. The harm to distant and alien people is relatively abstract and immaterial. Therefore, the incentives to retaliate are largely intangible—which in practice usually means low. Compare the relatively strong response in places such as Somalia, Bosnia, and Rwanda, where genocide and starvation can be brought home to ordinary citizens—literally, into their homes in the form of disturbing television images of severe and widespread suffering—with the usually tepid responses to more "ordinary" human rights violations. The importance of overcoming the abstract character of moral interdependence is also illustrated by the decisive spur to international action provided by prominent individuals such as Andrei Sakharov or Anatoly Shcharansky in the Soviet Union; Nelson Mandela, Steve Biko, or Desmond Tutu in South Africa; Fang Lizhi or Harry Wu in China; or Ken Saro-Wiwa in Nigeria. The Nobel committee has clearly tried to use its Peace Prize to mobilize international pressure by enhancing the prominence of human rights activists such as Bishop Tutu, Aung Ken Suu Kyi in Burma, and, most recently, José Ramos-Horta and Bishop Carlos Bello in East Timor.

In addition, retaliatory enforcement of international human rights norms is inherently problematic. Moral suasion, which responds directly to the nature of the international offense, is notoriously weak. Other means of retaliation, however, must be imported from different issue areas, such as trade and aid. This risks escalating the dispute. Furthermore, because the sanctions are not clearly and directly tied to the violation, their legitimacy may appear questionable. "Natural" linkage makes, for example, trade sanctions in response to trade disputes much less problematic than trade sanctions over human rights abuses.

Taken together, these observations on the character of power and interdependence in the post–cold war world suggest that substantial impediments to international action on behalf of human rights remain deeply rooted in the states system. The best we can hope for is slow, incremental, and uneven progress. But the fact that structural changes have not brought a new era of inevitable progress means that our policies may have an important impact on the fate of human rights.

DEMOCRACY AND HUMAN RIGHTS

The preceding chapters have emphasized responding to particular violations. Effective international human rights policies, however, must be no less about creating conditions that prevent violations. Recent foreign policy emphasis on democracy and markets thus deserves special attention, because electoral democracy and market economies are indeed part of virtually all rights-protective regimes. I will argue however, that major *differences* between human rights, democracy, and markets as systems of social organization and political justification make the recent American emphasis on "market democracy" appear significantly misplaced. This section addresses democracy. Markets are taken up in the next section.

The Democratic Idea[2]

"Democracy" is derived from the ancient Greek *demokratia*, literally, rule (*kratos*) of the people (*demos*). Democratic regimes are those in which the people rule.

It is conventional to distinguish substantive and procedural conceptions of democracy. In a substantively democratic regime, goods, services, and real opportunities are enjoyed "democratically," that is, by the masses on an egalitarian basis. The people may or may not do the work of ruling, but they are beneficiaries of a regime that rules in their name and their interest. A procedurally democratic regime fills its political offices through fair and open periodic elections. Such polities may or may not pursue egalitarian policies. Their democratic credentials rest on the authority of the government deriving from the sovereign choice of the people.

Jefferson's familiar formula—government of the people, by the people, and for the people—suggests a similar distinction. All democracies are governments *of* the people. Some (procedural) conceptions of democracy, however, emphasize government *by* the people. Other (substantive) conceptions stress government *for* the people.

Americans seem particularly inclined to think of democracy in procedural terms, assuming that fair and open elections will produce governments that pursue the popular will and interest. Although often true, it is always legitimate to "test" allegedly democratic procedures by their substantive outputs. For example, a standard complaint about elected governments in much of Central America has been that they have in practice protected the interests of a small minority. Furthermore, and most important for our purposes here, a procedurally democratic government may still systematically violate human rights.

Democracy and human rights have very different, and often competing, theoretical and moral foundations. Democracy is a fundamentally collectivist political theory that answers the question who should rule. Democracy empowers the people and seeks to realize their collective good. Human rights rest on an individualistic political theory that addresses how governments should rule. Human rights empower autonomous individuals and seek to assure that personal and societal goals are pursued within the confines of guaranteeing every individual certain minimum goods, services, and opportunities.

In theory and practice alike, protected individual interests often conflict with the wishes of the majority. Many people, both individually and in groups, want to use their political power to harm their enemies or to gain (often unfair) advantage for themselves. "The people," understood as the substantial majority of the population, often want to do some very nasty things to some of their "fellow" citizens, especially those they see as inferior or dangerously different. For example, racial discrimination has been popular with the majority in procedural democracies such as the United States.

The potential conflicts between human rights and democracy have been resolved in a political system that students of comparative politics usually call liberal democracy, or more precisely, the liberal democratic welfare state. This type of polity, which is the implicit model underlying the Universal Declaration of Human Rights and other international instruments, is liberal: the state is seen as an institution to create the conditions needed to realize the rights of its citizens (see Box 8.1). It is democratic: political authority arises from the sovereignty of the people. It is a welfare state: economic and social rights extend well beyond the right to property. And all three elements are rooted in the overriding and irreducible moral equality of all human beings and the political equality and autonomy of all citizens.

This mixed liberal democratic conception is reflected in the standard civics text formula "majority rule with minority rights." But it is essential to note that there is nothing distinctively "democratic" about minority rights. Quite the contrary, "minority rights"—the individual human rights of every citizen—are prior and superior to the democratic rights of the majority. Human rights define the range within which democratic decisionmaking is allowed to operate. In fact, human rights are fundamentally nonmajoritarian.

Human rights are concerned with each, rather than all. They aim to protect every person, against majorities no less than against minorities. Human rights ordinarily take precedence over the wishes of the people, no matter how intensely even the vast majority of society desires to abuse some individual or group. In fact, in procedurally democratic societies, where the majority is relatively well positioned to care for its own rights and interests, a (the?) principal function of human rights is to *limit* democratic decisionmaking.

Contemporary Western liberal democracies are liberal (rights-protective) states first. Citizens' rights provide the government's authority and the standard by which its achievements are to be judged. The sovereignty of

---

BOX 8.1 "Liberalism"

The terms "liberal" and "liberalism" pepper contemporary human rights debates. It is often difficult, though, to figure out the exact reference.

What we might call *ideological* liberals are those committed to a strong state role in society. These "liberals" tend to support active international human rights policies.

Economic liberals, in the classical nineteenth century sense of that term, emphasize heavy reliance on markets and minimal state involvement. Economic liberals usually are ideologically conservative. They also tend not to support strong and active international human rights policies, athough this is not demanded by the theory.

Political liberalism is rooted in a social contract tradition of political theory going back to Locke. It sees government primarily as an institution to realize the rights of its citizens. Depending on their attitude to economic and social rights, political liberals may or may not be economically or ideologically liberal. Political liberalism is compatible with both strong international human rights policies and isolationism.

Further confusion is by reference to market-oriented economics as "liberal"—in the classical economic sense. But it is also called "neo-classical," in reference to underlying economic theory. This position is not ideologically liberal. It is, however, neutral with respect to political liberalism: neo-classical economic theory is compatible with both utilitarian and rights-based political theories.

This market-oriented "liberalism," however, is very different from the "neo-liberal" or "Bretton Woods" international economic system, which was established after World War II and still influences contemporary international economic institutions. The neo-liberal model was based on Keynesian, not (neo-)classical, economic theory. It advocates tend to be ideologically liberal, and are motivated more by political than economic liberalism.

Finally, in discussing democratization it is common to talk of "liberalization," a process of political softening and opening distinct from (and short of) electoral democracy. Liberalization is neutral with respect to, and comes out of different sources than, the other "liberal" debates.

In this chapter I will use liberal, without scare quotes or further qualification, to refer to (rights-based) political liberalism. I will use "neo-classical" to refer to (market-oriented) economic liberalism. And I will endeavor to avoid reference to ideological liberalism.

---

the people derives from the individual rights of each person. And the scope of democratic politics is delimited by the human rights of every citizen.

These conceptual distinctions are important because "democracy" tends to be used in two very different senses in contemporary discussions. Sometimes the referent is electoral or procedural democracy. The other standard referent of "democracy" is the liberal democratic welfare state, which is defined more substantively (by its respect for internationally recognized human rights) than procedurally. But only liberal democracy is centrally and inherently committed to human rights. And that is because it is "liberal" (rights-based) rather than "democratic" (based on the will of the people).

For clarity, I will use the term "democracy" without qualification to refer to electoral democracies—regimes that regularly transfer political power through fair and open elections. And my emphasis will be on the ways in which democracy thus understood may fall short of the demands of internationally recognized human rights. The considerable virtues of democracy are well known and frequently touted. Democracy's limitations, however, have often been overlooked in international human rights discussions, especially in the United States.

Democratization and Human Rights

The post–cold war world has seen the continued spread and deepening of electoral democracy. Despite limits and failures, as Bill Clinton noted in his victory speech in November 1996, for the first time in history a majority of people on this planet live under democratically elected governments. This momentous achievement is a source of legitimate satisfaction. But even setting aside the more than 2 billion people who do not enjoy electoral democracy, we must not overestimate its human rights significance. In particular, we must not confuse decreased tolerance for old forms of repressive rule with support for, let alone institutionalization of, rights-protective regimes.

Extending the distinctions drawn earlier, we can distinguish three levels of political progress toward respect for internationally recognized human rights.

Liberalization involves a decrease in human rights violations and opening of political space for at least some previously excluded groups, which roughly means progress in civil and political rights short of democratization. China has undergone periodic limited liberalizations. Poland liberalized in the 1980s, initially under the pressure of Solidarity, before it democratized in 1990. South Korea liberalized in the mid-1980s before moving toward electoral democracy.

By *democratization*, I mean the process of establishing electoral democracy. Although it might be seen as a type of liberalization, the qualitative leap involved justifies a separate category. When "soft" authoritarian regimes allow truly fair and open elections (not just once, or if they win), the political system is fundamentally transformed.

A *rights-protective regime* (1) makes the protection of internationally recognized human rights a central element of its mission and justification, and (2) through extensive, intense, and sustained effort, has produced considerable success in realizing this aspiration. This is *liberal* democracy, a strong form of political liberalism. If one insists on using the language of democratization to describe transitions from electoral to liberal democracy, one might talk about the "deepening" of democratization—although respect for human rights, rather than the will of the people, deepens.

Note that only the middle of these three processes is centrally connected with democracy, understood in the core sense of rule of the people. The distinction between electoral and liberal democracy concerns not who rules but how (within what limits). Liberalization, too, is concerned with the limits on government rather than who rules.

Nonetheless, "democratization" is often used to cover all three kinds of change, on the assumption that they are phases of a single continuous and largely linear process of development. Such an overly convenient assumption, however, poses risks to effective and sustained international human rights policies.

Political development is not "naturally" driven toward a single end. Resistance to authoritarian rule is often not a transition to democracy, or anything else, but a reaction against particular injustices. Regimes that have liberalized often resist democratization. Even fair and moderately open elections may produce governments that violate human rights.

This is not only because elected governments sometimes have only limited control over the state. Many times the problem is that the people do not place a sufficiently high value on a rights-protective regime. For example, voters in Belarus in November 1996 approved a referendum that placed control of all branches of the government in the hands of President Alexander Lukashenko, who was already running the country without much concern for political liberties or civil rights. The election was procedurally flawed. But in contrast to tens of thousands of protesters in the streets that same week in both Croatia and Serbia—nearby countries also run by autocratic, populist demagogues engaged in new attacks on the opposition—Belarussians showed almost no popular resistance.

One of the most disturbing lessons of democratization in countries such as Belarus, Uzbekistan, Slovakia, and Bulgaria in the 1990s, as in much of Africa in the 1960s, is that voting often appears to people to be primarily a device for acquiring prosperity and a sense of control rather than a way to assure widespread protection of human rights. And I have not even mentioned cases of the majority oppressing a minority. Consider, for example, Croatia's revival of the symbols of the wartime Nazi-puppet regime, which massacred a half million Serbs, and its denial of full rights of citizenship to residents who do not have Croatian parents on both sides.

Electoral democracy may be a necessary condition for developing liberal democracy. Electoral democracy may even foster liberal democracy by allowing human rights advocates political space and opportunities.

But there is no natural, inescapable evolution. Electorally democratic governments may use their power in ways that violate, threaten, or fail to defend internationally recognized human rights. And especially in times of crisis or disillusionment, electoral democracy can be extremely vulnerable to populist, protofascist demagoguery.

Elections are only a device. They may have very different meanings in different political contexts. The crucial issue is not whether leaders are freely chosen or speak for the people but whether human rights are secure. Only when supported by rights-protective political attitudes and institutions will elections lead toward deeply liberal democratic regimes.

The danger, especially in U.S. foreign policy, is that we will forget that democratization is at best a good start on realizing human rights. Comments such as those of President Clinton suggest that rather than refocusing and redoubling our efforts to address continuing and evolving human rights challenges, including those in new (and old) democracies, Americans seem inclined to the convenient illusion that once elections have been held, the struggle for human rights—or at least our part in the struggle—is largely over.

MARKETS AND HUMAN RIGHTS

The gap between markets and economic and social rights is even greater than that between electoral democracy and civil and political rights. Markets seek economic efficiency, maximizing the total quantity of goods and services produced with a given quantity of resources. Although markets may produce more overall, they do not necessarily produce more *for* all. In fact, markets distribute goods and services unequally and without regard for individual needs, interests, and rights. Market distributions take into account only economic value added, which varies sharply across individuals and social groups. Free markets thus necessarily produce gross economic inequalities.

This is well known and is the basis of the welfare states that almost all Westerners now take for granted. The collectivity that benefits has an obligation to look after individual members who are disadvantaged in or harmed by those markets. The welfare state is a device to assure that *all* individuals are guaranteed certain economic and social goods, services, and opportunities irrespective of the market value of their labor.

Advocates of market reforms admit that some are harmed in the pursuit of collective gain. But, they argue, everyone benefits in the long run from the greater supply of goods and services. "Everyone," however, does not mean every individual. The referent is the *average* individual, an abstract collective entity. And even the average person is assured of significant gain only at some point in the future. In the here and now, and in the near future, many real, flesh and blood, individual human beings and families suffer.

Markets, for all the talk of individual initiative, ground a collectivist, "utilitarian" political theory. Like (pure) democracy, (free) markets are justified by arguments of collective good and aggregate benefit, not individual rights (other than, perhaps, the right to economic accumulation). Free markets are an economic analogue to a political system of majority rule without minority rights. The welfare state, from this perspective, is a device to assure that a minority that is disadvantaged in or deprived by markets is still treated with minimum economic concern and respect.

If human rights are what civilize democracy, the welfare state is what civilizes markets. If civil and political rights keep democracy within proper limits, economic and social rights set the proper limits of markets. Only when the pursuit of prosperity is tamed by economic and social rights—when markets are embedded in a welfare state—does a political economy merit our respect.

This is a particularly important point for U.S. foreign policy. We tend to forget how heavily the U.S. government is involved in regulating markets and attempting to counteract the social inequities they produce. Not even Ronald Reagan seriously proposed returning to a true free market economy. Twentieth-century liberal democracies are distinguished from "classical liberalism" or "free market capitalism" by redistributive policies that protect individual rights and seek social justice.

For all the gaps in its coverage, the United States has a huge welfare state. For example, workers and employers together are taxed more than one-seventh of an employee's income just to fund a single social welfare program: state-supported old age pensions for all (social security). Even Americans, who are more individualistic and antistatist than most Europeans, see their welfare state as an essential part of the American political ideal.

In American foreign policy, however, all one hears about is markets. When a nation is faced with the legacy of command economies, the allure of the market is perhaps understandable. But this leads to overlooking the drawbacks of market remedies. There is a disturbing parallel with cold war anticommunism. Excessive focus on the "problem" (communism; command economies) yields inattention to the "unintended" consequences of the "solution" (dictators; markets).

This is particularly true for American support of IMF-imposed structural adjustment programs (SAPs). SAPs almost always have immediate and detrimental short-term effects on the enjoyment of economic rights by large segments of the population. Reductions in state spending on education and health, retrenchments in public sector employment, reductions in real wages, and programs to privatize land leave the poor even more vulnerable than they were before. In addition, the political costs to governments forced to institute unpopular and often punitive cuts in social services may also disrupt the pace and process of political liberalization and democratization.

I do not want to belittle the problems faced in implementing economic and social rights. Nor would I deny the contribution of properly regulated markets. I do not even want to deny that some countries may face a tragic choice between growth and equity. But where victims of market-driven growth truly cannot be prevented (at a reasonable cost), they must be acknowledged, and mourned. Yet in their enthusiasm for sweeping away the old, Americans seem not to see, let alone be troubled by, the problems in the new—an attitude with eerie similarities to Reagan-era attitudes toward the homeless.

Both dimensions of the new market democracy rhetoric in effect seek to substitute a simple, collectivist, procedural device for the hard work of implementing individual rights for all. Having "won" the cold war, it would be a shame if we forgot what the moral struggle was really about: not markets or democracy but human rights. Sadly, this seems to be precisely the direction American foreign policy is heading.

INTERNATIONAL HUMAN RIGHTS POLICY IN A NEW WORLD ORDER

Even well-intentioned and well-designed international human rights policies face immense national and international barriers, as has been discussed earlier in considerable detail. Furthermore, human rights are only one part of foreign policy. In some circumstances, other policy objectives may require or justify cooperating with a repressive regime. In practice, however, external constraints and competing interests have too often served as excuses for inaction rather than as the basis for reasoned policy judgments.

We need to go beyond general rhetorical flourishes and give human rights a clear and explicit priority in the United States. We must *integrate* human rights into foreign policy rather than occasionally tack them on. Human rights, finally, must be treated as a genuine national interest.

The appropriate starting point, I would suggest, is to treat severe human rights violations as establishing a prima facie case for ending direct U.S. support and reducing many voluntary cooperative ties. This would shift the burden of proof to advocates of maintaining (or improving) relations with rights-abusive regimes. Rather than asking, in effect, whether the human rights situation is so bad that we can no longer allow business as usual, we should ask instead whether there are other, precisely defined, interests that are sufficiently important to excuse cooperating with a rights-abusive regime.

Establishing a (rebuttable) presumption against close relations with repressive regimes, however, is only a first step toward integrating human rights concerns into foreign policy. Because of limited funds, time, interest, and attention, international human rights policy must selectively focus on some countries. Four criteria should be central in choosing the cases that will receive special attention and action: severity, trends, responsibility, and efficacy.

Although the severity of human rights violations in a country must be a central concern, it should not be the sole criterion. We should also examine trends in patterns of respect for and abuse of human rights. For example, two dozen death-squad killings in a year in Guatemala in the mid-1980s would have represented a reduction of over 99 percent from the level of the early 1980s. It would have merited a different level of concern and a different type of response than in Costa Rica, which had almost entirely avoided the phenomenon of death squads.

Few systematic violations of even a single right can be stopped all at once. The criterion of severity responds to the universality of human rights. The criterion of trends recognizes the political particularities of establishing rights-protective practices. A focus on trends may also encourage an international response before the situation gets entirely out of hand.

In choosing countries for special attention, we should also consider the likely effects of our efforts. Foreign policy is not only about setting ends but also about matching means to those ends. Although symbolic acts, as has been noted, are important, we should also consider the actual short- or medium-term impact on human rights practices. As already stated, this may sometimes suggest the paradoxical strategy of targeting countries where human rights problems are less severe, because improvements there are less difficult. It may also suggest focusing on "friends" more than either on "enemies" or countries with which we do not have close relations, because we have greater influence with our friends.

We should also take into account our own responsibility for creating or fostering rights-repressive policies or regimes. This too may suggest a focus on "friends" or special efforts on behalf of recent enemies. Conversely, past support for recently removed repressive regimes may require a less-forceful public diplomacy than might otherwise be demanded.

Looking at trends, efficacy, and responsibility will lead to treating comparably severe violations differently in different countries. Rather than a sign of debilitating inconsistency, however, this is necessary and desirable. Consistency means treating like cases in like manner. "Like cases," however, are not specified simply by the number and type of human rights violations. Consider a legal analogy. Not every thief deserves the same punishment for the same crime. We also look, for example, at past behavior, typically treating first-time offenders more leniently than hardened criminals.

Severity, trends, influence, and responsibility provide only rough guidelines, which may point in different directions in particular cases. Nonetheless, they provide a relatively clear basis for constructing a coherent and defensible policy. The danger, though, is that "balancing" diverse and competing considerations may degenerate into incoherent, ad hoc decisions or partisan inconsistency. Unfortunately, this has been, and remains, the rule in U.S. international human rights policy.

The international human rights challenge for the United States (and other countries) is to develop a realistic, committed, morally sound international human rights policy and to truly integrate this into the rest of U.S. foreign policy. This has not, however, been a major concern of either the Bush or Clinton administrations or the Congress. And with no other country or organization asserting international leadership, we are likely to look back on the 1990s as a period of missed opportunities.

□ □ □

Appendix:
Universal Declaration
of Human Rights

General Assembly Resolution 217A (III), 10 December 1948.

Whereas recognition of the inherent dignity and of the equal and inalienable rights of all members of the human family is the foundation of freedom, justice and peace in the world,

Whereas disregard and contempt for human rights have resulted in barbarous acts which have outraged the conscience of mankind, and the advent of a world in which human beings shall enjoy freedom of speech and belief and freedom from fear and want has been proclaimed as the highest aspiration of the common people,

Whereas it is essential, if man is not to be compelled to have recourse, as a last resort, to rebellion against tyranny and oppression, that human rights should be protected by the rule of law,

Whereas it is essential, to promote the development of friendly relations between nations,

Whereas the peoples of the United Nations have in the Charter reaffirmed their faith in fundamental human rights, in the dignity and worth of the human person and in the equal rights of men and women and have determined to promote social progress and better standards of life in larger freedom,

Whereas Member States have pledged themselves to achieve, in co-operation with the United Nations, the promotion of universal respect for and observance of human rights and fundamental freedoms,

Whereas a common understanding of these rights and freedoms is of the greatest importance for the full realization of this pledge,

Now, therefore,

The General Assembly

Proclaims this Universal Declaration of Human Rights as a common standard of achievement for all peoples and all nations, to the end that every individual and every organ of society, keeping this Declaration constantly in mind, shall strive by teaching and education to promote respect for these rights and freedoms and by progressive measures, national and international, to secure their universal and effective recognition and observance, both among the peoples of Member States themselves and among the peoples of territories under their jurisdiction.

Article 1. All human beings are born free and equal in dignity and rights. They are endowed with reason and conscience and should act towards one another in a spirit of brotherhood.

Article 2. Everyone is entitled to all the rights and freedoms set forth in this Declaration, without distinction of any kind, such as race, colour, sex, language, religion, political or other opinion, national or social origin, property, birth or other status.

Furthermore, no distinction shall be made on the basis of the political, jurisdictional or international status of the country or territory to which a person belongs, whether it be independent, trust, non-self-governing or under any other limitation of sovereignty.

Article 3. Everyone has the right to life, liberty and the security of person.

Article 4. No one shall be held in slavery or servitude; slavery and the slave trade shall be prohibited in all their forms.

Article 5. No one shall be subjected to torture or to cruel, inhuman or degrading treatment or punishment.

Article 6. Everyone has the right to recognition everywhere as a person before the law.

Article 7. All are equal before the law and are entitled without any discrimination to equal protection of the law. All are entitled to equal protection against any discrimination in violation of this Declaration and against any incitement to such discrimination.

Article 8. Everyone has the right to an effective remedy by the competent national tribunals for acts violating the fundamental rights granted him by the constitution or by law.

Article 9. No one shall be subjected to arbitrary arrest, detention or exile.

Article 10. Everyone is entitled to full equality to a fair and public hearing by an independent and impartial tribunal, in the determination of his rights and obligations and of any criminal charge against him.

Article 11.-1. Everyone charged with a penal offence has the right to be presumed innocent until proved guilty according to law in a public trial at which he has had all the guarantees necessary for his defence.

2. No one shall be held guilty of any penal offence on account of any act or omission which did not constitute a penal offence, under national or international law, at the time when it was committed. Nor shall a heavier penalty be imposed than the one that was applicable at the time the penal offence was committed.

Article 12. No one shall be subjected to arbitrary interference with his privacy, family, home or correspondence, nor to attacks upon his honour and reputation. Everyone has the right to the protection of the law against such interference or attacks.

Article 13.-1. Everyone has the right to freedom of movement and residence within the borders of each state.

2. Everyone has the right to leave any country, including his own, and to return to his country.

Article 14.-1. Everyone has the right to seek and to enjoy in other countries asylum from persecution.

2. This right may not be invoked in the case of prosecutions genuinely arising from non-political crimes or from acts contrary to the purposes and principles of the United Nations.

Article 15.-1. Everyone has the right to a nationality.

2. No one shall be arbitrarily deprived of his nationality nor denied the right to change his nationality.

Article 16.-1. Men and women of full age, without any limitation due to race, nationality or religion, have the right to marry and to found a family. They are entitled to equal rights as to marriage, during marriage and at its dissolution.

2. Marriage shall be entered into only with the free and full consent of the intending spouses.

3. The family is the natural and fundamental group unit of society and is entitled to protection by society and the State.

Article 17.-1. Everyone has the right to own property alone as well as in association with others.

2. No one shall be arbitrarily deprived of his property.

Article 18. Everyone has the right to freedom of thought, conscience and religion; this right includes freedom to change his religion or belief, and freedom, either alone or in community with others and in public or private, to manifest his religion or belief in teaching, practice, worship and observance.

Article 19. Everyone has the right to freedom of opinion and expression; this right includes freedom to hold opinions without interference and to seek, receive and impart information and ideas through any media and regardless of frontiers.

Article 20.-1. Everyone has the right to freedom of peaceful assembly and association.

2. No one may be compelled to belong to an association.

Article 21.-1. Everyone has the right to take part in the Government of his country, directly or through freely chosen representatives.

2. Everyone has the right of equal access to public service in his country.

3. The will of the people shall be the basis of the authority of government; this will shall be expressed in periodic and genuine elections which shall be by universal and equal suffrage and shall be held by secret vote or by equivalent free voting procedures.

Article 22. Everyone, as a member of society, has the right to social security and is entitled to realization through national effort and international co-operation and in accordance with the organization and resources of each State, of the economic, social and cultural rights indispensable for his dignity and the free development of his personality.

Article 23.-1. Everyone has the right to work, to free choice of employment, to just and favourable conditions of work and to protection against unemployment.

2. Everyone, without any discrimination, has the right to equal pay for equal work.

3. Everyone who works has the right to just and favourable remuneration insuring for himself and his family an existence worthy of human dignity, and supplemented, if necessary, by other means of social protection.

4. Everyone has the right to form and to join trade unions for the protection of his interests.

Article 24. Everyone has the right to rest and leisure, including reasonable limitation of working hours and periodic holidays with pay.

Article 25.-1. Everyone has the right to a standard of living adequate for the health and well-being of himself and of his family, including food, clothing, housing and medical care and necessary social services, and the right to security in the event of unemployment, sickness, disability, widowhood, old age or other lack of livelihood in circumstances beyond his control.

2. Motherhood and childhood are entitled to special care and assistance. All children, whether born in or out of wedlock, shall enjoy the same social protection.

Article 26.-1. Everyone has the right to education. Education shall be free, at least in the elementary and fundamental stages. Elementary education shall be compulsory. Technical and professional education shall be made generally available and higher education shall be equally accessible to all on the basis of merit.

2. Education shall be directed to the full development of the human personality and to the strengthening of respect for human rights and fundamental freedoms. It shall promote understanding, tolerance and friendship among all nations, racial or religious groups, and shall further the activities of the United Nations for the maintenance of peace.

3. Parents have a prior right to choose the kind of education that shall be given to their children.

Article 27.-1. Everyone has the right freely to participate in the cultural life of the community, to enjoy the arts and share in scientific advancement and its benefits.

2. Everyone has the right to the protection of the moral and material interests resulting from any scientific, literary or artistic production of which he is the author.

Article 28.-1. Everyone is entitled to a social and international order in which the rights and freedoms set forth in this Declaration can be fully realized.

Article 29.-1. Everyone has duties to the community in which alone the free and full development of his personality is possible.

2. In the exercise of his rights and freedoms, everyone shall be subject only to such limitations as are determined by law solely for the purpose of securing due recognition and respect for the rights and freedoms of others and of meeting the just requirements of morality, public order and the general welfare in a democratic society.

3. These rights and freedoms may in no case be exercised contrary to the purposes and principles of the United Nations.

Article 30. Nothing in this Declaration may be interpreted as implying for any State, group or person any right to engage in any activity or to perform any act aimed at the destruction of any of the rights and freedoms set forth herein.

□ □ □

Discussion Questions

CHAPTER ONE

1. Why should Americans be concerned with human rights practices abroad? Why should *states* or intergovernmental organizations be concerned? Anyone under thirty probably takes it for granted that states pursue human rights in their foreign policies. As we have seen, however, this is historically unusual. Whether you think the traditional practice of not pursuing international human rights objectives is good or bad, it is important to understand the logic underlying it. How can it be justified? In your opinion, why were people in the past willing to treat human rights violations as a purely national affair?

2. Why have these traditional views been replaced? Consider the following possibilities:

> Changing moral sensibilities: *Are* our moral views all that much different from those of other generations? (If so, what does that suggest about the universality of human rights?) Or is it that we now feel more free to act on these values? If so, why? *Can* changes in ideas, by themselves, have such an impact on policy?
> Other changes in the character of international relations: Are these reasons for changes in views of human rights? Peace and prosperity. Growing international interdependence. Cold war and détente. Decolonization.
> Changes in *national* human rights practices: Or is it that we are now doing better at home, and naturally want to project that progress abroad?

3. We might also ask just how deeply changing views toward international human rights have penetrated. We talk often about international human rights, but action often falls far short of rhetoric. Why? Is it lack of *real* interest? Constraints on our ability to achieve our objectives? Competing objectives?

4. *Should* international agencies like the United Nations be involved in enforcing internationally recognized human rights? Why? What would be sacrificed by a greater international role? What would be gained? Can international organizations be trusted to make the sort of sensitive political choices involved in dealing with human rights?

169

5. If you think that there should be a larger international role, why do you think that this has not come about? What would be required to overcome the existing impediments? How costly—economically, politically, and in human terms—would this be? Would these costs be worthwhile? Do you think that change is likely in the next few years? The next few decades? What factors would lead one to expect continuity? What factors suggest change?

6. What kind of actor is best suited to pursue international human rights: individuals, NGOs, states, or intergovernmental organizations? What are the strengths and weaknesses of each?

CHAPTER TWO

1. *Are* there such things as human rights? Where do they come from? How would you go about trying to convince someone who answers these questions differently from you? Do you find my claim that human rights rest on a moral account of human possibility to be plausible? Persuasive? Satisfying? Why?

2. I emphasize differences between rights and other sorts of moral principles and practices. Do I overemphasize the differences? What are the ways in which rights are similar to considerations of righteousness (or utility)?

3. Should we really prefer to protect human rights when doing so conflicts with social utility? Should the rights of the individual or the few take priority over the happiness of the many? In particular, should *governments* act on any principle other than social utility?

4. How do we know what things are on a justifiable list of human rights? How would you go about trying to convince someone who proposes a radically different list? Would it be easier or harder if the list were less radically different?

5. What is the status of the principle of equal concern and respect, which I draw on to justify the list of human rights in the International Bill of Human Rights? Should this principle be preferred to others? What are some other plausible grounds that might underlie this particular list?

6. I proceeded on the assumption that some sort of justification of human rights is possible. Does it really make no difference why people believe that there are human rights?

7. Are economic, social, and cultural rights human rights? Why? What explains the general reluctance of many Americans to consider them *really* human rights? Are the reasons philosophical? Is anything more involved than the generally poor performance of the United States on assuring these rights? Just how different are such arguments from the old Soviet claims that civil and political rights are really not as important as economic, social, and cultural rights?

8. Does the "positive-negative" distinction really make no moral difference at all? Is there really no difference between killing someone and failing to help someone who then dies? Does it make any difference whether we are thinking about personal morality or the activity of governments?

9. What is the relation between philosophical theory and international legal norms in the case of human rights? Can we legitimately evade philosophical diffi-

culties by pointing to international consensus? What are the costs of such a strategy? What are the costs of *not* following the consensus? And speaking of consensus, am I correct about the *moral* irrelevance of consensus? Does it make no difference at all to the validity of a moral principle or proposition whether there is widespread agreement or disagreement about it?

10. *Should* human rights function as an international standard of legitimacy? If yes, what else, if anything, is required for international legitimacy? If a government meets all the other criteria but violates human rights, why should it be seen as *internationally* (rather than morally or nationally) illegitimate?

11. Sovereignty certainly has gotten in the way of international human rights policies. But is it really such a bad thing? Do you want other countries and international organizations inquiring into the human rights practices of *your* country? International anarchy has its obvious drawbacks, but do you *really* want a higher political authority telling your country how to behave?

12. Which of the three models of international human rights do you find most attractive (issues of their current descriptive accuracy notwithstanding)? Why? What are the greatest strengths of your preferred model? How and why might others find it defective?

13. Even if realists overstate their case, don't they have one? How frequently are states really able to pursue international human rights concerns? Have recent international changes made it harder or easier?

14. How often do states use "realism" as little more than an excuse for not doing things that they know they ought to do but simply don't want to be bothered with? Imagine personal moral relations if "realist" arguments were allowed. Are the differences between interpersonal and international relations really so extreme that we can allow such radically different standards to apply? Conversely, are the similarities so great that we can apply the same standards without major modifications across the two realms?

15. *Are* human rights ideas truly universal? Are the differences between cultures and countries really primarily concerned with secondary human rights issues? Do recent changes in international relations have anything to tell us about the universality of human rights? Consider, for example, the fall of the Communist bloc and democratization in much of the Third World. Then consider Islamic fundamentalism and the rise of nationalist ethnic hostilities.

16. Make a list of all the arguments you can think of that can be made for cultural relativism. Which of these actually refer to *cultural* factors and which to political, economic, or ideological factors? Are arguments of political relativism as persuasive as arguments of cultural relativism? Why? What about economic relativism? Is the distinction between culture, politics, and economics helpful or revealing? Why?

17. Are differences in human rights ideas, whatever their nature, relatively permanent and static, or are they fluid and changing? Does this make a difference to your evaluation of relativism?

18. If practices are changing (or even just capable of change), should international human rights policy be directed more to respecting the way they are now or trying to make them more consistent with international human rights standards? What are the strengths and weaknesses of each approach?

19. Suppose that there are indeed major cultural differences with respect to human rights in the world today. *Should* we take those into account? Why? Should we allow them to alter our international human rights policies and practices? If so, don't we in effect end up acting on other people's values? If not, what right do we have to impose our values on others?

CHAPTER THREE

1. When we talk about human rights violations, numbers of victims can take on a strangely abstract character. In order to make the suffering behind the numbers more concrete, try this simple exercise. Count all the people you know personally. For most people, the number will be several hundred. This is far fewer than the number disappeared in Argentina or Chile. It is about the number of people killed in a single day in June 1989 in Tiananmen Square in China. Now add all the people you know of (actors, writers, celebrities, people in the news). The total will probably be a few thousand. In Argentina, literally more people disappeared than you can even name! In the early 1980s in Guatemala and El Salvador, this many people were being killed every several months.

2. Are there situations in which torture or disappearances could be justified? (Don't answer too quickly, whatever your initial inclination.)

3. How can people become torturers? Even if they are not applying the electric shocks to the victims, how can people work in, for, or around institutions that regularly practice torture or arbitrary execution? Consider the following possibilities:

Sadism: They enjoy it.
Commitment: They believe it is necessary to achieve a higher good.
Self-interest: They see an opportunity to get ahead.
Coercion: They are forced to participate.
Cowardice: They find themselves in a system they are afraid to resist.
Denial: They try to convince themselves that things are other than they appear.
Inertia: They simply do it because it is there.

Does why people do it make a difference? Does it make a *moral* difference?

4. Chile and Uruguay had long and relatively well-established democratic traditions. Nonetheless, they endured over a decade of extraordinarily repressive military rule. How can this be explained? Although you probably lack the factual information to make a truly informed judgment, speculating on possible reasons can be useful, particularly if we want to use these cases to think about prospects for democracy elsewhere.

5. Is it easier to build or to destroy a democracy? Once it is destroyed, how (and how easily) can it be fixed? Does the way it was destroyed—and the length of time it took—have a significant impact on the prospects for recovery or repair? Does the particular way that democracy was (re-)instituted have an impact on its future prospects?

6. It obviously makes sense to distinguish between larger and smaller numbers of human rights violations. But does it make sense to distinguish between different types of violations? If so, which ones are especially heinous? Why?

7. Is there a qualitative difference between a regime that tortures people but feeds everyone well and one that allows people to suffer from malnutrition but tortures no one? Or between a regime that allows free political participation but requires everyone to work sixty-hour weeks and one that provides thirty-five-hour workweeks but no political participation? There are differences, certainly, and they are likely to be of considerable political importance. But are the differences of any *moral* significance?

8. Are the only important (moral) distinctions between human rights violations ultimately quantitative? This would seem to be the implication of the claim that all human rights are interdependent and indivisible. But is the moral difference really just the number of people and the number of rights violated?

9. However you have answered the preceding set of questions, you can construct a list of human rights violators and rank them from more to less severe. Having done that, what foreign policy implications can you draw? Suppose we concentrate on the worst cases. The reasons to do so are fairly obvious. But are there drawbacks? Suppose someone were to suggest that we actually should focus on *less*-severe violators because the chances for improving practices there are greater. Or consider the claim that we should focus on the trend in a given country. Even if we accept this, should an improving or a declining trend receive greater weight? What other relevant considerations can you think of? States clearly cannot concentrate on all human rights violators equally. But how should they choose priority cases? (We will return to these questions at the end of Chapter 8.)

10. How should new governments deal with former torturers, dictators, and the members of the repressive apparatus of the old regime? Suppose that there are no political constraints imposed by the continuing power of these forces. Who should be punished, for what, and how severely? How should vengeance, justice, mercy, and reconciliation be balanced? Now suppose that the old forces of repression do still hold considerable power. How far should the demands of justice be pressed? At what point does bowing to power corrupt or undermine the new political order? Is there a practical alternative to accepting the lesser of two evils? Are practical alternatives the only ones that should be acted upon?

11. Although economic, social, and cultural rights received some attention in this chapter, the central focus was on violations of civil and political rights. This reflects the focus of international discussions of human rights violations in the Southern Cone. Is that focus the best one? Was the distinctive character of human rights violations in the Southern Cone significantly connected with economic, social, and cultural rights? Even if the distinctive nature of the repression concerned civil and political rights, should there have been greater international attention to economic and social rights?

CHAPTER FOUR

1. You have read in this chapter about a large number of multilateral human rights regimes. What kind of overall evaluation would you draw? Clearly there is a reasonably large amount of international activity. What sort of impact has it had? Is that impact worth all the effort?

2. There is a diverse array of multilateral human rights bodies: global and regional, comprehensive and single issue, individual and situation oriented, political and legal. What are the strengths and weaknesses of each type? Is there, in your view, some best type? What is the relationship between the best and the possible in this area?

3. How would you assess international reporting schemes in particular? Be sure to ask not only what they have (and have not) accomplished, but also what the costs have been and what alternatives there are.

4. Make an inventory of alternative multilateral approaches that either have not yet been tried or in your view have not been adequately exploited. Then ask yourself why they haven't been used and whether these impediments are likely to persist.

5. I have suggested that international human rights procedures are likely to have their greatest impact where the situation is relatively good (or at least less bad). What do you think of this? What does it suggest about the most effective forms of international action? Are you comfortable with the idea of writing off the worst cases (which some may draw as the central policy implication of this argument)? Is there a practical alternative?

6. Multilateral human rights institutions concentrate heavily on civil and political rights. While there has been much general political talk in the UN about economic, social, and cultural rights, when it comes to treaties and monitoring systems, the focus has been largely on civil and political rights. (At the global level, the Committee on Economic, Social, and Cultural Rights is the exception that proves the rule, as is the ILO in single-issue regimes.) What are the reasons for this? Is this a defensible allocation of resources and attention? What kinds of things would have to change to bring about a more comprehensive system of international human rights monitoring?

7. Even when we consider only civil and political rights, there is a strong concentration on a relatively small number of rights, especially rights to nondiscrimination and particularly egregious violations of personal liberty and bodily integrity. There has been very little attention to the *political* aspects of civil and political rights. How can this be explained? How should it be evaluated? What are the alternatives, both theoretical and practical?

CHAPTER FIVE

1. Should we accept the description of postwar U.S. foreign policy as dominated by anticommunism? Suppose that we do. Was it a bad thing? Should anticommunism have had a less-overriding priority? Or was the problem that anticommunism was pursued with excessive zeal? Is there something special about an ideological (or moralistic) foreign policy that leads to such excess? If so, does that force us to reconsider some arguments of the realists?

2. Should the United States be able to define for itself which internationally recognized human rights it wishes to recognize or pursue? If so, why? If we can pick and choose, how can we justify an international human rights policy if others pick

and choose differently? If not, why? Why should the United States (or any other sovereign state) have to follow international human rights norms, no matter how widely accepted they are?

3. The United States has a relatively active and aggressive bilateral international human rights policy but has been reluctant to participate in most multilateral international human rights regimes. (It wasn't until April 1992 that the United States ratified the International Covenant on Civil and Political Rights, and even then it did not ratify the optional protocol.) Isn't this a double standard? Can it be justified? Why should other countries take U.S. international human rights policy seriously when the United States is so reluctant to open itself to the international human rights policies of other countries and multilateral agencies?

4. In reviewing the evidence of U.S. policy toward South Africa, Central America, and the Southern Cone, what strikes you more, the continuities or the changes between different U.S. administrations? When all is said and done, just how different was Carter's policy from that of either Ford or Reagan? Were the differences largely symbolic? Even if they were, how serious a criticism is that? Is symbolism a negligible part of foreign policy? Of international human rights policy?

5. The same question might be asked about the differences between the international human rights policies of the United States and the like-minded countries. When it comes to making the difficult choices, when it comes to sacrificing their own interests, just how different are countries such as Canada, Norway, and the Netherlands? Consider, for example, the differences between Dutch policy toward Indonesia and Suriname. Is the difference one of quality of merely a matter of degree?

6. Whether large or small, "real" or "symbolic," there are differences between the international human rights policies of these countries. How can these be explained? What are the factors considered in the chapter? What additional possible explanations can you advance?

7. Consider the emphasis of the like-minded countries on economic, social, and cultural rights. Is their approach better than or just different from that of the United States? Why? Does your answer change if you look at the issue from the perspectives of foreign policy, foreign aid policy, or international human rights policy?

CHAPTER SIX

1. The evidence from Eastern Europe in late 1989 suggests that the Chinese government was basically right in its political assessment: substantial liberalization would mean the end of Communist rule. Does this provide some justification for the Chinese crackdown? Why should some states but not others be allowed to preserve their social and political systems?

2. Why all the fuss over Tiananmen? China had for decades regularly engaged in massive repression and yet received only the most mild criticism. Why should killing a few hundred people in order to restore things to pretty much the way they were one year earlier make such a difference? Could one argue that the real

failure in international human rights policies toward China lay not in responses to Tiananmen but in acquiescence to decades of massive totalitarian repression?

3. Who was hurt by economic sanctions? To what extent do sanctions merely victimize innocent people a second time? Consider a more extreme case such as Iraq, where by some estimates thousands of children a month were dying from food shortages caused in large part by international sanctions. But if we don't use economic sanctions, aren't we in effect giving in to regimes that use their people as hostages? If leading opposition figures ask for sanctions, as was the case in South Africa in the 1980s, that may simplify our problem. But what about cases such as Iraq (or China), where the opposition has been silenced or eliminated?

4. What do you think the relative mix between different motives was in the case of Japanese policy? American policy? How would you evaluate these priorities?

5. How long should a country be punished for even a shocking act such as the Tiananmen massacre? At some point, the past needs to be forgotten—not buried, but set aside in foreign policy. How do we know when that is? Are there general standards or guidelines that we might develop or draw on?

6. I suggested that when U.S. allies had abandoned sanctions, that largely justified an American return to business as usual. Isn't this troubling? Should we really let others dictate to us when to stop (or start)? Aren't we obliged to follow our own judgments?

7. Which "bottom line" do you find most persuasive? Did China, literally, get away with murder? Or did it suffer unusually strong and sustained international punishment? Both?

8. Over and over we have seen repressive regimes release prisoners or improve their treatment as a response to international pressure. This may make us feel as if we have achieved something. But just how important is it? To the extent that such changes are our principal focus, as in the case of Amnesty International, doesn't this actually amount to a strategy of treating symptoms while ignoring causes?

9. What influence, though, do outside actors have on the deep structural causes of respect for and violation of human rights? It is clear that outside actors can often make things a lot worse. But how often have they made things systematically better? Can outsiders really do much more than apply bandaids to wounds while they wait for deeper social, economic, and political forces to transform local people's tolerance for repression?

10. Should businesses be in the "business" of improving human rights? If you believe that individuals and governments have a responsibility to do something about international human rights, why shouldn't businesses? If businesses don't have *any* international human rights responsibilities, why should states or individuals?

11. If businesses have no human rights responsibilities overseas, why do we impose them on businesses operating domestically? Ask the same question for individual citizens. And then for governments.

12. *Do* international human rights standards really leave enough room for incorporating Asian (or other foreign) values into national human rights practices?

13. Why shouldn't a government be able to enforce long-established traditions? Does the fact that they have to be imposed by force really make that much differ-

ence? Don't laws that protect internationally recognized human rights also have to be enforced and thus in some important sense be imposed? What is the difference?

CHAPTER SEVEN

1. How do you interpret the rapid switch from ethnic tolerance to violent ethnic mobilization in the former Yugoslavia? Clearly we are not dealing with "primordial" animosities, especially in the case of Serbs and Croats, who had no significant political contact with one another until the twentieth century. But what do you imagine the relative mix was between deep but repressed animosities and opportunistic manipulation of the sorts of differences that usually lead at worst to social and political discrimination? Which explanation is more frightening?

2. The evidence of the post–cold war era to date suggests a new willingness to act in response to genocide and humanitarian crisis. How do you interpret its significance for the future? What are the prospects for "spillover" into either action to prevent (not merely respond to) genocide or coercive action against other, more "ordinary" types of human rights violations?

3. Is there any moral or theoretical significance to the sharp gap in responses to genocide and other kinds of human rights violations? What *dangers* are posed to international human rights policies when we respond forcefully only to unusually photogenic suffering?

4. In recent years there has been much talk of a clash of civilizations and the development of anti-Islamic attitudes in the West, especially in the United States. How does Bosnia fit into such arguments? Some have charged that the West did not do more because the Bosnians were Muslims. Others have used Bosnia as an example of Western policies clearly distinguishing politicized Islamists from ordinary adherents of one of the world's great religions.

5. The former Yugoslavia has also been used in arguments over the place of race in contemporary Western foreign policies. Here the comparison is with Rwanda. Did the West do more to stop genocide in Croatia and Bosnia because the victims were white than in Rwanda, where the victims were black? Or was the crucial difference that the killing was so quick in Rwanda, where half a million died in the course of a few weeks?

6. Bosnia and Rwanda illustrate a willingness to respond to genocide *after* it has occurred. Why is there no comparable international willingness to respond to *prevent* genocide?

7. The war crimes tribunal for the former Yugoslavia, as well as the parallel process for war crimes in Rwanda, has finally introduced an element of personal international legal responsibility to human rights violations, at least in the case of genocidal warfare. This is obviously of great symbolic significance. But what is its practical value? In the particular cases? In the future? In answering these questions, try to recall the earlier discussions of the role of normative transformation and the relative strengths and weaknesses of individual petition procedures.

8. Do I present an unfair treatment of nationalism? What about the "good" side, embodied in values such as patriotism? More generally, aren't there values in

groups and group loyalties that I have systematically undervalued in the highly individualistic account in both this and the preceding chapter?

9. Isn't there a paradox, or worse, in my criticism of nationalism and my acceptance of states as the basis of the international human rights system?

CHAPTER EIGHT

1. How would you evaluate my argument that the structure of the international system remains fundamentally the same? Is a (more) multipolar system really as similar to a bipolar one as I suggest? Is the state really still as central as I claim? Is one interdependent area, such as economics or human rights, really likely to remain relatively insulated from other areas?

2. Trying to assess the future after a momentous change such as the end of the cold war is in part an exercise in figuring out what evidence we should be focusing on. I stressed evidence of continuity and called for limited expectations. Is there evidence of change that I ignored or downplayed?

3. "Current" cases date quickly. When I finished the final draft of the first edition of this book, Croatia had been replaced in the public eye by Bosnia, and Somalia was only beginning to receive considerable international publicity. When the draft was delivered to the publisher, the U.S. military was relatively well ensconced in Somalia. But Rwanda was known to most people (if at all) only for its mountain gorillas. And even fewer had heard of Chechnya. As I completed the revisions for this second edition, the Rwanda crisis had expanded into a broader crisis in the "lakes region" of Central Africa. Street demonstrations for democracy were taking place in Belgrade, Zagreb, and Rangoon. By the time you read this, other cases will be grabbing the headlines. Take two or three such cases and ask whether the international response shows evidence primarily of continuity or of change.

4. How would you evaluate the distinction drawn between liberalization, democratization, and creating a rights-protective regime? Am I correct in saying that this distinction points to important long-term concerns that should lead us to moderate some of the early optimism associated with the fall of the Soviet Union? Am I correct that this distinction is especially important for Americans, who tend to focus on the formalities of democratization, often to the exclusion of the real substance of protecting human rights?

5. Are markets, from a human rights point of view, really just (at best) the lesser evil? Am I correct in suggesting that questions of economic, social, and cultural rights have in recent years often gotten lost in the rush toward market-oriented economic reforms? Even if that is true, is this a necessary first step toward sustained progress on economic, social, and cultural rights? If it is, though, how can we assure that later steps are taken?

6. Why do Americans, who claim to be so individualistic, seem so attracted to democracy and markets, which as I have argued are fundamentally collective systems of political justification? What kind of individualism is it that Americans really value?

7. Can a viable international human rights policy be constructed by responding to violations according to the principles of severity, trends, responsibility, and efficacy? Are there other principles that are as important? Is this list too long? Is the problem of "inconsistency" really as easily resolved as I suggest?

8. Throughout this book, the focus has been on describing what has taken place. Even when prescriptive arguments have been advanced, the emphasis has been as much on the possible as on the desirable. Whatever one may have to say about such an approach in thinking about the past and the present, is it the best one for thinking about the future? Even if it is, doesn't it need to be supplemented by innovative, perhaps even visionary, thinking? What would that look like in the case of international human rights? What explains the distance between the desirable and the possible?

□ □ □

Notes

CHAPTER ONE

1. Participation in the league's Minorities System, however, was forced upon a defeated Germany and the new states of Central and Eastern Europe as the price of international recognition. The victorious powers refused to be covered, even in their European territories, let alone in their colonial empires. The countries of Latin America also refused to join. And the United States was not a member of the League of Nations.

2. Although no negative votes were cast, the Soviet Union and its allies abstained, claiming that insufficient emphasis was given to economic and social rights. South Africa abstained, because of the provisions on racial discrimination, as did Saudi Arabia, because of the provisions on gender equality.

CHAPTER TWO

1. This is not exactly correct. Although children are human beings, they usually are not thought to have, for example, a right to vote, on the grounds that they are not fully developed. But once they reach a certain age, they must be recognized to hold all human rights equally. Similarly, those who suffer from severe mental illness are often denied the exercise of many rights—but only until they regain full use and control of their faculties. Furthermore, both children and the mentally ill are denied the protection or exercise only of those rights for which they are held to lack the necessary requisites. They still have, and must be allowed to enjoy equally, all other human rights. And in the case of children, the 1989 Convention on the Rights of the Child seeks to clarify this special status, including rights to special protections.

2. Some other languages stress a different multiplicity of meaning in their parallel terms. For example, Spanish, French, and German all use terms—*derechos humanos, droits de l'homme, Menschenrechte*—that contain words meaning both law and rights. Were we working in one of these languages, our discussion at this point might take a slightly different route.

3. Alan Gewirth, *Human Rights: Essays on Justification and Application* (Chicago: University of Chicago Press, 1984).

4. Jack Donnelly, *Universal Human Rights in Theory and Practice* (Ithaca: Cornell University Press, 1989), chaps. 1–3.

5. For a more extensive development of this argument, which derives from the work of Ronald Dworkin, see Rhoda E. Howard and Jack Donnelly, "Human Dignity, Human Rights, and Political Regimes," *American Political Science Review* 88 (September 1986), pp. 801–817.

6. The common argument that some internationally recognized human rights (especially civil and political rights) cannot be implemented because of the demands of economic development advocates only a temporary, and regrettable, strategic sacrifice. The arguments I am interested in here claim that certain (more or less) permanent divergences from the norms of the Universal Declaration are intrinsically desirable.

7. Maurice Cranston, *What Are Human Rights?* (London: Bodley Head, 1973), pp. 66–67.

8. In what follows, I will focus on the "external" dimensions of sovereignty, that is, sovereignty as it appears in the relations of states. Here the emphasis is on the absence of any superior (sovereign) above the state and is thus on the sovereign equality of states. The "internal" dimensions of sovereignty concern the supreme authority of the state within its territory. Here the focus is on the legal and political superiority of the state over other actors. In the contemporary world, internal sovereignty is usually seen to rest on the state acting in the name and interests of the people: "popular sovereignty."

9. For an extended discussion of this idea, see Hedley Bull, *The Anarchical Society* (New York: Columbia University Press, 1977).

10. Robert Gilpin, "The Richness of the Tradition of Political Realism," in Robert O. Keohane (ed.), *Neo-Realism and Its Critics* (New York: Columbia University Press, 1986), p. 305.

11. Hans Morgenthau, *Politics Among Nations*, 2d ed. (New York: Alfred A. Knopf, 1954), p. 9.

12. George F. Kennan, "Morality and Foreign Policy," *Foreign Affairs* 64 (Winter 1985–1986), p. 206; and *Realities of American Foreign Policy* (Princeton: Princeton University Press, 1954), p. 48.

13. George F. Kennan, *The Cloud of Danger: Current Realities of American Foreign Policy* (Boston: Little, Brown, 1977), p. 45.

14. Herbert Butterfield, *Christianity, Diplomacy, and War* (London: Epworth Press, 1953), p. 11.

15. Robert J. Art and Kenneth N. Waltz, "Technology, Strategy, and the Uses of Force," in Art and Waltz (eds.), *The Use of Force* (Lanham, Md.: University Press of America, 1983), p. 6.

16. Kennan, "Morality and Foreign Policy," p. 207.

17. Perhaps the best version of this argument is Adamantia Pollis, "Liberal, Socialist, and Third World Perspectives of Human Rights," in Peter Schwab and Adamantia Pollis (eds.), *Toward a Human Rights Framework* (New York: Praeger, 1982). A revised version appears in Richard P. Claude and Burns Weston (eds.), *Human Rights in the World Community*, 2d ed. (Philadelphia: University of Pennsylvania Press, 1992).

18. Even then, however, the problem was not an underemphasis on economic rights but rather an exceedingly narrow list of economic rights, extending scarcely if at all beyond the right to property. One might even argue that the real problem

was an overemphasis on the (economic) right to property, to the detriment of (civil and political) rights such as freedom of association.

19. Rhoda Howard has labeled this perspective "cultural absolutism." See "Cultural Absolutism and the Nostalgia for Community," *Human Rights Quarterly* 15 (May 1993), pp. 315–318.

20. This may be just slightly too strong. Indigenous peoples who live in traditional societies relatively unchanged by states and markets may have a plausible claim to radically different treatment. Only a tiny fraction of the world's population, however, lives in such societies today.

CHAPTER THREE

1. Marcelo Cavarozzi, "Political Cycles in Argentina Since 1955," in Guillermo O'Donnell, Philippe C. Schmitter, and Laurence Whitehead (eds.), *Transitions from Authoritarian Rule: Latin America* (Baltimore: Johns Hopkins University Press, 1986).

2. Quoted in Amnesty International USA, *Disappearances: A Workbook* (New York, 1981), p. 9.

3. Guatemala was the first country to use disappearances systematically as a means of repression, in the 1960s. The practice seems to have been introduced into South America through the example of the Brazilian military in the late 1960s. For a good general introduction, see ibid.

4. Americas Watch, *Truth and Partial Justice in Argentina: An Update* (New York, 1991), p. 6. In Uruguay, however, as we will see, most of the disappeared reappeared. Chile fell somewhere in between. But the basic strategy was similar in the three countries.

5. Ian Guest, *Behind the Disappearances: Argentina's Dirty War Against Human Rights and the United Nations* (Philadelphia: University of Pennsylvania Press, 1990), p. 41.

6. V. S. Naipaul, *The Return of Eva Perón* (New York: Vintage Books, 1981), pp. 170, 162.

7. Lawrence Weschler, *A Miracle, a Universe: Settling Accounts with Torturers* (New York: Pantheon Books, 1990), p. 145.

8. John Simpson and Jana Bennett, *The Disappeared: Voices from a Secret War* (London: Robson Books, 1985), p. 225.

9. See ibid.

10. Quoted in ibid., p. 66.

11. In fact, one of the tragic ironies in Uruguay was that the Tupamaros had already been destroyed by the end of 1972, that is, before the coup. (See Weschler, *A Miracle, a Universe*, pp. 107–111; Martin Weinstein, *Uruguay: Democracy at the Crossroads* [Boulder: Westview Press, 1988], pp. 51, 203.) And in Chile there was no guerrilla threat at all.

12. Guest, *Behind the Disappearances*, p. 29.

13. See, for example, David Pion-Berlin, *The Ideology of State Terror: Economic Doctrine and Political Repression in Argentina and Peru* (Boulder: Lynne Rienner Publishers, 1989), pp. 119–122.

14. Lawyers' Committee for International Human Rights, *The Generals Give Back Uruguay* (New York, 1985), p. 57; Weschler, *A Miracle, a Universe*, p. 112; Inter-

Church Committee on Human Rights in Latin America, *Violations of Human Rights in Uruguay* (Toronto, 1978), p. 7; Weinstein, *Uruguay,* pp. 44, 52; Pion-Berlin, *The Ideology of State Terror,* p. 101.

15. Simpson and Bennett, *The Disappeared,* p. 110.

16. For a good brief overview of the activities of the Vicaría, see Americas Watch, *The Vicaría de la Solidaridad in Chile* (New York, 1987).

17. Lawyers' Committee for International Human Rights, *The Generals Give Back Uruguay,* pp. 32–35.

18. For a review of the entire process of prosecutions and pardons, as well as further information on the actions of the Menem government, see Americas Watch, *Truth and Partial Justice.*

19. See Weschler, *A Miracle, a Universe,* pp. 173–236.

20. Hannah Arendt, *The Human Condition* (Chicago: University of Chicago Press, 1958), p. 241.

21. From Zbigniew Herbert, "Mr. Cogito on the Need for Precision," quoted in Weschler, *A Miracle, a Universe,* p. 191.

CHAPTER FOUR

1. Stephen D. Krasner, "Structural Causes and Regime Consequences: Regimes as Intervening Variables," in Krasner (ed.), *International Regimes* (Ithaca: Cornell University Press, 1982), p. 2.

2. This section draws heavily on Howard Tolley's authoritative book, *The U.N. Commission on Human Rights* (Boulder: Westview Press, 1987).

3. Optional procedures for complaints by one state against another have never been used. The other major activity of the Human Rights Committee is to issue "general comments" that seek to interpret particular provisions of the covenant or to improve the reporting process. A second optional protocol, on abolition of the death penalty, has not yet entered into force.

4. The 1990 International Convention on the Protection of the Rights of Migrant Workers and Members of Their Families envisions a similar procedure. By mid-1995, however, the convention had only two parties.

5. These racial designations, however, did not necessarily have any connection to previously existing facts. For example, in 1956 and 1957, Sophiatown, a black freehold section of Johannesburg, was rezoned white and the residents forcibly removed. In 1966, District Six of Capetown was declared white, although the population was 90 percent Coloured. Over 3.5 million blacks were removed from white areas, and more than a million were forced to relocate within designated black areas great distances away from their actual home.

6. This was no coincidence. In fact, one could largely plot economically worthless land by looking at a map of the Homelands. For example, Bophuthatswana was made up of nineteen separate pieces, and KwaZulu contained twenty-nine major and forty-one minor pieces of unconnected territory. And mineral rights were not even formally placed under the control of the Homeland governments.

7. Figures on European commission and court activities in the following paragraphs are from Council of Europe, Yearbook of the European Convention on Human Rights, 1995, vol. 38 (The Hague: Martinus Nijhoff, 1997), pp. 47, 49, 219, 220.

8. The principal source for the remainder of this section is Cecilia Medina Quiroga, *The Battle of Human Rights: Gross, Systematic Violations and the Inter-American System* (Dordrecht: Martinus Nijhoff, 1988).

9. Ibid., p. 312.

10. For a discussion of national human rights NGOs in Chile, see Chapter 3.

11. For a detailed account of Argentina's efforts in the United Nations, see Ian Guest, *Behind the Disappearances: Argentina's Dirty War Against Human Rights and the United Nations* (Philadelphia: University of Pennsylvania Press, 1990), pt. 2.

12. See Robert Pastor, *Condemned to Repetition: The United States and Nicaragua* (Princeton: Princeton University Press, 1987), pp. 149–151.

13. Quoted in Helsinki Watch Committee, *The Moscow Helsinki Monitors: Their Vision, Their Achievement, the Price They Paid, May 12, 1976–May 12, 1986* (New York, 1986), p. 5. The following discussion draws principally on this report.

14. We should also note that repression of human rights activists in CSCE countries was not entirely restricted to the Soviet bloc. In Turkey, twenty-three members of the Executive Committee of the Turkish Peace Association, formed in response to the security provisions of the Helsinki accords, were imprisoned for their activities.

CHAPTER FIVE

1. For a slightly different but generally consistent periodization, see David P. Forsythe, *The Internationalization of Human Rights* (Lexington, Mass.: Lexington Books, 1991), pp. 121–127.

2. The domestic and international sides of this arrogance come together in the reluctance of the United States to ratify international human rights treaties. Only in 1992, more than a quarter century after it was adopted, did the United States even ratify the International Covenant on Civil and Political Rights. And even then, there was no serious consideration given to ratification of the International Covenant on Economic, Social, and Cultural Rights.

3. The willingness, even eagerness, to engage in a vitriolic public campaign of vilification of countries such as Cuba, Nicaragua, and the Soviet Union further suggests that such arguments were not worth taking seriously.

4. There is now a fairly substantial quantitative social scientific literature on this topic. David Carleton and Michael Stohl, "The Foreign Policy of Human Rights," *Human Rights Quarterly* 7 (May 1985), pp. 205–229, present a case for no linkage. David Cingranelli and Thomas Pasquarello ("Human Rights Practices and the Distribution of U.S. Foreign Aid to Latin American Countries," *American Journal of Political Science* 29 [August 1985], pp. 539–563) argue for a modest but statistically significant relationship. Some of the most sophisticated work is being done by Steven Poe and his collaborators. See, for example, Steven C. Poe and C. Neal Tate, "Repression of Human Rights to Personal Integrity in the 1980s: A Global Analysis," *American Political Science Review* 88 (December 1994), pp. 853–872; Steven C. Poe and Rangsima Siriangsi, "Human Rights and U.S. Economic Aid During the Reagan Years," *Social Science Quarterly* 75 (September 1994), pp. 494–509; and Steven C. Poe et al., "Human Rights and U.S. Foreign Aid Revisited: The Latin American Region," *Human Rights Quarterly* 16 (August 1994), pp. 539–558. For a much more anecdotal

account by a former participant in the process, see Stephen B. Cohen, "Conditioning U.S. Security Assistance on Human Rights Practices," *American Journal of International Law* 76 (April 1982), pp. 246–279.

5. Liisa Lukkari North, "El Salvador," in Jack Donnelly and Rhoda E. Howard (eds.), *International Handbook of Human Rights* (Westport, Conn.: Greenwood Press, 1987), pp. 125–126.

6. Most independent observers put the figure significantly higher. See, for example, Lawyers' Committee for International Human Rights and the Watch Committees, *The Reagan Administration's Record on Human Rights in 1985* (New York, 1986), pp. 53–54. Americas Watch estimated almost 2,000 murders by death squads and the security forces in 1985. See also North, "El Salvador," p. 119, and Americas Watch, *El Salvador's Decade of Terror: Human Rights Since the Assassination of Archbishop Romero* (New Haven: Yale University Press, 1991).

7. This section is a revised version of the introductory section of Rhoda E. Howard and Jack Donnelly, "Confronting Revolution in Nicaragua: U.S. and Canadian Responses," Carnegie Council on Ethics and International Affairs, (New York, 1990).

8. Lars Schoultz, *National Security and United States Policy Toward Latin America* (Princeton: Princeton University Press, 1987), p. xi.

9. Jeane J. Kirkpatrick, "Dictatorships and Double Standards," *Commentary* 68 (November 1979).

10. The Committee of Santa Fe, *A New Inter-American Policy for the Eighties* (Washington, D.C.: Council for Inter-American Security, 1980), p. 37.

11. See, for example, Americas Watch Committee and the American Civil Liberties Union, *As BAD as Ever: A Report on Human Rights in El Salvador* (New York, 1984).

12. Americas Watch, *Annual Report, June 1984–June 1985* (New York, 1985), p. 4.

13. Cynthia Brown (ed.), *With Friends like These: The Americas Watch Report on Human Rights and U.S. Policy in Latin America* (New York: Pantheon Books, 1985), p. 20. Compare the Watch Committees and Lawyers' Committee for Human Rights, *The Reagan Administration's Record on Human Rights in 1986* (New York, 1987), pp. 49, 92–99, and *The Reagan Administration's Record on Human Rights in 1987* (New York, 1987), p. 106. On the Reagan administration's systematic misrepresentation of the facts, see Americas Watch, *Managing the Facts: How the Administration Deals with Reports of Human Rights Abuses in El Salvador* (New York, 1985).

14. This is not to suggest that human rights ought to have been at the top (or even necessarily that they ought not to be at the bottom). My purpose here is simply to describe the place of human rights concerns in the policies of the two administrations.

15. Christopher Coker, *The United States and South Africa, 1968–1985: Constructive Engagement and Its Critics* (Durham, N.C.: Duke University Press, 1986), p. 105.

16. Another Dutch institutional innovation of interest is the independent Human Rights Advisory Committee, created in 1983 to provide advice to the foreign minister on practical issues of human rights policy. The advisory committee has taken its independence very seriously, even issuing unsolicited advice to the minister and, in 1984 in the case of Suriname, advice that the minister explicitly said that he did not want to receive.

17. The two quoted passages were taken from Olav Stokke, "Norwegian Aid: Policy and Performance," in Stokke (ed.), *European Development Assistance* (Oslo: Norwegian Institute of International Affairs, 1984), pp. 328–329; and Olav Stokke, "The Determinants of Norwegian Aid Policy," in Stokke, *European Development Assistance*, p. 170.

18. Quoted in Charles Cooper and Joan Verloren van Themaat, "Dutch Aid Determinants, 1973–85: Continuity and Change," in Olav Stokke (ed.), *Western Middle Powers and Global Poverty: The Determinants of the Aid Policies of Canada, Denmark, the Netherlands, Norway, and Sweden* (Uppsala: Almquist and Wiksell International, 1989), p. 119.

19. For example, in 1974 the program countries of the Netherlands were Indonesia, India, Pakistan, Bangladesh, Sri Lanka, North Yemen, Nigeria, Tunisia, Kenya, Tanzania, Upper Volta, Zambia, Sudan, Egypt, Colombia, Suriname, Netherlands Antilles, Peru, Cuba, Jamaica, and Turkey. By 1984, Nigeria, Turkey, Tunisia, Peru, Cuba, Colombia, and Jamaica had been removed from the list, the programs in Upper Volta and Zambia had been expanded to broader regional programs for the Sahel and Southern Africa, and a Central American regional program, with special emphasis on Nicaragua, had been introduced. Historical (that is, colonial) ties explain the inclusion of Indonesia, Suriname, and the Netherlands Antilles. Pakistan provided geopolitical balance to India, and Kenya provided ideological balance to Tanzania, which was selected on social justice and human rights criteria.

20. Peter Baehr, Hilde Selbervik, and Arne Tostensen, "Responses to Human Rights Criticism: Kenya-Norway and Indonesia-the Netherlands," *Human Rights in Developing Countries: 1995* (The Hague: Kluwer Law International, 1995), p. 79. The discussion in this paragraph and the next draws heavily on this article.

21. The behavior of the like-minded countries in multilateral human rights forums has also been in sharp contrast to that of the United States. These countries have given multilateral human rights a high priority in their foreign policies, in contrast to the at best secondary emphasis of the United States. For example, Canada and the Netherlands played leading roles in the revival of the Commission on Human Rights in the late 1970s and early 1980s. Although the Carter administration supported these efforts, the Reagan administration did its best to undo them and to turn the commission into an instrument in the new cold war.

22. Jan Egeland, *Impotent Superpower—Potent Small State: Potentialities and Limitations of Human Rights Objectives in the Foreign Policies of the United States and Norway* (Oslo: Norwegian University Press, 1988), pp. 3, 5.

23. Ibid., p. 15.

24. *Statements and Speeches* 82/12, Ottawa: Bureau of Information, Department of External Affairs. Quoted in Howard and Donnelly, "Confronting Revolution in Nicaragua."

25. Egeland, *Impotent Superpower*, p. 23.

26. Norway and the Netherlands are usually the world's two leading aid providers on a per capita basis, providing more than 1 percent of GNP in foreign aid. In recent years, the United States has provided less than one-fifth of 1 percent. For example, in 1986 Norway, a country of 4.2 million people, provided $800 million in foreign aid, whereas the United States, with 240 million people, provided

$9.8 billion. The United States, with nearly sixty times the population, provided only about twelve times as much aid.

27. Students of comparative politics usually refer to this as a "corporatist" system. Each well-defined segment of society—each "corporate" group—is seen as *entitled* to have its interests taken into account, even if it is at the moment politically out of power. The United States, by contrast, tends to operate with a more "winner take all approach," as the early years of the Reagan revolution demonstrated particularly clearly.

CHAPTER SIX

1. Fang Lizhi, "Declaration to Support Democratic Reform in Mainland China," *World Affairs* 152 (3) (Winter 1989–1990), pp. 136–137.

2. *World Affairs* 152 (3) (Winter 1989–1990), p. 138.

3. Jonathan D. Spence, *The Search for Modern China* (New York: W. W. Norton, 1990), p. 742.

4. Despite the immense media attention it received in the West, however, the statue was not the essence of the Tiananmen democracy movement. Rather, it was a late and rather desperate gesture calculated to appeal to the United States more than to the Chinese people. Given the pervasive belief in Chinese distinctiveness and superiority—which often crosses over into xenophobia and is effectively manipulated by the government—any Chinese who would have responded positively to this ostentatiously foreign symbol certainly were already mobilized behind the students.

5. Assuming a growth rate of one-third raises the cost to over $15 billion. China also lost access to about $1 billion in World Bank loans for the better part of a year. Assessing the impact on private funding is more complex. Commercial borrowing was stagnant from 1987 through 1992. Direct foreign investment stagnated from 1988 through 1990, grew some in 1991, and then took off dramatically in 1992 (Nicholas R. Landy, *China in the World Economy* [Washington, D.C.: Institute for International Economics, 1994], tables 3.6 and 3.7). Structural economic and legal factors lie at the root of these lulls, which predate Tiananmen. Nonetheless, most observers had expected a surge in foreign investment in late 1989 and 1990. This seems to have been delayed until 1991–1992, at a cost to China of another few billion dollars.

6. The discussion of Japanese policy here draws heavily on K. V. Kesavan, "Japan and the Tiananmen Square Incident," *Asian Survey* 30 (July 1990), pp. 669–681, and David Arase, "Japanese Policy Toward Democracy and Human Rights in Asia," *Asian Survey* 33 (October 1993), pp. 935–952.

7. Actual Japanese loan disbursements to China, however, did drop from a high of $670 million in 1989 to $539 million in 1990 and to $424 million in 1991 (almost exactly the 1987 level), in contrast to the large increases anticipated when the new five-year aid plan was approved in August 1988. See Landy, *China in the World Economy*, table 3.5b. Thus, even Japan's most reluctant sanctions had immediate and direct economic costs to China of perhaps $2 billion.

8. Peter Van Ness, "Australia's Human Rights Delegation to China, 1991: A Case Study," in Ian Russell, Peter Van Ness, and Beng-Huat Chua, *Australia's Human Rights Diplomacy* (Canberra: Australian National University, Australian Foreign Policy Papers, 1992), p. 83.

9. China considers Tibet an integral part of its territory. Others consider it an occupied country. In either case, the distinctive Tibetan culture and religion has been under sustained and often violent attack for more than forty years.

10. David M. Lampton, "America's China Policy in the Age of the Finance Minister: Clinton Ends Linkage," *China Quarterly* 139 (September 1994), p. 615.

11. Quoted in Bruce Stokes, "Playing Favorites," *National Journal* (March 26, 1994), p. 714.

12. Thomas Friedman, in the next day's *New York Times*, quoted in Lampton, "Age of the Finance Minister," p. 597.

13. Ann Kent, "China and the International Human Rights Regime: A Case Study of Multilateral Monitoring, 1989–1994," *Human Rights Quarterly* 17 (February 1995), pp. 1–47.

14. Nihal Jayawikcrama, "Human Rights Exception No Longer," in George Hicks (ed.), *The Broken Mirror* (N.p.: n.p., 1990), p. 362, quoted in Kent, "Multilateral Monitoring," p. 15.

15. Quoted in Kent, "Multilateral Monitoring," p. 13.

16. Kent, "Multilateral Monitoring," p. 21.

17. Quoted in Kent, "Multilateral Monitoring," p. 12.

18. Kent, "Multilateral Monitoring," p. 12.

19. "U.S. Interference Protested," *Beijing Review* 32 (June 12–25, 1989), p. 10. Note that the scheduled June 12–19 issue did not appear.

20. Ding Xinghao, "Managing Sino-American Relations in a Changing World," *Asian Survey* 31 (December 1991), p. 1168.

21. Kent, "Multilateral Monitoring," p. 21.

22. *Economist*, October 26, 1966. For the curious, I will note that the firm was Mobil. In the text, however, I use the anonymous "the company" to underscore the generic nature of the issues being raised.

23. Quoted in Stokes, "Playing Favorites," p. 713.

24. Bilahari Kausikan, "Asia's Different Standard," *Foreign Policy* 92 (1993), p. 37.

CHAPTER SEVEN

1. Of a population of about 23 million in the early 1990s, over 9 million (roughly two-fifths) were Serbs and about half as many were Croats.

2. Sabrina Petra Ramet, *Balkan Babel: Politics, Culture, and Religion in Yugoslavia* (Boulder: Westview Press, 1992), p. 51.

3. Lawrence Freeman, "Why the West Failed," *Foreign Policy* 97 (Winter 1994–1995), p. 59, quoted in Thomas G. Weiss and Cindy Collins, *Humanitarian Challenges and Intervention* (Boulder: Westview Press, 1996), p. 84.

CHAPTER EIGHT

1. Speech of April 13, 1991, at Maxwell Air Force Base, *Vital Speeches of the Day* 57, no. 15 (May 15, 1991), pp. 450–452.

2. This section draws heavily on my paper "Human Rights, Democracy, and U.S. Foreign Policy," which will appear in a volume on international human rights edited by David Forsythe.

□ □ □

Suggested Readings

CHAPTER ONE

Although the literature on human rights has become rather large in the past decade, there are few good general introductory overviews of international human rights policies. David P. Forsythe, *Human Rights and World Politics* (Lincoln: University of Nebraska Press, 2d ed., 1989) emphasizes U.S. foreign policy, but there are also good discussions of international law and organization and theoretical and ideological perspectives on human rights. Also useful is R. J. Vincent, *Human Rights and International Relations* (Cambridge: Cambridge University Press, 1986). Vincent offers good discussions of the theory of human rights, cultural relativism, and the implications of human rights for contemporary international theory and practice (although the chapter on East-West relations is now dated). Jack Donnelly, *Universal Human Rights in Theory and Practice* (Ithaca: Cornell University Press, 1989), is somewhat narrower in focus. All three of these books, however, are somewhat dated. Peter R. Baehr, *The Role of Human Rights in Foreign Policy* (New York: St. Martin's Press, 1994) is current but somewhat more basic. Richard Pierre Claude and Burns H. Weston (eds.), *Human Rights in the World Community* (Philadelphia: University of Pennsylvania Press, 2d ed., 1992), is the best general collection of essays currently available.

Students in particular are likely to find much useful information in Walter Laqueur and Barry Rubin (eds.), *The Human Rights Reader* (New York: New American Library, 2d ed., 1989). A very different, but quite comprehensive, volume is Edward Lawson (ed.), *Encyclopedia of Human Rights* (New York: Taylor and Francis, 1991). Attention should also be drawn to *Human Rights Quarterly.* This interdisciplinary journal is generally considered to be the best scholarly journal in the field, but its articles are typically quite accessible to the average reader.

Those interested in the activities of human rights NGOs can get a pretty good sense of the range and diversity of their activities through the *Human Rights Internet Reporter.* For a good analytical overview, see Laurie S. Wiseberg and Harry M. Scoble, "Recent Trends in the Expanding Universe of NGOs Dedicated to the Protection of Human Rights," in Ved P. Nanda, James R. Scarritt, and George W. Shepherd, Jr. (eds.), *Global Human Rights: Public Policies, Comparative Measures, and NGO Strategies* (Boulder: Westview Press, 1980).

191

On Amnesty International, see Marie Staunton and Sally Fenn (eds.), *Amnesty International Handbook* (Claremont, Calif.: Hunter House, 1991). This short and very accessible book includes information for those interested in becoming actively involved in the work of Amnesty International. They may also write to Amnesty International USA, 322 Eighth Avenue, New York, N.Y. 10001 or call (212) 807–8400 or (800) 55AMNESTY.

Relatively current information on human rights conditions is available in the annual reports of both Amnesty International and Human Rights Watch, as well as in their irregular reports and press releases, which are readily available in many large libraries. The annual report of the United States Department of State is also a useful source of information (although sometimes, especially during the cold war, biased by American foreign policy concerns).

CHAPTER TWO

The single most important, and most cited, theoretical work on human rights is Henry Shue, *Basic Rights: Subsistence, Affluence, and U.S. Foreign Policy* (Princeton: Princeton University Press, 1980). Shue provides a subtle and powerful argument for the equal and overriding priority of rights to security, subsistence, and liberty; an extended discussion of the duties that flow from these rights; and a sensitive application of these theoretical ideas to U.S. foreign policy. (A shorter version of the core of the argument is available in Shue's essay "Rights in the Light of Duties," in Peter G. Brown and Douglas MacLean [eds.], *Human Rights and U.S. Foreign Policy: Principles and Applications* [Lexington, Mass.: Lexington Books, 1979].) For an alternative perspective on economic, social, and cultural rights, see Maurice Cranston, "Are There Any Human Rights?" *Daedalus* 112 (Fall 1983), pp. 1–18, and Hugo Adam Bedau, "Human Rights and Foreign Assistance Programs," in Brown and MacLean, *Human Rights and U.S. Foreign Policy.*

The most ambitious effort to develop a contemporary philosophical theory of human rights is Alan Gewirth, *Human Rights: Essays on Justification and Applications* (Chicago: University of Chicago Press, 1982). Gewirth's main argument, however, is dense and rather technical (although some of the later essays in the volume do provide accessible applications of the theory). For critiques of Gewirth and good examples of other philosophical perspectives, see J. Roland Pennock and John W. Chapman (eds.), *Human Rights* (New York: New York University Press, 1981).

Chapters 1 and 2 of Jack Donnelly, *Universal Human Rights in Theory and Practice* (Ithaca: Cornell University Press, 1989), present a more modest, and much more accessible, theory. For a good book-length discussion that emphasizes the similarities between rights and other grounds of action (in contrast to Donnelly's emphasis on the special features of rights), see James W. Nickel, *Making Sense of Human Rights: Philosophical Reflections on the Universal Declaration of Human Rights* (Berkeley: University of California Press, 1987). Chapter 1 of R. J. Vincent, *Human Rights and International Relations* (Cambridge: Cambridge University Press, 1986), provides a good, if necessarily brief, overview of some of the central theoretical issues. Vincent's "The Idea of Rights in International Ethics," in Terry Nardin and David R. Mapel (eds.), *Traditions of International Ethics* (Cambridge: Cambridge University Press, 1992), usefully links ethical issues with international relations theory in the case of human rights.

The literature on cultural relativism and human rights is large. Chapter 3 of Vincent's *Human Rights and International Relations* provides a good general overview of the issue. For a further development of the weak relativist position defended in this chapter, see Donnelly, *Universal Human Rights in Theory and Practice*, parts 2 and 3 (especially chapters 3 and 6). A very similar argument, applied to contemporary Africa, is developed in chapter 2 of Rhoda E. Howard, *Human Rights in Commonwealth Africa* (Totowa, N.J.: Rowman and Littlefield, 1986). For a radical relativist account, see Alison Dundes Renteln, "The Unanswered Challenge of Relativism and the Consequences of Human Rights," *Human Rights Quarterly* 7 (November 1985), pp. 514–540. (Renteln develops this argument in much greater detail in *International Human Rights: Universalism Versus Relativism* [Newbury Park, Calif.: Sage Publications, 1990].) A slightly less radical relativist argument is presented in Adamantia Pollis and Peter Schwab, "Human Rights: A Western Construct with Limited Applicability," in Pollis and Schwab (eds.), *Human Rights: Cultural and Ideological Perspectives* (New York: Praeger Publishers, 1980).

There are several useful readers that deal entirely or principally with issues of cultural relativism. I list them here in chronological order of publication: UNESCO, *Human Rights: Comments and Interpretations* (London: Allan Wingate, 1949); Pollis and Schwab (ed.), *Human Rights: Cultural and Ideological Perspectives;* Kenneth W. Thompson (ed.), *The Moral Imperatives of Human Rights: A World Survey* (Washington, D.C.: University Press of America, 1980); Claude E. Welch, Jr., and Virginia A. Leary (eds.), *Asian Perspectives on Human Rights* (Boulder: Westview Press, 1990); Jan Berting et al. (eds.), *Human Rights in a Pluralist World: Individuals and Collectivities* (Westport, Conn.: Meckler, 1990); Abdullahi Ahmed An-Na'im and Francis M. Deng (eds.), *Human Rights in Africa: Cross-Cultural Perspectives* (Washington, D.C.: Brookings Institution, 1990); Abdullahi Ahmed An-Na'im (ed.), *Human Rights in Cross-Cultural Perspectives: A Quest for Consensus* (Philadelphia: University of Pennsylvania Press, 1991).

CHAPTER THREE

Readers interested in more information on the Southern Cone should probably begin with Ian Guest, *Behind the Disappearances: Argentina's Dirty War Against Human Rights and the United Nations* (Philadelphia: University of Pennsylvania Press, 1990). Guest, a journalist who covered the United Nations Commission on Human Rights for a number of years, begins with an account of the repression following the coup in Argentina. His telling of the story is particularly powerful because of the effective use of personal accounts of some of the victims. Guest then moves on to the halting efforts of the United Nations to deal with disappearances in Argentina (and elsewhere), followed by an extended discussion of U.S. policy during both the Carter and the Reagan years. Somewhat narrower, but even more moving for being a first-person account by a journalist victim of the Dirty War, is Jacobo Timerman, *Prisoner Without a Name, Cell Without a Number* (New York: Knopf, 1981).

John Simpson and Jana Bennett, *The Disappeared: Voices from a Secret War* (London: Robson Books, 1985), is another useful example of political journalism, providing detailed information on the internal politics of the Dirty War. A much more idiosyncratic, but penetrating, analysis by a cynical external observer can be found in V. S. Naipaul, *The Return of Eva Perón* (New York: Vintage Books, 1981). For a more general discussion of disappearances as a technique of human rights violations, see Amnesty International USA, *Disappearances: A Workbook* (New York, 1981). Pamela Lowden, *Moral Opposition to Authoritarian Rule in Chile, 1973–1990* (New York: St. Martin's Press, 1996) provides a useful study of resistance to military rule. For an excellent study of the human rights movement in Argentina, see Alison Brysk, *The Politics of Human Rights in Argentina: Protest, Change, and Democratization* (Stanford: Stanford University Press, 1994). On human rights and democratic politics in authoritarian regimes in Latin America, a useful starting point is Elizabeth Jelin and Eric Hershberg (eds.), *Constructing Democracy: Human Rights, Citizenship, and Society in Latin America* (Boulder: Westview Press, 1996).

The horror of the Dirty War is difficult to capture fully even in good journalism (let alone in dry academic prose). Literary representations can thus be particularly useful. Among fictional accounts, perhaps the best is Lawrence Thornton, *Imagining Argentina* (New York: Doubleday, 1987), a novel in the "magic realist" tradition of García Marquez. Among poets, one might begin with Marjorie Agosin, *Zones of Pain/Las Zonas del Dolor* (Fredonia, N.Y.: White Pine Press, 1988), a short bilingual collection of poems on the human consequences of military rule in Chile.

Another journalistic account, Lawrence Weschler, *A Miracle, A Universe: Settling Accounts with Torturers* (New York: Pantheon Books, 1990), is perhaps the best place to begin further reading and reflection on the difficult process of overcoming the legacy of repression. The second half of the book, which began as two articles in the *New Yorker,* is a brilliant and moving discussion of the system of repression in Uruguay and the politics of the amnesty referendum. The first half, which deals with Brazil and thus is, strictly speaking, outside the scope of this chapter, is also valuable.

Readers interested in additional country case studies of the sort presented in this chapter should consult Jack Donnelly and Rhoda E. Howard (eds.), *International Handbook of Human Rights* (Westport, Conn.: Greenwood Press, 1987). Although a number of the chapters have become somewhat dated, there is no other readily available source of such case studies. Although not entirely comparable, a useful two-country comparative study is Hilde Hey, *Gross Human Rights Violations: A Search for Causes. A Study of Guatemala and Costa Rica* (The Hague: Martinus Nijhoff, 1995).

CHAPTER FOUR

The bulk of the literature on international human rights regimes is written by international lawyers. As a result, much of it is more technical and legalistic than the average reader of this book would desire. Three comprehensive edited volumes, however, should be noted: Karel Vasak and Philip Alston (eds.), *The International Dimensions of Human Rights* (Westport, Conn.: Greenwood Press, 1982); Theodor Meron (ed.), *Human Rights and International Law: Legal and Policy Issues* (Oxford: Clarendon Press, 1984); and Hurst Hannum (ed.), *Guide to International Human Rights Practice* (Philadelphia: University of Pennsylvania Press, 2d ed., 1992). These volumes, which are structured primarily in terms of particular international organizations, cover all the international human rights regimes discussed in this chapter. For a legal approach focusing more on the work of lawyers, with a special emphasis on the United States, see Frank Newman and David Weissbrodt (eds.), *International Human Rights: Law, Policy, and Process* (Cincinnati: Anderson Publishing Co., 1990).

Two good summary overviews of the human rights work of the United Nations in its first four decades are David P. Forsythe, "The Politics of Efficacy: The United Nations and Human Rights," in Lawrence S. Finkelstein (ed.), *Politics in the United Nations System* (Durham, N.C.: Duke University Press, 1988), and Tom J. Farer, "The United Nations and Human Rights: More Than a Whimper, Less Than a Roar," *Human Rights Quarterly* 9 (November 1987), pp. 550–586. (An abbreviated version of the Farer essay can be found in Richard Pierre Claude and Burns H. Weston [eds.], *Human Rights in the World Community* [Philadelphia: University of Pennsylvania Press, 1989].) The best comprehensive overview of United Nations activities is Philip Alston (ed.), *The United Nations and Human Rights: A Critical Appraisal* (Oxford: Clarendon Press, 1992). Howard Tolley's *The United Nations Commission on Human Rights* (Boulder: Westview Press, 1987) is the definitive book on this central institution of the global human rights regime. It also provides a good general account of the ups and downs of the human rights work of the United Nations. For a somewhat more jaundiced perspective, focusing on the problem of political bias, see Jack Donnelly, "Human Rights at the United Nations, 1955–1985: The Question of Bias," *International Studies Quarterly* 22 (September 1988), pp. 275–303.

Burns H. Weston, Robin Ann Lukes, and Kelly M. Hnatt, "Regional Human Rights Regimes: A Comparison and Appraisal," in Claude and Weston (eds.), *Human Rights in the World Community*, provides a useful brief summary. For more depth, consult A. Glenn Mower, Jr., *Regional Human Rights: A Comparative Study of the West European and Inter-American Systems* (New York: Greenwood Press, 1991). Although often highly technical, Cecilia Medina Quiroga, *The Battle of Human Rights: Gross, Systematic Violations and the Inter-American System* (Dordrecht: Martinus Nijhoff, 1988), is an excellent resource on the Inter-American regime. On the Helsinki process, see Arie Bloed and Pieter Van Dijk (eds.), *Essays on Human Rights in the Helsinki Process* (Dordrecht: Martinus Nijhoff, 1985). For an extended study of the impact of regional human rights law on domestic practice in Europe, see Robert Blackburn (ed.), *The Impact of the European Convention on Human Rights in the Legal and Political Systems of Member States* (London: Mansell, 1996).

CHAPTER FIVE

Stanley Hoffmann, "Reaching for the Most Difficult: Human Rights as a Foreign Policy Goal," *Daedalus* 112 (Fall 1983), pp. 19–49, provides an excellent and subtle discussion of some of the fundamental problems and possibilities in pursuing human rights in foreign policy. Equally useful as a general introduction to the issue is Charles Frankel, *Human Rights and Foreign Policy* (Headline Series, no. 241, October 1978). Another good, short introductory discussion, with an especially thorough presentation of the means available for use on behalf of human rights, is Evan Luard, *Human Rights and Foreign Policy* (Oxford: Pergamon Press [for the United Nations Association of Great Britain and Northern Ireland]). (An abbreviated version of this essay is available in Richard Pierre Claude and Burns H. Weston [eds.], *Human Rights in the World Community* [Philadelphia: University of Pennsylvania Press, 1992].)

Arthur Schlesinger, Jr., "Human Rights and the American Tradition," *Foreign Affairs* 57 (3) (1979), pp. 503–526, presents a lively version of a standard, mainstream U.S. liberal approach. Richard Falk ("Ideological Patterns in the United States Human Rights Debate: 1945–1978," in Natalie Kaufman Hevener [ed.], *The Dynamics of Human Rights in U.S. Foreign Policy* [New Brunswick, N.J.: Transaction Books, 1981], and chapter 2 of *Human Rights and State Sovereignty* [New York: Holmes and Meier, 1981]) offers a more radical view. William F. Buckley, Jr., "Human Rights and Foreign Policy: A Proposal," *Foreign Affairs* 58 (Spring 1980), pp. 775–796, presents a clear statement of the traditional conservative approach. Jeane J. Kirkpatrick, "Dictatorships and Double Standards," *Commentary* 68 (November 1979), pp. 34–45, is the authoritative presentation of the Reagan position. Tracy Strong, "Taking the Rank with What Is Ours: American Political Thought, Foreign Policy, and Questions of Rights," in Paula R. Newburg (ed.), *The Politics of Human Rights* (New York: New York University Press, 1980), provides an excellent, and somewhat more neutral, discussion of human rights ideas in the American tradition of political thought. Although all these articles were written in response to Jimmy Carter's introduction of human rights into the mainstream of U.S. foreign policy, they remain valuable statements of the basic perspectives that still dominate American discussion. The same is true of Hans Morgenthau's essay *Human Rights and Foreign Policy* (New York: Council on Religion and International Affairs, 1979), a classic statement of the realist perspective. For another classic realist analysis, see Henry A. Kissinger, "Continuity and Change in American Foreign Policy," in Abdul Aziz Said (ed.), *Human Rights and World Order* (New York: Praeger Publishers, 1978).

Said (ed.), *Human Rights and World Order*, is just one of several edited volumes on human rights and U.S. foreign policy produced in the later 1970s. The best is Peter G. Brown and Douglas MacLean (eds.), *Human Rights and U.S. Foreign Policy: Principles and Applications* (Lexington, Mass.: Lexington Books, 1979). This volume combines theory and policy analysis in a stimulating way. Although many of the examples, as well as the case studies in the final part of the volume, are now pretty dated, most of the volume remains surprisingly timely. David P. Kommers and Gilburt D. Loescher (eds.), *Human Rights and American Foreign Policy* (Notre Dame, Ind.: University of Notre Dame Press, 1979), and Hevener, *The Dynamics of Human Rights in U.S. Foreign Policy*, have held up a bit less well, but many of the individual essays remain worth reading.

David Heaps, *Human Rights and U.S. Foreign Policy: The First Decade, 1973–1983* (New York: American Association for the International Commission of Jurists,

1984), is perhaps the best short historical overview of U.S. policy. It also sharply draws the contrast between the Carter and the Reagan approaches. The discussion of U.S. policy in David P. Forsythe's introductory text *Human Rights and World Politics* (Lincoln: University of Nebraska Press, 2d ed., 1989) is excellent. For more detail, see A. Glenn Mower, Jr., *Human Rights and American Foreign Policy: The Carter and Reagan Experiences* (Westport, Conn.: Greenwood Press, 1987). The chapters on the United States in David P. Forsythe, *The Internationalization of Human Rights* (Lexington, Mass.: Lexington Books, 1991), are extremely useful. Forsythe's *Human Rights and U.S. Foreign Policy: Congress Reconsidered* (Gainesville: University of Florida Press, 1988) is the only extended discussion of the much understudied congressional role in U.S. international human rights policy.

For essays dealing with some of the basic theoretical and practical problems of linking human rights and foreign aid, see Brown and MacLean (eds.), *Human Rights and U.S. Foreign Policy*. Stephen B. Cohen, "Conditioning U.S. Security Assistance on Human Rights Practices," *American Journal of International Law* 76 (April 1982), pp. 246–279, provides a detailed account of the loopholes and inadequacies in the U.S. policy process. Two articles by David Carleton and Michael Stohl ("The Foreign Policy of Human Rights: Rhetoric and Reality from Jimmy Carter to Ronald Reagan: A Critique and Reappraisal," *Human Rights Quarterly* 7 [May 1985], pp. 205–229, and "The Role of Human Rights in U.S. Foreign Assistance," *American Journal of Political Science* 31 [November 1987], pp. 1002–1018) show that there is little statistical correlation between the human rights practices of recipient states and U.S. foreign aid disbursements. Also useful is David P. Forsythe, "U.S. Economic Assistance and Human Rights: Why the Emperor Has (Almost) No Clothes," in David P. Forsythe (ed.), *Human Rights and Development: International Views* (London: Macmillan, 1989).

Roberta Cohen, "Human Rights Diplomacy: The Carter Administration and the Southern Cone," *Human Rights Quarterly* 4 (May 1982), pp. 212–242, is the best brief discussion of this subject. Ian Guest, *Behind the Disappearances: Argentina's Dirty War Against Human Rights and the United Nations* (Philadelphia: University of Pennsylvania Press, 1990), provides much more detail, covering both the Carter and the Reagan years. Lars Schoultz's book *Human Rights and United States Policy Toward Latin America* (Princeton: Princeton University Press, 1981) is one of the few works that looks in detail at the actual operation of the U.S. foreign policy process in the field of human rights. On U.S. policy toward South Africa, see Christopher Coker, *The United States and South Africa, 1968–1985: Constructive Engagement and Its Critics* (Durham, N.C.: Duke University Press, 1986).

There has been very little written on human rights and foreign policy in countries other than the United States. The three principal exceptions are Robert O. Matthews and Cranford Pratt (eds.), *Human Rights in Canadian Foreign Policy* (Kingston and Montreal: McGill-Queen's University Press, 1988); and Jan Egeland, *Impotent Superpower—Potent Small State: Potentialities and Limitations of Human Rights Objectives in the Foreign Policies of the United States and Norway* (Oslo: Norwegian University Press [distributed by Oxford University Press], 1988); and David Gillies, *Between Principle and Practice: Human Rights in North-South Relations* (Toronto: University of Toronto Press, 1997). The Matthews and Pratt volume is particularly useful for its comprehensive scope, covering the domestic Canadian policy context and Canadian policy in both multilateral and bilateral contexts. On the aid policies of the like-minded states, see Olav Stokke (ed.), *Western Middle Powers and Global Poverty: The Determinants of the Aid Policies of Canada, Denmark, the Netherlands, Norway, and Sweden* (Stockholm: Almquist and Wiksell International, 1989). Wolfgang S. Heinz, "The Federal Republic of Germany: Human Rights and Development," and Peter R. Baehr, "Human Rights, Development and Dutch Foreign Policy: The Role of an Advisory Committee," in Forsythe (ed.), *Human Rights and Development,* are useful brief discussions of countries that have adopted some unusual institutional mechanisms.

The general issue of the justifiability of humanitarian intervention, although not pursued in this chapter, is worth additional reading and reflection. The starting point for contemporary discussions is Michael Walzer, *Just and Unjust Wars* (New York: Basic Books, 1977), pp. 53–63, 101–108. Walzer argues that in a world of sovereign states, humanitarian intervention is likely to be morally justifiable only in extremely narrow and rare instances. See also Michael Walzer, "The Moral Standing of States: A Response to Four Critics," *Philosophy and Public Affairs* 9 (Spring 1980), pp. 209–229. For a variety of less restrictive accounts, see the critics to whom Walzer responds in "The Moral Standing of States," and Terry Nardin and Jerome Slater, "Non-Intervention and Human Rights," *Journal of Politics* 48 (February 1986), pp. 86–96. For an argument that comes to conclusions similar to Walzer's, but primarily through legal and political rather than moral analysis, see Jack Donnelly, "Human Rights, Humanitarian Intervention, and American Foreign Policy: Law, Morality and Politics," *Journal of International Affairs* 37 (Winter 1984), pp. 311–328. (An abbreviated version of this essay is available in Richard Pierre Claude and Burns H. Weston [eds.], *Human Rights in the World Community* [Philadelphia: University of Pennsylvania Press, 1989].)

CHAPTER SIX

Perry Link's *Evening Chats in Beijing: Probing China's Predicament* (New York: W. W. Norton, 1992) is an immensely engaging attempt to capture the political climate of Tiananmen and the ideas and aspirations of many Chinese democrats. Andrew J. Nathan is the leading American scholar of Chinese democracy. See, for example, *Chinese Democracy* (New York: Knopf, 1985). For his brief account of Tiananmen, see "Chinese Democracy in 1989: Continuity and Change," *Problems of Communism* 38 (September-October 1989), pp. 16–29. On human rights in China more generally, see Ann Kent, *Between Freedom and Subsistence: China and Human Rights* (Hong Kong: Oxford University Press, 1993), and R. Randle Edwards, Louis Henkin, and Andrew J. Nathan, *Human Rights in Contemporary China* (New York: Columbia University Press, 1986). Jonathan D. Spence's *The Search for Modern China* (New York: W. W. Norton, 1990) is a very long but lively book that strives to set 1989 in a broad historical context.

David M. Lampton, "America's China Policy in the Age of the Finance Minister: Clinton Ends Linkage," *China Quarterly* (1994), pp. 597–621, provides an excellent, detailed but brief review of Clinton's China policy, focusing on the 1994 MFN decision. Robert G. Sutter, *Shaping China's Future in World Affairs: The Role of the United States* (Boulder: Westview Press, 1996) is a dry but accessible general survey of U.S.-Chinese relations, with an emphasis on the post–cold war era. The UN response is covered in detail in Ann Kent, "China and the International Human Rights Regime: A Case Study of Multilateral Monitoring, 1989–1994," *Human Rights Quarterly* 17 (February 1995), pp. 1–47. David Arase, "Japanese Policy Toward Democracy and Human Rights in Asia," *Asian Survey* 33 (October 1993), pp. 935–952, sets Japan's post-Tiananmen policy in a broader regional context.

For an unusually subtle Chinese defense by the director of the Department of American Studies at the Shanghai Institute of International Studies, see Ding Xinghao, "Managing Sino-American Relations in a Changing World," *Asian Survey* 31 (December 1991), pp. 1155–1169. More typically vitriolic and xenophobic official Chinese defenses can be found in numerous issues of *Beijing Review*. For 1989, for example, see the issues of June 12, p. 10; July 3, pp. 9–10; July 10, pp. 18–21; July 17, pp. 18–19; July 31, p. 10; and November 20, pp. 38–40. John F. Cooper, "Peking's Post-Tiananmen Foreign Policy: The Human Rights Factor," *Issues and Studies* 30 (October 1994), pp. 49–73, reviews in detail the evolution of China's response. China's official White Paper is *Human Rights in China* (Beijing: Information Office of the State Council, 1991).

For generally positive assessments of engagement strategies toward China, see James Shinn (ed.), *Weaving the Net: Conditional Engagement with China* (New York: Council on Foreign Relations Press, 1996); David Shambaugh, "Containment or Engagement with China? Calculating Beijing's Responses," *International Security* 21 (Fall 1996); and Joseph S. Nye, Jr., "The Case for Deep Engagement," *Foreign Affairs* 74 (July-August 1995), pp. 90–102. Thomas A. Metzger and Ramon H. Myers (eds.), *Greater China and U.S. Foreign Policy: The Choice Between Confrontation and Mutual Respect* (Stanford: Hoover Institution Press, 1996) deals primarily with the question of Taiwan but contains a useful short chapter on human rights by Merle Goldman.

Two unusually clear and subtle presentations of the "Asian values" position are Bilahari Kausikan, "Asia's Different Standard," *Foreign Policy* 92 (1993), pp. 24–41, and Fareed Zakaria, "Culture Is Destiny: A Conversation with Lee Kuan Yew," *Foreign Affairs* 73 (March/April 1994), pp. 109–126. Kim Dae Jung, "Is Culture Destiny? The Myth of Asia's Anti-Democratic Values," *Foreign Affairs* 73 (November/December 1994), pp. 189–194, is a brief response by a leading Korean politician and former human rights activist. James C. Hsiung (ed.), *Human Rights in an East Asian Perspective* (New York: Paragon House Publishers, 1985), is a good collection of essays with a generally relativist orientation. Peter R. Baehr et al., *Human Rights: Chinese and Dutch Perspectives* (The Hague: Martinus Nijhoff, 1996), is an interesting recent collection, based on a symposium held in Beijing. James T. H. Chang (ed.), *Human Rights and International Relations in the Asia-Pacific Region* (London: Pinte, 1995) is a good introduction to some of the current theoretical and practical issues connected with the "Asian challenge." The essays by Joseph Chan ("The Asian Challenge to Universal Human Rights") and Yash Ghai ("Asian Perspectives on Human Rights") present subtle discussions that should appeal to readers who find my presentation extreme or one-sided.

CHAPTER SEVEN

The conflict in the former Yugoslavia is so recent that much of what is available now will seem preliminary or dated by the time this book is in wide circulation. For more background information, see Sabrina Petra Ramet, *Balkan Babel: Politics, Culture, and Religion in Yugoslavia* (Boulder: Westview Press, 1992), and Robert Donia and John V. A. Fine, *Bosnia and Hercegovina: A Tradition Betrayed* (New York: Columbia University Press, 1994). Anna Cataldi (ed.), *Letters from Sarajevo: Voices of a Besieged City* (London: Element Books, 1994) provides a powerful glimpse into the human dimensions of this tragic war. Robert M. Hayden, "Constitutional Nationalism in the Formerly Yugoslav Republics," *Slavic Review* 51 (Winter 1992), pp. 654–673, is an interesting study of the development of nationalist ideas in the former Yugoslavia. Charles Gati, "From Sarajevo to Sarajevo," *Foreign Affairs* 71 (1992), pp. 64–78, places the conflict in a broader regional context.

Philip Rieff, "The Lessons of Bosnia: Morality and Power," *World Policy Journal* 12 (Spring 1995), pp. 76–88, provides a thoroughly negative reading of the international response that sharply contrasts with my much more positive assessment. Along these more critical lines, see also David Rieff, *Slaughterhouse: Bosnia and the Failure of the West* (New York: Simon and Schuster, 1995); Thomas Cushman and Stjepan G. Mestrovic (eds.), *This Time We Knew: Western Responses to Genocide in Bosnia* (New York: New York University Press, 1996); and Human Rights Watch/Helsinki, *The Fall of Srebrenica and the Failure of U.N. Peacekeeping* (New York: Human Rights Watch, October 1995).

CHAPTER EIGHT

Much of the literature on the post–cold war era has been either very general or extremely topical. Therefore, the suggested readings for this chapter are minimal. David P. Forsythe, "Human Rights in a Post–Cold War World," *Fletcher Forum of World Affairs* 15 (Summer 1991), pp. 55–70, one of the earliest attempts to make sense of the human rights implications of the end of the cold war, is still useful. Two excellent readers addressed to broader issues that influence the international politics of human rights are Thomas G. Weiss (ed.), *Collective Security in a Changing World* (Boulder: Lynne Rienner Publishers, 1993), and Graham Allison and Gregory F. Treverton (eds.), *Rethinking America's Security: Beyond Cold War to New World Order* (New York: W. W. Norton, 1992).

Sara Steinmetz, *Democratic Transition and Human Rights: Perspectives on U.S. Foreign Policy* (Albany: State University of New York Press, 1994) is a useful attempt to address the foreign policy problems posed by democratic transitions.

Glossary

American exceptionalism is the belief that the United States is culturally and politically different from, and usually superior to, other countries. It can be traced to the colonial period and the biblical image of the city on the hill. In the area of human rights, it tends to be expressed in the common American view that the United States in some important sense defines international human rights standards.

Anarchy, the absence of political rule, is characterized by the lack of authoritative hierarchical relationships of superiority and subordination. In international relations, anarchy refers to the fact that there is no higher authority above states. Anarchy, however, need not involve chaos (absence of order). Thus, international relations has been called an anarchical society, a society in which order emerges from the interactions of formally equally sovereign states.

Apartheid, an Afrikaans term meaning "separateness," was the policy of systematic, official racial classification and discrimination in South Africa. Building on a long tradition of racial discrimination, white South African governments in the 1950s and 1960s developed an unusually extensive, highly integrated system of official discrimination touching virtually all aspects of public life and many aspects of private life as well. The policy was officially renounced following a (whites only) plebiscite in March 1992.

The **categorical imperative** is Kant's fundamental principle of morality. Kant argues that there is one and only one fundamental moral principle: Act so that you always treat other people as ends, never as means only. This principle is an imperative (a command), and it is categorical (it applies without exception, in all times, places, and circumstances). It is a classic example of deontological ethics, moral systems that focus on the inherent character of an act (and the intentions of the actor) rather than on the consequences of acts.

Civil and political rights are one of two principal classes of internationally recognized human rights. They provide protections against the state (such as rights to due process, habeas corpus, and freedom of speech) and require that the state provide certain substantive legal and political opportunities (such as the rights to vote and to trial by a jury of one's peers). They are codified in the International Covenant on Civil and Political Rights and in Articles 1–21 of the Universal Declaration of Human Rights (see Table 1.1).

Cold war is the term used for the geopolitical and ideological struggle between the Soviet Union and the United States following World War II. It began in earnest roughly in 1948, waxed and waned over the following forty years, and finally ended with the collapse of the Soviet bloc in 1989.

Cosmopolitan and **cosmopolitanism** refer to a conception of international relations that views people first and foremost as individual members of a global political community ("cosmopolis") rather than as citizens of states.

Disappearances are a form of human rights violation that became popular in the 1970s. Victims, rather than being officially detained or even murdered by the authorities or semiofficial death squads, are "disappeared," taken to state-run but clandestine detention centers. Torture typically accompanies disappearance, and in some countries the disappeared have also been regularly killed.

Economic, social, and cultural rights are one of two classes of internationally recognized human rights. They guarantee individuals socially provided goods and services (such as food, health care, social insurance, and education) and certain protections against the state (especially in family matters). They are codified in the International Covenant on Economic, Social, and Cultural Rights and in Articles 22–27 of the Universal Declaration of Human Rights (see Table 1.1).

Ethnic cleansing is the genocidal "purification" of the population of a territory through murder and forced migration. The term entered international political vocabularies to describe the strategy and practices of Serbian separatists in the former Yugoslavian republic of Bosnia-Herzegovina during the civil war of 1992–1995.

The **1503 procedure** is an investigatory procedure (established by ECOSOC Resolution 1503) of the United Nations Commission on Human Rights that deals with situations of gross, persistent, and systematic violations of human rights.

The **Helsinki process** is an informal description of the human rights activities undertaken within the Conference on Security and Cooperation in Europe (CSCE). The term derives from the Helsinki Final Act of 1975, which defined the terms of reference of the CSCE.

Human rights, the rights that one has simply because one is a human being, are held equally and inalienably by all human beings. They are the social and political guarantees necessary to protect individuals from the standard threats to human dignity posed by the modern state and modern markets.

The **International Bill of Human Rights** is the informal name for the Universal Declaration of Human Rights and the International Human Rights Covenants, considered collectively as a set of authoritative international human rights standards. This title underscores the substantive interrelations of these three documents.

The **International Human Rights Covenants** comprise the International Covenant on Economic, Social, and Cultural Rights and the International Covenant on Civil and Political Rights, which were opened for signature in 1966 and entered into force in 1976. Along with the Universal Declaration of Human Rights, these are the central normative documents in the field of international human rights.

An **international regime** is a set of principles, norms, rules, and decisionmaking procedures accepted by states (and other relevant international actors) as binding in an issue area. The notion of a regime points to patterns of international governance that are not necessarily limited to a single treaty or organization.

Internationalist and **internationalism** refer to a conception of international relations that stresses both the centrality of the state and the existence of social relations among those states.

The **like-minded countries** are a group of about a dozen small and medium-sized Western countries, including Canada, the Netherlands, and the Nordic countries. They often act in concert in international organizations and generally pursue foreign policies that are more "liberal" than those of the United States, Japan, or the larger Western European countries. The like-minded countries particularly emphasize development issues, and they have tried to play an intermediary role between the countries of the South and the larger northern countries.

A **nongovernmental organization (NGO)** is a private association of individuals or groups that engages in political activity. International NGOs carry on their activities across state boundaries. The most prominent international human rights NGOs include Amnesty International, Human Rights Watch, the International Commission of Jurists, and the Minority Rights Group.

Nonintervention is the international obligation not to interfere in matters that are essentially within the domestic jurisdiction of a sovereign state. This duty is correlative to the right of sovereignty and expresses the principal practical implications of sovereignty, viewed from the perspective of other states.

Peacekeeping involves the use of lightly armed multilateral forces to separate previously warring parties. Peacekeeping is distinguished from collective security enforcement by a limited mandate, an effort to maintain neutrality, and reliance on the consent of the parties in whose territory peacekeepers are placed.

Quiet diplomacy is the pursuit of foreign policy objectives through official channels, without recourse to public statements or actions. A standard mechanism for pursuing virtually all foreign policy goals, it became a political issue in the United States in the late 1970s and 1980s, when conservative critics of the policy of the Carter administration and defenders of the policy of the Reagan administration argued that U.S. international human rights policy toward "friendly" (anticommunist) regimes should in most cases be restricted *solely* to quiet diplomacy.

Realism (realpolitik) is a theory of international relations that stresses international anarchy, human egoism, the priority of power and security, and the need to exclude considerations of morality from foreign policy.

A **relativist** believes that values are not universal but are a function of contingent circumstances. **Cultural relativism** holds that morality is significantly determined by culture and history. Marxism is another form of **ethical relativism,** holding that values are reflections of the interests of the ruling class. **Radical relativism** sees culture as the source of all values.

Sovereign and **sovereignty** refer to the absence of obligation to a higher authority. International relations over the past three centuries have been structured around the principle of the sovereignty of territorial states.

Statist and **statism** refer to a theory of international relations that stresses the centrality of sovereign states. Realism is usually associated with a statist theory of international relations.

A **treaty** is an agreement between states that creates obligations on those states. Treaties are one of the two principal sources of international law, along with custom (regularized patterns of action that through repeated practice have created expectations and thus acquired an obligatory character). The two most important international human rights treaties are the International Covenant on Economic, Social, and Cultural Rights and the International Covenant on Civil and Political Rights.

The **Universal Declaration of Human Rights** is a 1948 General Assembly resolution that provides the most authoritative statement of international human rights norms. Together with the International Human Rights Covenants, it is sometimes referred to as the International Bill of Human Rights.

Universalism is the belief that moral values such as human rights are fundamentally the same at all times and in all places. It is the opposite of relativism.

Utilitarianism is a moral theory (most closely associated with Bentham and Mill) that holds that the right course of action is that which maximizes the balance of pleasure over pain. This is the most common form of consequentialist ethics, which focus on the consequences of acts rather than their inherent character.

Index